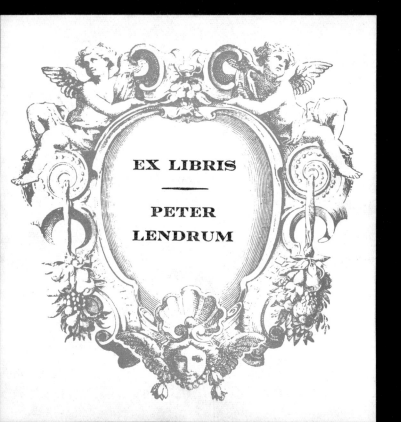

EX LIBRIS

—

PETER
LENDRUM

BROOKS'S
A SOCIAL HISTORY

BROOKS'S

A Social History

EDITED BY

Philip Ziegler

AND

Desmond Seward

CONSTABLE · LONDON

First published in Great Britain 1991
by Constable and Company Limited
3 The Lanchesters, 162 Fulham Palace Road
London W6 9ER
Copyright © Brooks's Club 1991
ISBN 0 09 470770 7
Set in 11pt Sabon by
Servis Filmsetting Limited, Manchester
Printed in Great Britain by
St Edmundsbury Press Limited
Bury St Edmunds, Suffolk

A CIP catalogue record for this book
is available from the British Library

Contents

Contents

Illustrations

Preface

I T is now more than twenty-five years since Lord Spencer prepared his history of Brooks's. Another formal study of that kind is hardly called for. Much has happened to the Club, however, since Spencer's book was written; most notably the merger with the St. James' and the advent of the Dilettanti with their extraordinary collection of paintings. The nature of the Club and its membership has changed, superficially to a striking extent, fundamentally perhaps less so. It seemed to us that it would be worth while to persuade some of the many writers who are members of Brooks's to contribute essays which, chronologically and thematically, would cover the history of the Club and some of the more interesting and entertaining aspects of its day-to-day existence. We hoped that such a study would reveal how much besides the building does indeed survive of the Brooks's that existed two, three, or for that matter, nine or ten generations ago.

We believed that such a book would not merely be valued by members but would possess some wider interest as a study of political and social history. No club which could boast eighteen out of twenty members of the Cabinet in 1830, sixteen out of sixteen in 1834, thirteen out of fifteen in 1852, eight out of fourteen in 1886 and twelve out of twenty-five even as late as 1905, can be denied some political significance; while any social anthropologist wishing to study the customs and practices of the unreconstructed Whig could not find a more propitious field for his venture.

We have not sought to impose uniformity on the contributors; the differences of style and approach seemed to us to add an extra appeal to the volume. Nor did we seek to make the book comprehensive, though we believe that not much of importance in the history of Brooks's has been omitted. This is a collection of casual though related essays – alike only in that they are well-written and well-informed. As such we think that it is appropriate to the Club itself.

Peter Fyson was Chairman of Brooks's when this book was conceived; Kenneth James when it was published; both of these, and John Ogden as Chairman of the Library Committee, supported the enterprise with enthusiasm and helped immeasurably to bring it to fruition. To them, and to the various Managers over the last two years, the editors owe a great debt of gratitude. We are as much indebted to the contributors, who found time in their often alarmingly overcrowded lives to do a considerable amount of research and writing with no reward beyond that of helping an institution to which they were all attached. Graham Rust, who provided the painting for the jacket, was quite as generous in his efforts. Georgina Stonor, through her knowledge of the Club's archives, was able to guide the various essayists to the most useful sources. Michael Roberts, Secretary of Brooks's, and his staff provided invaluable logistic support.

It remains only to thank Brooks's itself: for providing both a home-from-home in which all the contributors have constantly taken pleasure, and a subject worthy of their talents.

P.Z.   D.S.

PART I

The World of Brooks's

John Plumb

THE British population began to increase at a slow but steadily accelerating speed from the middle of the eighteenth century. Between 1690 and 1750 it had certainly grown a little, but not enough to have a significant effect on the age structure of the population or its prosperity. The reasons for this growth are complex – the age of marriage dropped, giving a larger period of child-bearing, while both overseas trade and the home market showed strong growth, though not continuous, for there was a bad depression in agriculture during the 1730s. Even so, Britain produced more food of greater variety than ever before. There were corn shortages and corn riots but, unlike Europe, no famines. The growing middle and upper-middle classes fed well and that protected lives. Inoculation, again amongst the upper classes rather than the population as a whole, did something to diminish the scourge of smallpox, and certainly the upper classes, and even the middle class, were less louse-ridden than their ancestors. And there were probably other profound, yet obscure, reasons at work, because Europe's population also grew, as indeed did China's.

The growth in Britain after 1750 was sufficient to affect the age structure of population too: more children were born; more children lived. Steadily the middle-aged and the old were outnumbered by the young. It was young men who founded Brooks's and the average age of members must have been much lower in the first decade of its existence than it has ever been since.

Even so, the population of Britain was small considering the size of the country. London, the largest city in Europe, was still close to the countryside. The outlying villages, Kensington, Chelsea, Marylebone, Islington, Newington, Bethnal Green and Wapping, were becoming linked to Westminster and the City, yet green fields, dairy farms and smallholdings for vegetable growers or just open spaces of common land were within easy reach of the City or the West End. Boswell in the 1760s, drunk with the wonder of London, usually walked wherever he was going, hence his need to have his shoes cleaned twice a day, an item of expenditure which he carefully budgeted for, even in his most desperate financial plights, for the streets were infamously filthy with mud and dung and clogged with wagons, hackney carriages and private coaches. Most founder members of Brooks's would sometimes have walked like Boswell or more often made use of a sedan chair with its four strong Irishmen, who could shout and bully the crowds and outdistance most carriages, even the hackneys.

Throughout the century, London expanded: squares, crescents, ovals, up they went, or terrace after terrace of plain, elegant, Georgian houses; everywhere there was a sense of movement, growth, prosperity, in spite of dreadful slums with their abject poverty and vicious diseases. Much of this hardship and destitution, however, was fading out of sight, for the great divide between East End and West End had begun, blocked by the City itself which slowly emptied of people as the century progressed. The pleasures of life were to be found in the West End – the theatres, the concert halls, the sparkling shops of Bond Street, above all the great houses of the nobility where entertaining never stopped; a little further on were the gardens of Vauxhall and Ranelagh where the whores, the pimps, the hucksters drew in, as did Hyde Park, the hopeful young bourgeois, hell bent on apeing their betters.

Dominating the west of London were the great institutions of government which essentially belonged to the landed aristocracy, the lawyers and the City financiers – the most important were the King's palaces, St. James's, Kensington, and in George III's day, Buckingham House: equally significant were Whitehall and Parliament near by and, not least, the Inns of Court – an irresistible world of power and money. The frenetic excitement of the young Boswell was not idiosyncratic except in its excess. In the third quarter of the eighteenth century euphoria amongst the upper-class young everywhere abounded. By 1776 their dazzling, beckoning world began to darken as the bickerings with the American colonies turned into a savage and cruel war; a war whose disastrous results brought the world to which Brooks's belonged into crisis, a world where the urbanity and easy compromises of Charles James Fox had to be brushed aside by the harsher patriotism of Pitt. The upper-class talk of reform took on the taint of treason.

Between 1760 and 1780, the time of Brooks's growth and formal establishment in St. James's Street, the voice of the young was becoming louder and more dominant but even louder and more visible was the young aristocracy. The Seven Years War against France, followed as it was by the war with America and the revolutionary turmoil in France, led to a great increase in both the Navy and Army and also the establishment of country militias. This coincided with an explosion in military uniforms, many exotic, some bordering on fantasy, all colourful – reds, whites, blues and buffs, plastered with gold braid, gold knots, gold epaulettes and from time to time bedecked with fur, especially on the head. For a time, the young rioted in their fancy dress and thoroughly enjoyed their parades at the Horse Guards or in Hyde Park, but soon it became chic at Brooks's to follow the fashion set by Beau Brummell, quiet colours, extremely elegantly cut, tailored close to the figure. Either way status was revealed – through clothing.

Although numerically the landed aristocracy had grown little by 1760, it had become richer; its assets were easily turned into credit as banks grew and mortgages became easier. As Horace Walpole wrote, everyone was 'into bricks and mortar' – looking back to Italy, to Palladio and beyond to Rome and Greece; they expressed their confidence in their world by building huge houses that might last to eternity. They moved hills, blocked rivers, dug lakes, created forests, snapped up trees, shrubs and flowers from China to Peru: a whole new garden culture grew up – explorers searched the globe. Kew, established for exotics by Frederick, Prince of Wales, created a rapid growth of nurserymen throughout the land, eager to develop and spread Kew's new wonders.

Excited by the aristocracy and landed gentry, the middle classes, full of passionate class emulation, became avid gardeners also. City merchants and their wives became as addicted to window boxes as East Berliners to house plants. At this period the landed classes were enclosing the common lands of their villages at an astonishing rate, changing the face of the countryside. On occasion, they shifted a village if it spoilt the vista and built a model replacement, often in the new bastard-cottage Gothic style. And their newly created landscapes provided innumerable architectural opportunities for temples, pagodas, grottoes, hermitages (with hermit) and artificial ruins. They knew that the future belonged to them. Until the guillotine began its labours, hardly a shadow darkened the beckoning future. After the French Revolution, the aristocratic future was haunted with democratic demons.

The young aristocratic men and women who created the fashions in art and architecture and its attendant decorative delights were a very small body of people. There were only about 180 aristocratic families in England in the 1760s, groups of them closely related because the British aristocracy, like its European counterparts, tended to be endogamous, and even when they married out, it was largely to rich heiresses with fortunes founded either in land, finance, or the law. Of course there were spectacular mis-matches: some due to an uncontrollable onrush of passion, like the Duke of Chandos's marriage with an innkeeper's daughter; others more mundane, such as Lord Carteret making an honest woman of his mistress of forty-three years standing; betwixt and between, Charles James Fox's marriage to Mrs Armistead. Most of the members of Brooks's married their own kind and kept within the circles of the rich and titled. The membership of Brooks's itself reflected the structure of aristocratic marriages – occasionally an outsider of great charm and distinction such as Sheridan was, not without difficulty, elected, but Sheridans were almost as rare in Brooks's as inn-keepers' daughters among duchesses. In 1780 Brooks's sported fifteen dukes. The founders of Brooks's were aristocratic, and they were of one generation. Although Charles Fox was incredibly young at sixteen, his swarthy complexion and coal-black chin made him look much older; the rest of the membership was about twenty-five; all were under thirty.

Their heavy drinking has been exaggerated – a study of the surviving wine bills for supper taken at Brooks's shows a relatively modest consumption – this is in line with the existing wine books of the seventeen-eighties of my college. Dons, according to Gibbon, were sodden with wine, and unscholarly social historians have dismissed them as a drunken lot. In fact they rarely drank a bottle a head, even during a long evening of cards or gossip. The same is true of Brooks's sessions at the gaming table: *pace* Rowlandson, they did not end in drunken incapacity.

Far more dangerous than heavy drinking was their uncleanliness – Chatsworth and Blenheim had a bathroom and maybe one or two other great houses had them too, but mostly the landed gentry and the aristocracy were content to wash their hands occasionally and sluice their faces. Linen and, increasingly, cotton shirts were changed often, sometimes twice a day; hence their wearers were less lousy than their ancestors, but they stank, as did the club. There were no water closets, only a cesspit that was baled out when it was full. Even though they did not have to endure the health hazards of their ancestors, they had enough – typhoid, typhus, appendicitis, consumption, etc., etc. All members of Brooks's experienced the death of brothers, sisters, friends to an extent we should find horrifying – and surely this must have heightened their lust for life and strengthened their obsession to enjoy all that life had to offer.

However, Brooks's as a health hazard did not compare with the world outside. There dung – human and animal – everywhere abounded. Chamber pots were emptied, the contents flung into the street. Every alley-way or convenient corner was befouled. There were local orders to prevent offal and waste being thrown into the street but they were harder to enforce than to make. Streets were not only filthy but full of traffic jams and incredibly noisy, probably worse than today. Few of the rich walked, except in Bond Street or St. James's Street where shopkeepers, eager to attract customers, kept their pavements clean – a habit which was steadily to grow as Brooks's matured. By the end of the century the West End was cleaner, better paved and better lit – vile maybe even by the depressing standard of today but getting better not worse.

London was not only filthy, it was a violent city with growing crime rates; violence was endemic, street fights commonplace. Youthful mobs paraded the streets and were often egged on by discontented journeymen, discharged sailors and demobilized soldiers to try through riots to better their lot. The mobs that yelped for 'Wilkes and Liberty' or burned breweries and opened prisons during the Gordon riots were the worst that London has ever known: terrible even for a society used to riots and violence. We think of the eighteenth century as a world of elegance and enlightenment but, in fact, it was a world of sadism and violence. Bear-baiting might have almost died out, but bull-baiting, dog fights, cock fights, bare-fisted boxing until the loser was knocked unconscious, were daily delights of a society that rushed to Tyburn in their thousands for the public hangings. By contrast the Sunday treat of viewing and jeering at the mad in Bedlam seems almost humane.

This world of violence and pain was in no way alien to the founder-members of Brooks's. Unless they had the good fortune to be educated at home by an easy-going parson-tutor, they had been regularly flogged at school by their seniors or their masters for the slightest breach of arcane etiquette. And many members knew about riot – Harrow and Eton were given to such excesses: boys shut in or expelled their masters; they sometimes barricaded their own quarters and caused general mayhem and destruction – rather like rioting prisoners today. As with violence, so with sex. Many young men became libertines at school. The public school habit of putting two boys together in a small bed (which only died out towards the end of the century) did not encourage chastity; and when they roamed the nearby fields and river banks, both the housemaids and the country girls were regarded as fair game for rough sport. Eighteenth-century society was a mixture of indulgence and intolerance, creating a sense of insecurity which was controlled by coded behaviour that enabled groups of young men to recognize each other as belonging to the same private world, to essentially the same tribe. It was not only dress that was important, but also formal and informal manners, shared attitudes to travel, schools, wives, lovers. Clubs satisfied a deep psychological need for rich young men, or for mature men for that matter.

Their shared education had been prolonged by the development of the Grand Tour which started in a low key in the seventeenth century. By 1730 the numbers going to Europe were increasing fast. Most young men went immediately after school, a few delayed by going to Oxford and Cambridge for a year or so, and some, especially the Scots, attended by their tutors and valets, even went to Leiden University before viewing the rest of Europe. Not all young aristocrats enjoyed a Grand Tour – younger brothers, the sickly, the mad, and of course all sisters, stayed at home – but by the 1760s it was almost unthinkable for a family of considerable social and political influence not to send its heir on the Grand Tour. Most went to France and Italy. A few, especially those with an eye to politics and diplomacy, took in Germany, especially the King's German dominions. Bolder parents, abetted by adventurous tutors, allowed their sons to push on to Russia in the north or from Italy to Greece and the Middle East. The Grand Tour was extremely expensive because the boy required a large entourage – a tutor always, and usually servants. The seriously rich either took their own coach or hired one at Calais: the merely rich went by post-chaise. Whenever they settled for a time they required valets: additional local tutoring was essential for fencing and dancing lessons and for language teaching. Often their travelling tutors were men of great distinction, so not cheap. One of the early members of Brooks's – the Duke of Buccleuch – took Adam Smith, the economist, as his tutor. The heir to the Earl of Pembroke, Lord Herbert, was under the tutorage of Archdeacon Coxe, one of the most important historians of late eighteenth-century Britain.

The regime imposed on Lord Herbert was a curious mixture of methodical and time-consuming activity spiced with licence. Lord Pembroke insisted on a rigorous time-table: detailed reports had to be sent to him on the first, tenth and thirtieth of every month: for every activity, whether it was mathematics, history, geography, French or dancing, riding the great horse, fencing or even billiards, the time employed had to be reported. Even the times of the boy's regular purges were laid down – camomile tea every morning before breakfast. Hair had to be cut every month on the second day of the full moon; young Lord Herbert was given a highly-regulated education. At the same time, Lord Pembroke expected, indeed encouraged, Herbert to lose his virginity and strongly recommended a young mistress of his own who, by repute, had grown into an attractive middle-aged lady. Herbert preferred, it seems, to plan his own *rite de passage*.

Fathers were alive to the risks of unsuitable marriages and, as modern parents fear drugs, they were terrified of gambling and excessive drink. Woe betide the tutor that let either get out of hand. Although fathers, tutors and sons constantly bickered about money, the young aristocrats were rarely short of credit if not cash. Besotted with Roman antiquities and Italian painting, they plundered the art market. Very few came back without crates of art – good, bad or indifferent: genuine or faked. Naturally the young men who, like Sir Francis Dashwood or William Weddell, had already inherited their estates, spent heavily, to the great advantage of Britain's heritage. Taste for the visual arts became the mark of a gentleman – not surprisingly one of the earliest clubs was the Society of Dilettanti.

A common education and the common personal experience that went with it were important factors in creating an attitude to life that stimulated young men to club together. But there were others. The social background of the founders of Brooks's was landed and aristocratic, as it was so to remain for members during most of its history: and in consequence, as with all classes, their leisure activities were another shared experience.

In Queen Anne's reign fox-hunting was largely a local pastime, organized by a local gentleman who bred the hounds for his friends and the neighbouring farmers, but by the time Brooks's was founded it had become more clearly defined and professionalized, with carefully-bred hounds and hunters. The shires were dominated by clubs such as the Quorn, the Cottesmore or the Meynell, patronized by young aristocrats, hard-drinking, hard-living, gamblers all, with a lust for danger. Shooting too had become more formalized and more exclusive, protected by game laws which had been enacted in Parliament by the grandfathers of Brooks's founders. And so, too, had horse-racing. The Jockey Club had established its authority over the sport, regulated its calendar and done its best to stamp out the grosser forms of corruption. All the grand classic races dated from the last decades of the century – Colonel St. Leger was a member of Brooks's and so, too, was Lord Derby. It became like cricket – sport organized by the aristocracy and landed gentry but whose audience was drawn from all classes.

Cricket flourished, as did horse-racing, because of the splendid opportunities it offered for gambling. Indeed, cricket provides an infinite variety of betting opportunities, more than any other sport invented by man. Gambling in eighteenth-century England amazed foreign travellers; its addicts ranged from the abject poor to the extravagantly rich. And, after all, it was, initially, the *raison d'être* of Brooks's. Gambling induced excitement to an intense degree – like motor racing or any other reckless activity – but Brooks's as a gambling house had this advantage: the money gambled went from one member's pocket into another's; at least, members were not being swindled by hustlers, bought jockeys or doped horses.

Gambling was in a sense in the family and some gentlemen were remarkably steady winners. When Lord Carlisle was building Castle Howard, about one-third of his income came from his steady winnings at the card table, just about meeting his costs. Few were as constantly lucky or clever as Carlisle but, equally, few experienced the wild roller-coaster existence of Fox at the gaming table. He lost and won over the years hundreds of thousands but, of course, on balance went down and down: so far down that his friends had to bail him out.

There was another reason for this reckless outburst of gambling: the rich were far richer than they had been in the seventeenth century and their cash flow less capricious, for there was a growing number of prosperous and well-established banks both in London and, increasingly, in the provinces, to give them credit or arrange a mortgage. One noble family after World War II was still paying off a mortgage first contracted in the 1790s (of course, frequently reserviced – like a Third World debt). In such a world the presence of Brooks's, with its high stakes and day-long and night-long sessions, was almost irresistible.

The world by the 1780s was becoming even more dominated by the young. That William Pitt should become Prime Minister at twenty-four was far less astonishing to his peers than to later generations. In many ways the last half of the eighteenth century exhibited a growing youth culture. This was true not only of Britain but of France too. The young relish the new and are full of enthusiasm not only for ideas but also, and alas, for ideologies. From 1760 to 1790 was a heady time for a young man to be alive – indeed, intoxicating.

The King was very young: George III was just twenty-two at his accession. He, too, wished to exert himself and was determined to get rid of his detested grandfather's ageing ministers. The King loathed his grandfather so much that he hated to spend a night in any palace George II had used. The King might work at St. James's but Buckingham House, as it was then, was where he slept – Kensington Palace and Hampton Court were taboo. Fortunately George II had scarcely used Windsor and

George III doted on Kew where his parents had lived. After years of planning he built a huge neo-Gothic palace, a testimony to his own and his parents' love for the place. Alas, Queen Victoria blew it up.

Although his court lacked brilliance and was short on style, at least it was delectably lively in comparison with George II's. Like his father Frederick, Prince of Wales, George III loved music; true, his taste was monotonous, Handel was his favourite composer. He took great delight in painting and founded the Royal Academy. He was the first monarch since Charles II to patronize the sciences, especially astronomy and botany. He was a compulsive book collector. This was the environment in which the Prince Regent, whose friends adorned Brooks's, grew up. Encouraged by the court, it was one of the most creative periods of British art and architecture – the quality of the art can be appreciated by glancing at the Dilettanti's superlative Reynoldses in the Subscription Room. Sitting there and looking across at Boodle's is one of the most pleasing vistas of eighteenth-century urban architecture.

The achievements of great painters and architects were a part of the physical world in which our founders grew up. There was a change in architecture during the formative period of Brooks's but not a fundamental one; the neo-classical appealed more to the young, but it was a change of key rather than a revolution. Fortunately the founder members of Brooks's were dead before the artistic horrors of the mid-nineteenth century could assail their sensitivities. The beginnings of Brooks's also witnessed the first and only time in which British painting, especially its portraiture, reached the quality of the French and the Italian even though it did not surpass it.

Although there was a great deal of common experience – and many common attitudes to life – amongst our founders, there was an area in which they became more bitterly divided than their immediate ancestors, namely politics, where the factions in the ruling classes became increasingly bitter. Again, it was partly the conflict of generations. In 1760, George II's ministers and some of the leading figures in opposition had been in and out of office since the fall of Sir Robert Walpole in 1742, and indeed some had held office throughout his career. Men such as the Duke of Newcastle had been at the heart of politics for well over forty years. They had enjoyed patronage as well as power, and so felt themselves to be as essential for the stability of the State as any *nomenklatura*. Their position was more vulnerable than they realized.

What followed the accession of George III was a crumbling of old strategies – and old alliances. Political issues, never absent from British life, became more strident: the peace treaty with France in 1763; the attacks on Wilkes over the publication of his famous, or infamous, No. 45 of *The North Briton*; followed by the outcry concerning the use of General Warrants, and the bleeding sore of the repeated elections for the County of Middlesex, when the government majority in the House of Commons overturned, time and time again, Wilkes's legitimate election to that seat in Parliament. These matters focused political debate, bred violence and became the concern of thousands of men and women outside formal politics.

Naturally the young at Brooks's who had a vested interest in the control of power, Fox and his friends, became passionately involved in day-to-day politics – the old Whig machine broke up, groups formed, coalesced, dissolved. It was the politics of issues, however, rather than the clash of fundamental ideologies that divided men, hence there was a great deal of slipping from one side to another, especially if the plum of patronage was large enough to ease the conscience. Even Fox, in 1783, found himself with Lord North as a bedfellow. There emerged, however, a radical group of Whigs of which Fox was the acknowledged leader – many of whom were members of Brooks's – who, reluctantly maybe, accepted the Independence of America; who wished to reform not only the Court with its antiquated Civil List, but also the House of Commons itself; who detested the slave trade which Fox, as an old man, brought to an end; and who welcomed the early, optimistic days of the French Revolution, even though later they were sickened by the Terror. This group had a very important effect on the image that Brooks's was to maintain over the generations, that of old-fashioned Whiggism which believed in constitutional monarchy, in strengthening the powers of the House of Commons, and in modest extensions of the electorate, yet rarely, if ever, departed from its conservative convictions.

Charles James Fox was not a good politician: he did not pursue power or principle with single-minded dedication. Nor did he have the luck that all politicians need: his luck in politics proved as capricious as at cards.

And yet when members of Parliament knew that Fox was to speak they crowded into the Chamber. What Fox could do, as no other of his generation, was to clothe in magnificent rhetoric the convictions which sprang from the warmth and generosity of his own heart. He could stir the most sluggish of his supporters and sow seeds of doubt even in those most bitterly prejudiced against his principles. Pervading all of his speeches was a sense of magnanimity. Perhaps that was the secret of his greatness, both in private and public: quickly responsive, warm-hearted to a fault, generous. The virtues of Fox were rare in politics and uncommon in life. In Brooks's, at least, Fox found some congenial spirits and so strong was his personality that memories of Fox have given Brooks's much of its own individuality – the open-mindedness of old Whiggery based on unshakeable constitutional principles.

The Birth of Brooks's

John Jolliffe

S URPRISING though it may seem, Brooks's was not born at Brooks's. The Club takes its name from William Brooks, one of the managers employed by William Almack to run his establishment at 49 Pall Mall, who broke away in 1778, taking with him all the members of Almack's (the Macaronis) who were willing to follow him. Almack himself had opened his doors fourteen years earlier, in 1764, and the Club acquired its name when it moved, with Brooks, to the building which he commissioned Henry Holland to design, and which has been its home ever since. Another of Almack's managers, Edward Boodle, followed suit four years later and established the club which faces Brooks's across St. James's to this day.

Like the members themselves, Henry Holland had started young. At the age of twenty-six, with the help of his father, who owned property in Fulham and Kensington, he had leased from Lord Cadogan eighty-nine acres of land between Knightsbridge and the Thames, and he proceeded to develop in particular what is now Sloane Street and Cadogan Place. Brooks's was not only a plum job in itself, but it put him in touch with patrons who later gave him enormous commissions. These ranged from Carlton House and the Brighton Pavilion for the Prince of Wales, to the remodelling of Althorp for Lord Spencer, and much work for the young Duke of Bedford both in Bloomsbury and at Woburn. Especially at the latter, Holland developed a number of architectural trends from France; and his biographer Dorothy Stroud tells us that his interest in that direction was stimulated by the general sympathy with French ideas and ideals which was to be found among the early members of Brooks's in their more lucid moments, especially after the Treaty of Versailles in 1793. His marriage to the daughter of Capability Brown gave him further useful contacts in the world of Brooks's. His work was later echoed elsewhere, and so it may be said to have been at least partly through Brooks's that he achieved such a significant influence on domestic architecture on the grand scale in England in the last quarter of the eighteenth century.

Brooks began his career as a valet, and when his employer was overwhelmed by debt and was considering retiring to Boulogne, Brooks told him he need do nothing of the kind: 'The fact is, having put by a little money, and seeing what was likely to happen, I found an opportunity of buying up your lordship's debts. I have therefore the happiness, at this moment, to be your lordship's only creditor.' 'Brooks, you should go into the House of Commons,' came the reply. 'I will put one of my boroughs at your disposal.' Brooks's reaction was worthy of Jeeves at his loftiest. 'Thank you, my lord, but the opportunities you have given me will avail me to serve you better by a club.'

James Hare, who had been proposed at Almack's by Charles James Fox in 1771, wrote at the time of the move that 'Brooks opens his new house and invites all or as many as Please to come from the Club in Pall Mall. Almack desires us to stay but as there can be no reason for preferring a bad old house to a good new one, I imagine Brooks will be victorious'. Hare was typical of the founders, a Member of Parliament for twenty-five years, and Ambassador at Warsaw between 1779 and 1782, who lost a fortune at gambling.

When the original twenty-seven Macaronis had banded together, their average age was twenty-five. They elected a further 141 members before the end of 1764, and by the time of the move the numbers had increased to 333. The popular image of Brooks's in its early days is of a gambling hell on an astronomical scale. This was indeed one aspect of the lives of some of the members, and being lurid and sensational it is the most widely known. One of the best stories in this particular field is recorded of a Mr Thynne, probably the brother of the third Viscount Weymouth, who was a founder member. According to the club records, 'having won only £12,000 during the last two months, he retired in disgust March 21 1772; and that he may never return is the ardent wish of members.' The gambling was also to the great disadvantage of Brooks himself, who could not resist the pleas of some members to advance them money to pay their debts. He was not always repaid or well treated, and he died only four years later a relatively poor man. Horace Walpole commented that 'the gaming is worthy of the decline of our Empire.' But many of the members occupied themselves in a more worthwhile fashion as well, or instead. Who were they, and how did they spend their days?

The original twenty-seven included the Duke of Portland, who became Lord Lieutenant of Ireland in 1782, and formed a government in the following year. It lasted only a few months, but he became Prime Minister again from 1807 to 1809. There was also the Duke of Roxburghe, who found it necessary to sell his library in 1812 for £23,000, giving rise to the foundation of the Roxburghe Club, for which the qualification was the ownership of a significant collection of books. There was Sir George Macartney, who led an embassy to Pekin in 1792 and brought back many Oriental curiosities, among them a collection of plants including what came to be called the Macartney Rose. There was the Duke of Gordon, afterwards Lord Keeper of Scotland, and his younger brother Lord William; and Lord Tavistock, eldest son of the Duke of Bedford, who died after a hunting accident three years later. There were five other future peers of lesser account, and five future members of the House of Commons. The rest were gentlemen about whom nothing of interest is known, with the exception of the super-eccentric Squire Mytton, of Pontyscownyd, whose wild practical jokes and escapades of many kinds were eventually immortalized by Edith Sitwell in *English Eccentrics*.

Describing Brooks's as 'the most famous political club that will ever have existed in England', Sir George Otto Trevelyan adds that it was not political in origin: 'The Duke of Grafton and Lord Weymouth are shown side by side with the Dukes of Portland and Richmond'. Fox, who was elected in the second year of the Club's existence, fifteen years later proposed his arch political rival, the younger William Pitt, whose principal haunt was White's. One of the first rules of the Club, which shows what store it set by *esprit de corps*, was that any member who joined any other club, with the exception of White's, was struck off from Brooks's. As regards the domestic arrangements, dinner was served from half-past four till seven, when the bill was brought in; and supper was available from eleven till half-past midnight. Anyone present during any part of the 'meal hours' paid his share of the total of wine consumed. Dinner itself cost eight shillings, and supper six. The annual subscription was initially four guineas, raised to eight in 1779, the year after the move. The ballot for election was held between 11 p.m. and 1 a.m., and one blackball excluded.

Of the early members, those who were not among the original twenty-seven, but who were elected before the end of 1764, included some notable and distinguished characters. The third Duke of Richmond, who succeeded his father at the age of fifteen, was a good example of a grandee who in early life was a strong reformer but like many others was appalled by the Terror and swung back to a position of strong opposition to the original generous spirit of the French Revolution. A great-grandson of Charles II, and therefore fourth cousin of Louis XV, he was sent as ambassador to Paris aged thirty in 1765, the year after joining Brooks's, having served at the Battle of Minden six years earlier. On the outbreak of the War of Independence he declared that 'the resistance of the American colonists was neither treason nor rebellion, but perfectly justifiable in every possible political and moral sense'. On the other hand, he was later reminded in the House of Lords by the first Lord Thurlow, the Lord Chancellor, whom he had taunted with low birth, that he, Richmond, owed his seat there to 'being the accident of an accident'. His sister was Charles Fox's mother, and George III is reported to have said of him that 'there was no man by whom he had been so much offended and no man to whom he was so much indebted'. At the age of twenty-four he opened a free school of painting and sculpture, with Cipriani and Joseph Wilton as teachers. Horace Walpole described him as 'intrepid and tender, inflexible and human, beyond example'; and in many ways he epitomizes the generous, cultivated and open-hearted side of the spirit of Brooks's. It is a tribute to the club in its earliest days that Horace Walpole himself, who was by no means hard up for access to a lively social life, became a member, at the age of forty-seven, along with two of Doctor Johnson's greatest friends, frequently mentioned by Boswell, in the shape of Mr Bennet Langton and Mr Topham Beauclerk. Four years younger than Richmond, but elected in the same year, 1764, was another patron of the arts, the second Lord Palmerston, father of the future Prime Minister. He was a pall-bearer at the funerals of both Garrick and Reynolds, and the latter gave him in his will 'second choice of any picture painted by him'.

To turn to the world of military and colonial command, almost none of the original members went through more dramatic adventures than another older man, General Lord Pigot, who was forty-five when the club was founded, and had by then already served as Governor of Madras for eight years. In 1775 he was again appointed Governor and returned to Madras to find that the Rajah of Tanjore, with whom he had made a treaty during his previous term of office, had meanwhile been officially robbed of his territories, which had been transferred to the Nabob of Arcot. Violently resentful of this betrayal of his treaty, Pigot was kept under house arrest by the new authorities, and guarded by a battery of artillery. The Court of the East India Company eventually decided to restore him to office but first to recall him and all the members of the Council in Madras for a full inquiry in London. But before this could happen, Pigot died in captivity, and at his inquest the jury recorded a verdict of murder against all who had been concerned in his arrest, four of whom were later fined £1,000 each. Among other distinctions the Governor had acquired the Pigot Diamond, which was sold after his death and later bought by Ali Pasha for the vast sum of £30,000. On being mortally wounded in 1822 he ordered that to prevent its falling into the hands of his enemies it should be crushed to powder in his presence, 'which was done'. The unfortunate Pigot died in 1777, and therefore never had the pleasure of setting foot in the new Brooks's. But his fiery attachment to principle, and contempt for personal danger, are again characteristic of many of the early members.

The other famous soldier who joined in the first year was a man who is often held up to ridicule and censure for his surrender at Yorktown. But Lord Cornwallis had little option in circumstances that were largely outside his control. He later had the distinction of resigning as Viceroy of Ireland in 1801 when the King refused to grant Catholic Emancipation, for fear, as he put it, of handing Ireland over to the House of Savoy. Four years later, Cornwallis was sent to India to try to conclude a lasting peace with the native rulers, but died later in the same year at Ghazipore. Then as now, funeral panegyrics need to be taken with a pinch of salt, but there is much truth in the words of Dean Milman of St. Paul's, when the memorial to Cornwallis was put up there. 'As Lord Lieutenant of Ireland, of Ireland in her most critical days, he alone stood above the base means used to achieve that necessary work, the Union. Amid the wide wreck of honour, he was still the soul of honour.' The Dean added that 'he strove to rule India not as a conquered country, but as a province of our empire; for the benefit of our subjects, as for the interests of their masters. . . . He laboured with primitive wisdom to repress the dominant grasping rapacity and insolent contempt of our native subjects.' Not altogether the words in which such a tribute would be paid today, but the message is clear, and if not the whole truth, is perhaps not entirely misleading.

General Burgoyne, whose defeat and surrender of the British Army at Saratoga was reckoned by Sir Edward Creasy to be among the fifteen Decisive Battles of the World, was another member elected in 1764. He had the courage to denounce Clive in Parliament in 1773, and to be one of the Managers of the Impeachment of Warren Hastings in 1789. There were other members with more conventional rural interests, such as Sir Charles Bunbury, the 'Father of the Turf' and founder of the Jockey Club, who tossed a coin with Lord Derby to decide which of their names should be given to the race which they were planning to establish, and had his revenge by winning the first running of it with Diomed in 1780. And there was the formidable Colonel Peter Beckford, MP for Hexham and the author of a famous treatise on hunting.

Brooks's was never a doctrinaire institution, though most of the members who took any part in politics, which included almost all the landowning element in the club, were to some degree or other in opposition to the King's party, and therefore attached willy-nilly to the Prince of Wales. Many of them may not have been entirely admirable characters, but, as has been seen, they mostly had an element of courage and independence in their natures, even if it sometimes ran to seed in profligacy, and they were unwilling to toe the line set by what might be regarded as the establishment of the day. The ways in which they put their principles into practice has often aroused derision, and the next chapters will show some striking anomalies. But for the century and a half following the birth of the Club, they continued, in varying degrees, in the same vein, allowing for the great changes in the times. The loyalty to Brooks's of a few leading families – Russells, Cavendishes, Howards,

Ponsonbys, Vernons, Spencers, Whitbreads – provided a core round which there grew up a largely civilized but always loosely co-ordinated circle, echoes of whose tolerance, good humour and goodwill survive there to this day.

Charles James Fox (1749–1806), the 'patron saint' of Brooks's. He wears the Whig colours of blue and buff, inspired by the uniform of George Washington's Continental Army. From a miniature after Opie at Brooks's

Brooks's as designed by Henry Holland in 1776, showing a version of its original portico

The Brooks's of Charles James Fox

Richard Ollard

THE Brooks's of Charles Fox is a tautology. If the Club is held to be more than the material entity of its bricks and mortar, its books and pictures, its wine and its furniture, its not inconsiderable value as a piece of real estate ripe for redevelopment as one of those charming office blocks with which we are so familiar, it is surely the personality, the image, the myth, dare one say the cult, of Charles Fox that best defines it. The Brooks's of Charles Fox is Brooks's *tout court*.

I am here speaking of spiritual truths spiritually discerned. While not agreeing with a senior member, now no longer with us, who described the Club as having become like London Airport, one does see that the membership in its numbers, its conversation, its habits, its antecedents is easily distinguished from that to which Charles Fox was elected a year after the formal constitution of the Club in 1764. That body was almost excessively ducal: and those who were not dukes were members of the landed aristocracy. It was Charles Fox himself who perhaps opened and certainly widened the chink in the curtain wall of lineage through which so many of us have entered.

For Fox whom we are accustomed to see in paintings, in sculpture, and in the memoirs and histories of his time as the personification of Whig aristocracy was not, in his family origins, either a Whig or an aristocrat. The founder of the family, his grandfather Sir Stephen Fox, had begun life as a choirboy at Salisbury Cathedral. Entering the Royal Household by way of the Stewards Room he had caught the eye of the Earl of Clarendon, then Sir Edward Hyde, as the one man who could manage the desperate domestic finances of the exiled court of Charles II in the 1650s.

After the Restoration place and promotion followed. Wisely Sir Stephen avoided the dangerous limelight of politics in that violent age. He retained, however, his eye for a balance sheet and employed it, naturally enough, in his own as well as his master's interests. Finding himself in his late seventies without a male heir to his fortune (his seven sons and the wife who bore them had predeceased him) he boldly married a lady some fifty years his junior and fathered a further two sons and two daughters. The elder son, Stephen, married the heiress of the great West Country Cavalier family of Strangways and became Earl of Ilchester. The younger, Henry, made a runaway marriage with Lady Caroline Lennox, daughter of the Duke of Richmond and granddaughter by the Duchess of Portsmouth of Charles II. The second son of this romantic union was christened Charles James, the clearest proclamation of his antecedents in that Stuart absolutism against which he was later to fulminate.

Henry Fox, it may safely be asserted, set no store by the political idealism for which his son was to be so widely admired. But he did inherit his father's appetite for public money without the older man's extraordinary talent for acquiring it without making enemies or even attracting unfavourable notice. No politician of the century has left so universal a reputation for single-minded avarice as Charles Fox's father. So cheerful a buccaneer generally wins a degree of grudging admiration for getting away with it. But even in the works of Whig hagiography such as Sir George Otto Trevelyan's *Early History of Charles James Fox* Henry Fox is given short shrift. The only undoubted merit allowed him is in his domestic affections. He was an adoring and faithful husband throughout a long marriage and a loving if too indulgent father.

His indulgence comes in handy for his son's hagiographers. To this can be ascribed the disorderly life, the financial irresponsibility, the tactical readiness to abandon principles – or at least to disavow what had appeared to be principles up to the day before yesterday – that have to be explained away if this great Parliamentarian is to take the high place assigned to him in the Whig pantheon. It certainly explains the reputation that he earned at Eton as introducing habits of luxury and expense. Eighteenth-century fathers were not inclined to liberality towards adolescents. Actually to encourage them in habits of conspicuous consumption as Henry Fox did, even in drinking and womanizing, was unheard of. That Charles Fox should have been elected at the age of sixteen to Brooks's where playing high and drinking deep were the main if not the sole occupations, was altogether consistent with his father's scheme of upbringing. It says much for Charles Fox's character and his good taste that he was not coarsened or besotted by the formidable excesses that, thanks to this bizarre youth-training scheme, became habitual to him. Henry Fox had done all he could to spoil his brilliant and attractive son and had not succeeded. On the credit side he had provided a background of family affection then uncommon in the upbringing of rich children, perhaps the most valuable and appropriate gift to one whose tenderness of heart seems always to have amazed the smart, sceptical, supercilious world in which he moved. Twenty years later Gibbon, by then himself a member of Brooks's, crystallized this recognition of 'the powers of a superior man, as they are blended in his attractive character with the softness and simplicity of a child. Perhaps no human being was ever more perfectly exempt from the taint of malevolence, vanity or falsehood.'

It is in this geniality, this unaffected, unpatronizing spirit of welcome, that Charles Fox personified all that is most agreeable in Brooks's. Its most eminent reflection in my day was the beaming countenance of Newman, for many years Hall Porter. But hardly less conspicuous a representative of it was the elegant figure of Sir John Wheeler-Bennett, forever seated on the sofa below the stairs over which Charles Fox presides from the *piano nobile*, forever wearing a carnation in his buttonhole, forever cheerful and warming.

It may be remarked in passing that Fox at no period in his life, even in his foppish youth, achieved such neatness. From the outbreak of the American War of Independence he habitually wore a blue coat and a buff waistcoat, the colours of George Washington's Continental Army, which, by this adoption, became the colours of the Whig party. In the winter of 1777, the great question at Brooks's was 'Have you heard the good news from Saratoga?' where General Burgoyne (a member) had surrendered to the Americans in October.

But we must return to our sources. Gibbon, though by no means averse to the pleasures of the town, cannot but raise the intellectual tone of any institution with which he is associated, except by his own account the

University of Oxford to which he was introduced at as absurd an age as that at which Fox entered Brooks's. Fox was not his proposer but it can hardly be doubted that his support was whole-hearted and that at this time (1776) he had become the moving spirit of the Club. Garrick had been elected in 1773, Sheridan was to follow in 1780, Burke in 1783, Sir Joshua Reynolds in 1785. All these were members of that distinguished body centred on Dr Johnson to which Fox himself had been elected in 1774. Known absolutely and without qualification as The Club, it had been founded in the same year as Brooks's on principles of unashamed literary and artistic élitism. To this the deepest springs of Fox's nature responded. His love of literature, especially of poetry, was his ruling passion. It had begun earlier than his addiction to gambling and was to last longer than his preoccupation with politics. Its strength triumphed over the slovenliness and disorder of his habits of life. 'I am a very painstaking man.' Such an avowal from the bulging roué of the portraits seems almost ridiculous. But it is true. He read the ancient authors with a sensibility that sometimes moved him to tears but he read them with a scholarship that commanded the respect of his learned correspondents. His appetite, his range, was enormous. French, Spanish and Italian authors from the Renaissance to his own day, English literature of every age down to the early Wordsworth for whom he did not much care enriched a diet of which Horace, Homer, Virgil and Euripides were the staple.

He was not alone in such tastes. Even among the founding Dukes was that greatest of bibliophiles whose name is commemorated by the Roxburghe Club. But one can hardly imagine the enthusiasts for faro and hazard electing the great antiquary and numismatist Richard Payne Knight until Fox had reconciled them to the company of cultivated men who were not also great nobles. With Fox as his proposer he became a member in 1788.

The greatest of all the members proposed by Fox and elected in 1781 was the young man who was to outplay him for stakes even higher than the fortunes he lost in the Great Subscription Room. Pitt now faces him across the hall above the chat and the comings and goings of our less Olympian age, as he so often faced him across the jeers and catcalls of St. Stephen's. A less brilliant debater than Fox, Pitt did not come behind him in felicity of expression or in love and knowledge of the ancient authors. Like many of his contemporaries in the Club he also belonged to Boodle's and to White's, the last of which he seems to have preferred. Indeed there is a disgraceful story of an attack on his coach as it was making a triumphant progress up St. James's. Just as it came level with Brooks's, roughs armed with bludgeons and broken poles smashed up the coach and hurt the servants. Pitt himself and his brother, who was with him, were with difficulty got into the safety of White's. Several members of Brooks's were seen to be among the attacking party. In a violent age when duelling was generally approved of and excess in drink not found disgusting, such incidents are hardly surprising. But it is easy to understand why Pitt found the clubs on the other side of St. James's more congenial. Fox we may be sure was not party to this hooliganism. Although he fought several duels, he was never the challenger and personal animosity towards political opponents or rivals was not in character, except in the case of Shelburne.

Yet though Pitt was only nominally a member of the Brooks's of Charles Fox, the fact that he was even that is perhaps worth stressing. Their fathers had been bitter political enemies struggling for power. Charles's proposal of William was a civilized departure from an unedifying past and a generous recognition of extraordinary quality. Their reputation as speakers is to a great extent mediated to us by a select few of those who listened to them. Neither of them has left a substantial prose legacy, as Burke has. Pitt indeed never so far as we know considered abandoning politics for literature as Fox certainly did from about 1797. Even then he placed oratory, the art in which he had reached the front rank, third behind poetry and history.

It was history that he resolved to write, a history of the Revolution of 1688. The subject was congenial enough and his own close family connections with Charles II and James II might have been thought to equip him with insights into the principal characters. The Duchess of Portsmouth had lived on till 1734, a mere fifteen years before his own birth. His mother had been taken to see her in France and had found her perfectly in possession of all her faculties. Fox's deceptive habits of intellectual industry – 'I am a very painstaking man' – were admirably suited to historical research. He used the Peace of Amiens to work in the

French archives, transcribing the dispatches of Barillon, Louis XIV's ambassador in London. His readiness of language would, one might have thought, make composition easy to him. But those who have not tried it little know how daunting a blank sheet of paper can be. Fox wrote his history, as one of his friends said, 'drop by drop'. At his death there were only a couple of introductory chapters which his favourite nephew Lord Holland published in 1808 under the title of *A History of the Early Part of the Reign of King James II*. Such a minute area of investigation suggests a sort of Regency version of a Ph.D. thesis. The whole reign, after all, did not last four years. But those who turn to this work for thoroughness of analysis or exactitude of judgement will be disappointed. His own royal ancestors are characterized, if that be the word, in phrases such as 'the levity of Charles the First and the mercenary meanness of the last two Princes of the House of Stuart'. Monck, the crucial figure in stopping the merry-go-round of governments in 1659–60, was, we are told, a man 'than whom a baser could not be found in its [the Army's] lowest ranks. Personal courage appears to have been Monck's only virtue.' The brass-band fortissimi of Whig historiography drown curiosity and interest. And there is more than a hint of a complacent self-portrait in the terms in which Sir William Temple is praised for his withdrawal from public life:

> The remainder of his life he seems to have employed in the most noble contemplations and the most elegant amusements; every enjoyment heightened, no doubt, by reflecting on the honourable part he had acted in publick affairs and without any regret on his own account (whatever he might feel for his country) at having been driven from them.

This is, we may suppose, Fox at St. Ann's Hill, coming seldom to Brooks's and seldomer to the House of Commons.

Lord Holland, himself elected to the club in 1794, has sketched an attractive picture of his uncle's life there at that time. 'His studies were not directed to any particular object. Such was the happy disposition of his mind that his own reflections, whether supplied by conversation, desultory reading or the common occurrences of a life in the country were always sufficient to call forth the vigour and exertion of his faculties . . .

How various his employments whom the world
Calls idle!

was an accurate description of the life he was then leading.'

The benign, large-minded, infinitely good-natured image of the great libertarian at sunset is convincing. But there were other elements in his mentality that must have made it easier for him to enjoy the confidence and popularity of his fellow members of thirty years earlier. The apostle of free speech had successfully moved the prosecution of a journalist on the grounds that his article constituted a libel 'on the aera of the glorious Revolution'. The thought-police are not less the thought-police for being controlled by persons professing liberal sentiments. There is no getting away from the fact that Fox was a thorough-going partisan. Even as late as the halcyon time described by his nephew he was still capable in his history of denouncing the wickedness of the political witch-hunts of the Popish Plot without admitting any degree of Whig responsibility for this ugly conspiracy. It is not that he feels any intellectual repugnance at passing judgements. They are thick on the page and thick in the colours in which they are laid on.

Fox's first employment at the outset of what everyone foresaw as a brilliant ministerial career was as a Junior Lord of the Admiralty. The naval connections of the Club were throughout his time considerable. Captain Augustus Hervey, elected in 1764, had been brought up as a friend of the Foxes. His mother, the famous beauty Molly Lepell, remained all her life on affectionate terms with Charles's father. But Augustus, who had commanded a ship of the line under Byng at the battle which resulted in the loss of Minorca, had been honourably outspoken in his defence of his chief and critical of the administration that sought to make him the scapegoat for their own misjudgements. He had written privately to Henry Fox, then Secretary of State, and had been revolted by the unscrupulous determination of the ministry to save its own skin by refusing clemency to an officer they had placed in an all but impossible position. He never forgave Henry Fox. His own career was by no means confined to salt water. The energy of his amours was remarkable even by the standards of his fellow members. But where he stands alone in the annals of the Club is in having been bigamously married to the same lady as another member, the Duke of Kingston, also elected in 1764. The scandal, which led ultimately to a trial, was on the larger-than-life scale that was part of his personal style. A year before the Battle of Mahon he had given passage to a couple of tigers in his ship, a present from the Bey of Tunis to the Emperor.

A far more distinguished sea officer in the intake of 1764 was George Brydges Rodney. A much older man than Charles Fox (the exact date of his birth is uncertain but he was baptized in 1718) their paths were to cross at points important to both of them. It is difficult to believe that they had much in common except for a spectacular talent for mismanaging their personal finances. Both men had frequent cause to bless the immunity from imprisonment for debt that was then one of the privileges of membership of Parliament. But Sir George was so unfortunate as to lose his seat at a point when his affairs were, in spite of outstanding professional success, at a very low ebb. He was driven to take refuge in France where, to his consternation, he became aware of the imminent outbreak of war in the spring of 1778. The story of the chivalrous intervention of Marshal the Duke of Biron is well known. He told Sir George's friends 'that he heard my stay in Paris was occasioned by the want of a remittance to discharge the Debts I must necessarily have contracted. That his purse was at my service, and begg'd that I would make use of it, that whatever sums, even to two thousand pounds might be necessary, he would immediately pay . . .'

This is Rodney's own account of an instance of that *vrai douceur de vivre* that Talleyrand praised more eloquently than he exemplified. The Biron family tradition has the old Marshal – he had been severely wounded at Dettingen thirty-five years earlier – driving to Versailles to ask Louis XVI's permission to release this formidable potential enemy from his embarrassments. '*Je vous envie d'avoir eu cette idée,*' the monarch is said to have replied, '*elle est française et digne de vous.*' Whatever be the truth of this inspiring scene it seems probable that it was Biron's nephew, the Duke of Lauzun, himself elected a member of Brooks's in 1783 the minute the war was over, who drew Rodney's plight to his uncle's attention. Lauzun had been in London till the approach of hostilities recalled him to his regiment with which he was to serve in America. With the Duke of Orleans (*Philippe Egalité*) he was one of the two members of Brooks's to be guillotined in the Revolution, so joyfully hailed by Charles Fox and so presciently characterized by Burke.

Once back in England Rodney was secured from arrest by the granting of lodgings in Cleveland Row within the royal penumbra of St. James's Palace. Money was raised – no one knows how – to pay the debt of honour to Marshal Biron, and the note of hand with Rodney's signature vigorously scratched out by his benefactor still survives. It was not until October 1779 that a suitable command could be found for so senior an officer. Once again he could re-enter Brooks's. But in December he had gone on board his flagship at Spithead and on Christmas Eve when the wind at last came fair he sailed down Channel, charged in the first place with the relief of Gibraltar, where the garrison was reduced to a diet of thistles and dandelions, and then to fly his flag as Commander-in-Chief in the West Indies. His brilliant success was the first in a war of failures periodically heightened by disaster. The vigorous security which he had enforced not only enabled him to relieve Gibraltar without the enemy having guessed the destination of the large convoy of supply ships he was escorting. It also enabled him to pick up a large Spanish convoy, to capture its powerful escort and to destroy a great part of the fleet that was carrying on the blockade.

The huzzas of his countrymen were not echoed in his club. Fox's friends there included the newly elected Keppel, till that summer Commander-in-Chief of the Channel Fleet and a Commissioner of the Admiralty, and Pigot, an admiral who shared with Fox the splendours and miseries of the faro table but had not so far hoisted his flag at sea. All of them pursued Lord Sandwich's conduct of Admiralty affairs with a virulence that was not abated by the mastery and vigour displayed in these operations. Keppel, indeed, whose relations with Rodney had had their ups and downs, sent him a private letter of congratulation. The government for its part was anxious to make political capital out of Sir George's initial victories and his continuing success in holding a much superior force at bay in the West Indies. Sir George himself was eager to resume his parliamentary career. 'A man in our country is nothing without being in Parliament,' he had written to his wife. But no doubt the reinsurance against the bailiff's men of the prize money and pensions that were now on the horizon was an even more powerful consideration. In the general election of October 1780 he was returned together with, but ahead of, Fox for Westminster, the constituency that came nearest in the unreformed House of Commons to a popular franchise.

But no temporary access of popularity could save the government from the consequences of its political and military blunders in America. The surrender at Yorktown was the real end of the road though it was not till March 1782 that Lord North resigned and George III was forced to swallow the pill of Fox taking office. Keppel came in with him as First Lord and on 2 May had the unenviable task of writing to Rodney to tell him that he was to be summarily relieved of his command by Charles Fox's crony Admiral Pigot. This act of factious irresponsibility was swiftly to be shown up for what it was. Three weeks earlier Rodney had won the great victory of The Saints (so called after the Saintes passage between Dominica and a group of islets known as *les îles saintes*), capturing the French flagship and accepting the surrender of the Commander-in-Chief. In the opinion of Sir Samuel Hood, Rodney's second in command, the victory, great as it was, could have been annihilating had the Commander-in-Chief not been so childishly delighted at entertaining de Grasse in his stern gallery as to call off the pursuit of the routed enemy. But there was no doubting the resounding and timely effect of this unlooked for success.

News of it reached the Admiralty at 2 a.m. on 18 May. Keppel had read the despatches by eight, and after writing to Lady Rodney and informing the King his first concern was to cancel the hero's recall. He and his colleagues hurriedly sent off a King's Messenger to Plymouth to stop Pigot from sailing. The man made good time – twenty-eight hours. But unluckily for the ministers, Pigot had sailed at the very moment that the messenger had been galloping out of London. A fast cutter was sent after Pigot's ship but failed to catch her. There was nothing for it but to let events take their course. The greatest naval victory ever won by a member of Brooks's was to be a grave embarrassment to its political patron saint.

Rodney's despatch was immediately published in the *Gazette* and the thanks of both Houses voted at once. Keppel moved them in the Lords and was seconded by the arch-enemy of Fox and his friends, the fourth Earl of Sandwich, who took the opportunity of asking if there were any truth in the rumours of Rodney's recall. Connoisseurs of ministerial evasion will savour Keppel's reply: 'What was thrown out by the noble Earl on that head proceeded from the vague report and fable of the day. There was no official evidence of the existence of such a thing before the House, and it was therefore improper to dwell upon it.'

Pigot's inadequacy to his position has been pithily described by Hood, who remained as second-in-command. He had had no experience as a flag officer and precious little as a captain. His contribution to the service was crowned by taking out with him his young son Hugh, who rose to be a Captain notorious for his cruelty and was ultimately murdered in the most grisly of all naval mutinies, that aboard the *Hermione*. The Admiral himself was not re-employed and returned, one presumes, to the pleasures of Brooks's, to which by 1785 Lord Sandwich had been elected on renouncing political life. Rodney secured a peerage and managed through the efforts of his son to maintain a precarious solvency. Charles Fox once again resigned office, this time because he could not endure serving with Shelburne, and Brooks's gained what the government lost. It was a cheerful, intemperate, selfish, good-natured place. But it was by no means the temple of political virtues and Charles Fox would surely have been the first to laugh at being cast as its Sarastro.

Brooks's of the Reform Bill

Philip Ziegler

THE 1830s saw the apotheosis of Brooks's as a political club. Lord Clarendon grumbled in 1841 that one might as well go to Brooks's as to a meeting of the Cabinet for all the difference there was between them. He had become a member of the government in 1840 and joined Brooks's the following year. Whether he made his disapproving comment before or after he joined the Club is uncertain; if the former then it presumably shows that while he disliked doing business at Brooks's, he found it still more unsatisfactory to be excluded from such deliberations.

It had not been always so. After the brief-lived and misnamed Ministry of All the Talents in March 1807 the Whigs spent twenty years in opposition. Supporters of, let alone members of the Portland, Perceval and Liverpool administrations rarely joined Brooks's, and even if, for family connections or other reasons, they did belong, their attendance was rare. It was unlikely that they would meet with overt hostility – but the atmosphere was not congenial. There was no rule stating that a member of Brooks's had to be a Whig and some of them had little interest in politics, but the prevailing spirit was so strongly supportive of the opposition, that only the most insensitive Tory would not have felt ill-at-ease within its portals.

If the Church of England was later said to be the Tory party at prayer, Brooks's was the Whig party at dinner or the gambling tables. It is remarkable how in the first half of the nineteenth century the name of Brooks's was used by diarists and letter-writers as being almost synonymous with Whiggery; if Greville or Creevey remarked that

Brooks's felt this or were indignant about that, they recognized no distinction between an impression formed in the club itself or gleaned in the Palace of Westminster, or Lansdowne or Devonshire House. Party meetings were more likely to occur in the houses of the senior Whigs than in Brooks's, but twice in the 1820s formal meetings were held in the club and by the end of the Napoleonic Wars dinners regularly took place there at the start of every session. Lord Duncannon, the Whig Whip, was also one of the most prominent Managers of the club – the two roles had no need to be associated but it was generally accepted that they complemented each other nicely and no one was surprised or disapproving when the party committee rooms were established at Brooks's during political elections. Brooks's, wrote Austin Mitchell, was the 'social centre for the Whig party, just as White's club was for the Tories and Boodle's for the country gentlemen and independents, and it was almost an informal political headquarters . . . to enrol in the club was tantamount to enlisting in the party.'

Though superficially homogeneous, the Whigs of Brooks's were no more harmonious than any other opposition group which was united in wishing to defeat the government and take office, but divided on what it would do when once in power. The spectrum of membership ranged from the most prudent conservatives, who regretfully accepted the need for a measure of parliamentary reform but felt that it should be gradual and as small as possible, to firebrands like Sir Francis Burdett, who had twice been imprisoned for seditious activities. It was always difficult to say at what point the left wing of the Whig party shaded into radicalism, but with a few exceptions, such as Joseph Hume, the radicals – for social and economic reasons as much as political – were not members of Brooks's. Burdett, however, as a young man was quite as vociferous and extreme as any radical and must have been viewed with some distaste by the more sedate members of the club and the Whig party.

In the 1820s the main division showed itself between those who believed that the only acceptable government was one that was purely Whig and abhorred the possibility of any compromise, and those who were prepared to serve in a coalition provided that it would support the principle of Catholic Emancipation and not entirely rule out the possibility of a measure of parliamentary reform. The difference, previously latent, came to a head in 1827 when Lord Liverpool succumbed to an apoplectic fit. No new government could last without the support of Canning, and Canning would serve under nobody, so with great reluctance George IV invited him to form a ministry. The Duke of Wellington and the high Tories refused to serve under a man whom Lord Londonderry had described as a 'charlatan parvenu' and who was notoriously unsound on Catholic Emancipation. The way was clear for some sort of liberal/conservative coalition, and overtures were made to Brooks's. Bitter argument ensued. The purists, under Grey and Althorp, refused to join any government which was not pledged to parliamentary reform. The trimmers, or those like Brougham with an eye to their own career, were ready to take Canning's good will on trust and accept office on almost any terms. In the middle a group of moderates under Lansdowne wavered fretfully, standing out now for one thing, now the other.

Negotiations with Canning finally broke down when a meeting of the leading Whigs at Lansdowne House concluded that they should not join the ministry unless, at the very least, the government of Ireland was handed over to those sympathetic to Catholic Emancipation. Lansdowne prepared to set off for Bowood, relieved that the matter was settled. He reckoned without Brougham. With the help of Robert Wilson, that maverick genius convened at Brooks's a meeting of forty or so members of the House of Commons who he knew were disposed to agree with his views on taking office. 'We had a row at Brooks's,' he told Creevey, '(which I own I created) and the negotiation is on again!' Brougham denounced the confabulations at Lansdowne House and insisted that the long-term interests of Whiggery would best be served by their joining Canning's coalition. Auckland was sent round to try to change Lansdowne's mind; he did not meet with too hostile a reception but it took a further visitation by the Duke of Devonshire to convince the malleable marquess where his true duty lay. Finally the moderate Whigs rallied to the coalition, while Grey and his resentful rearguard were left in opposition. 'Never was so scandalous a step as that of Brooks's', stormed Lord Holland, while Althorp referred resentfully to the 'insurrection at Brooks's', which had done 'the great injury of destroying Party in the country'. To Lord Essex it was not so much the deed itself as the manner of its doing which offended. 'At a *club* to settle a business of this nature!' he protested: '. . . Devonshire House, Bedford House, and Lansdowne or Burlington House are the places where men of high principle and character should be assembled to form an endeavour to advise their sovereign.' As to Grey, he was said by Greville to be in such a state of irritation that he would hardly speak to any of his old friends and declared that he would never set foot in Brooks's again (a resolution that did not last long). Six out of fifteen members of Canning's Cabinet (or seven out of sixteen if William Lamb as Chief Secretary in Ireland be included) were members of Brooks's, but only three of these could properly be described as Whigs: Anglesey, Charles Wynn, Lamb and Palmerston being to different degrees sympathetic to Whig causes but all considered by the party whips as men not necessarily to be counted on in a crisis.

This emphasis on politics might cause anyone to think that Brooks's was no more than an appendage to the Houses of Parliament and could readily have been transferred to Westminster if the accommodation had been available. So the Club sometimes appeared, particularly from across the road at White's. Yet even the most inveterate politicians among the members considered Brooks's as being above all a place where one met one's friends, ate, drank, gambled and then ate and drank some more, lounged about, wrote letters, and discussed the matters of the day – literary or theatrical; historical or philosophical; shooting, hunting or racing; but by no means confined to politics. No club would be narrowly political which boasted among its members such celebrated wits and diners-out as 'Conversation' Sharpe, Henry Luttrell, Lord Alvanley, Samuel Rogers or Scrope Davies; savants such as James Mackintosh, the philosopher and jurisprudentialist, David Ricardo the economist (elected in 1818 and probably the first member of Jewish blood), Henry Fox Talbot, the father of photography, Lord Stanley, President of the Linnaean and Zoological Societies and proud sponsor of the 'Stanley crane'; and writers of the calibre of Macaulay, Bulwer Lytton, Richard Ford, author of the *Handbook of Spain*, or Richard Neville, the editor – titular, at least – of Pepys's diaries. Lady Bessborough described to

'Promised Horrors of the French Invasion' – Fox flogs Pitt and White's is stormed.
From a cartoon of 1796 at Brooks's

PILLARS of the CONSTITUTION.

'Coming Home from Brooks's'. From a cartoon of 1809 by Gillray at Brooks's

Granville Leveson Gower her dismay at seeing so many of the more eligible younger men 'fall into that sink of sin and sea-coal, all absorbed in Whist and Brooks's,' and complained that so many of 'those who make society pleasant prefer a club and their rubber to everything else'. Tom Moore, the Irish poet who literally sang for his supper at most of the grandest houses in London, was another member who, though vaguely Whig from a sense of allegiance to his great patron and benefactor, Lord Lansdowne, in fact cared not a fig for politics. He used Brooks's as a place where he could breakfast in congenial surroundings (breakfast being a movable feast, on one occasion at least being taken after midday), meet friends and, very occasionally, eat a solitary supper. On 7 February 1830 he found himself reduced to this expedient and had just ordered his cutlet when he was approached by a 'Mr Stevenson' (probably, in fact, 'Boots' Stephenson, known by this nickname because he was the last man to wear Hessian boots) 'who had been commissioned by the Duke of Sussex to throw his drag-net at Brooks's for any stray guest he could catch for an impromptu dinner at Kensington'. Moore abandoned his cutlet and went rejoicing from the club; to judge by the memoirs of the time he was not the only bachelor or grass-widower who would haunt Brooks's an hour or so before dinner in the hope of being invited to some sufficiently attractive table.

Moore had been approached by Sir Ronald Ferguson on 1 June 1829 and urged to let his name be put forward for membership of Brooks's, with Lord Duncannon as proposer and Ferguson as seconder. He said that he would 'consider it'. Consideration cannot have taken long, and the electoral process must have been extremely rapid, for a mere fortnight later he was going 'to Brooks's to pay my 21 guineas – a costly honour'. (In 1815 the entrance fee had been raised to nine guineas and the subscription to eleven. In 1828 it was decided to channel a guinea a year from the subscription into a sinking fund to finance alterations or improvements to the club. This was presumably additional to the regular subscription, hence Moore's having to pay twenty-one rather than twenty guineas.)

As a protégé of Lansdowne and a friend of Ferguson and Duncannon, Moore would not have been likely to encounter many difficulties in the way of his election. Two years later Richard Sheil, the politician and dramatist, sounded Moore out about the possibility of his too becoming a member. Moore promised to speak to some of 'the leading members of the club' and was soon able to assure Sheil that his candidature would pose no problem. A look at the *Memorials of Brooks's* suggests who those 'leading members' might have been. The same names recur regularly among those who proposed or seconded members. Between 1810 and 1831 the immensely rich Whig grandee Earl Fitzwilliam led the list with sixty-four nominations, his son Lord Milton adding a further ten. Next came Moore's own seconder, the soldier turned Whig politician Sir Ronald Ferguson, who appeared thirty-eight times, a shade ahead of Lord Lansdowne with thirty-six. Lord Duncannon with thirty-one, Lord Cowper with thirty, Lord Althorp twenty-nine, the Duke of Norfolk twenty-eight, Lord Holland twenty-four, Lord Sefton twenty-one and Lord George Cavendish twenty, were also prominent. The figures are approximate since it is sometimes difficult to work out which member of a family is referred to, but it is obvious that a dozen or so members, all Whig, all rich, almost all noble, and all to some extent engaged in the political struggle, controlled entry to the club. Sheil was proposed by Sefton, seconded by Duncannon, and was a member within three weeks of his overture to Moore. This somewhat autocratic and expeditious system of election contrasts interestingly with the practice at Moore's other club, the Athenaeum. There, in 1830, when a new election was called for, 1,100 candidates put their own names forward, with a statement of what they felt to be their credentials, and a committee then sifted through the list and selected the hundred whom they felt to be most meritorious. Melbourne might have had membership of Brooks's in mind as well as the Order of the Garter, when he rejoiced that, in that case at least, there was 'no damned merit in it'.

Canning's uneasy coalition did not long survive the death of its leader in August 1827. Goderich came, winced and rapidly departed. The King turned to the Duke of Wellington and the Whig element resigned, with Lamb, Dudley, Palmerston and Charles Grant following a few months later. With the exception of Anglesey, who remained as Lord Lieutenant of Ireland, and Lord Rosslyn, the Tory Lord Privy Seal, Brooks's was once more united in opposition. Lord Holland acted as honest broker between the various groups and achieved a satisfactory assurance that orthodox Whigs, trimmer Whigs and former Canningites would all be prepared to serve under Grey in an administration pledged to Catholic Emancipation and a measure of parliamentary reform. On the first point Wellington cut the ground from under their feet by himself pushing through an emancipation bill – 'Went to Brooks's yesterday and found all the Whigs very merry at the Catholick news,' commented Greville; on the second he saved the Whigs' bacon by turning his face obdurately against even the smallest measure of reform. The death of George IV removed the most potent barrier between the Whigs and office; the general election that followed William IV's accession showed a marked swing away from the Tories; on 16 November 1830 Wellington resigned. After so many years in the wilderness, the Whigs had at last returned to power.

'Such a day at Brooks's!' rejoiced John Campbell. 'Who could have foreseen it? This room presents at this moment a new and striking spectacle. It is filled with the new Ministers and their adherents, and great numbers are sitting around the tables writing lists of the new Ministers for their friends in the country.' Those who believed that the advent of the Whigs would mean insurrection or, at the least, the overthrow of the landed interest, should have drawn some comfort from the news that was being dispatched by the evening post. Grey's Cabinet was richer, more aristocratic and its members owned more land than any since the eighteenth century. The Duke of Richmond and 'Goody' Goderich provided an uneasy right-wing presence and did not belong to Brooks's, the other eighteen out of the twenty members of Grey's Cabinet had either joined the club already or were shortly to do so.

It did not, of course, follow that every member of Brooks's was a committed supporter of Grey's government. There would have been very few members of the club in 1830 who did not accept that some reform of Parliament was necessary, or at least inevitable, but this surface unity covered many gradations of opinion, from the more conservative element, who believed that the smallest possible changes should be made and those only for cosmetic reasons, to the root-and-branch reformers like Lord Durham and Lord John Russell, who wished fundamentally to reshape the political map of Britain. There were other unquiet spirits too, notably Richard Sheil and Daniel O'Connell, the twin heroes of Irish liberation, whose interest in Westminster politics was confined mainly to their impact on Irish affairs and who viewed the Whig panjandrums with whom they rubbed shoulders every day with suspicion and some dislike.

O'Connell, a braggart and bully if also a demagogue of genius and a man of great courage, both moral and physical, proved a particularly turbulent member of Brooks's. In April 1835 he caused great offence when he described his fellow member, Lord Alvanley, as 'a bloated buffoon'; uttering the insult first in the House of Commons and then at a political meeting in the country. Alvanley demanded satisfaction and, when this was denied him, asked the Managers of Brooks's to call a general meeting to discuss the matter. In the end O'Connell's son Morgan, also a member of Brooks's, accepted the challenge on his father's behalf and the Managers seem to have avoided taking any position on the issue. This respite was short-lived; a few months later Sir Francis Burdett in his turn proposed the expulsion of O'Connell on the grounds of his gross and scandalous abuse of his political opponents and his refusal to give satisfaction to those whom he had insulted. There was much debate about what action the club should take. There were good arguments on both sides, Greville considered: 'On the one side, of the perilous example of a club taking cognizance of acts of its members, private or political, which do not concern the club, or have no local reference to it – a principle, if once admitted, of which it would be next to impossible to regulate and control the application, and [which would] probably be productive of greater evils than those it would be intended to remedy. On the other hand, the case of O'Connell is altogether peculiar . . .' In the end the Managers concluded that the peculiarity of O'Connell's case was not so extreme as to justify overthrowing the general principle. O'Connell was not expelled and Burdett later resigned, though probably as much because his political sympathies had moved far to the right as in pique at the pusillanimity of the Managers.

O'Connell himself, like others who are free with abuse, felt injured if it was directed at himself. When Tom Moore wrote an Irish melody mocking his pretensions, O'Connell ostentatiously cut him for several months. Indeed, the atmosphere of Brooks's can rarely have been the more congenial for O'Connell's presence. Though members were not prepared to press for his expulsion, many were unwilling to pass the time of day with him. 'Figure to yourself at this moment,' wrote Creevey, 'O'Connell and myself seated at the same table writing, very near each other, and no one else in the room, and yet no intercourse between us, tho' formerly we always spoke. This is no matter of choice with me . . . but after his abuse of Lord Grey, I made up my mind never to speak to him again.'

Burdett became as much a bugbear of Brooks's as his Irish enemy. When in 1837 he stood in the Tory interest for Westminster against the radical J.T. Leader, Greville told Disraeli that 'All Brooks's moved heaven and earth for Leader.' They did not achieve much by so doing, Burdett won comfortably. Probably some of 'all Brooks's' were by no means dissatisfied at their failure. Though Leader himself was a member of Brooks's from 1835 and throve in the somewhat rarified atmosphere which prevailed there, not many radical Members of Parliament would have said as much. The 1830s were marked by an ever more serious divergence between the Whigs – with whom the Canningites could now be considered reintegrated – and the radicals, who generally supported the government against the Tories but did not thereby feel precluded from criticizing them fiercely and at times voting against them.

Until the Reform Bill was passed a fair semblance of unity was maintained. The bill's gestation was a protracted process. Grey himself remained away from the club while the bill was being drafted so as to avoid being led into indiscretion – rather as a modern Chancellor might avoid mixing with his cronies in the weeks before his budget. Althorp, Durham and John Russell – the three men primarily responsible for working out the details – did not go as far as that, but they kept their own counsel to a remarkable extent. When Russell finally unveiled their proposals in the House of Commons on 1 March 1831, the extent of the bill – sixty boroughs abolished, a further forty-seven reduced to a single member – came as much as a shock to the radicals and the Whigs from Brooks's as to the Tories opposite. Though conservatives like Melbourne and Palmerston had their doubts, the party remained united as the bill was passed in the Commons, then defeated in the Lords, resubmitted after an election in which the Whigs and radicals had made substantial gains, then mauled so badly by the Lords in committee that it had to be withdrawn. When the leaders of the party insisted that either the King must create enough peers to force the bill through the House of Lords or they would go into opposition and defeat whatever government he might put in their place, the moderate Whigs began to quaver. Even then, however, only the Duke of Richmond actually broke ranks and refused to sign the memorandum to the King.

At first the King refused to succumb to this threat and accepted the government's resignation. 'Brooks's club is full of weeping and gnashing of teeth, so little was the party prepared for this sudden catastrophe,' wrote the exultant Raikes, one of the few Tories who were members of the club, though he was more often to be found at White's. If weeping indicated sorrow and gnashing rage, it was the latter that predominated when William IV called on the Duke of Wellington to form a ministry and himself pass a measure of reform very similar if not identical to that put forward by the Whigs. 'In the evening there was a most violent meeting of Whigs at Brooks's,' recorded Raikes, 'when the virulence of the speeches, particularly that of Mr Stanley, the Irish secretary, who got upon the table, showed the exasperated feelings of the party.' Raikes in fact got it wrong; Stanley, with the help of Althorp, was largely responsible for persuading the meeting that the important thing was to get the bill passed; if Wellington chose to tarnish his honour by taking on the charge himself, then the opposition could only acquiesce. The Whigs left Brooks's with the regretful determination to let the Tories pass the bill. Next day, however, it became clear that they no longer necessarily spoke for reformist Britain. In the House of Commons the careful arguments of Stanley and Althorp were swept away in an explosion of fury; with high Tories and radicals united in opposition to this ignoble shuffle. Wellington admitted defeat; the King accepted the inevitable; enough peers rallied to the bill to make it unnecessary to swamp the House of Lords by a large creation; on 4 January 1832 the bill passed its third reading and became law.

Once the Reform Bill was passed, the main cohesive factor in the Whig-radical alliance disappeared. The unpleasantness and tension that ensued were among the principal factors that drove Grey to resign. He wished a letter he wrote to Lord Ebrington setting out his intentions to be widely diffused among his colleagues and so left a copy 'lying on the table at Brooks's for publick inspection'. It was one of the last occasions on which a Whig prime minister would assume that if the members of Brooks's were told of something then the party could be said to know it too. Not that Melbourne's first administration seemed any less Whig than its predecessor. Eighteen out of twenty members of Grey's Cabinet had also belonged to Brooks's; in the case of Melbourne the figure was sixteen out of sixteen. Partly because the government rested on such a narrow base, there were general forebodings about its future. 'Peel looked gayer and easier than all Brooks's put together,' noted Greville, but in fact ministers stumbled on quite satisfactorily until the death of Lord Spencer, with the consequent disappearance of his son Althorp to the House of Lords, gave William IV an excuse to dismiss them and invite Robert Peel to form a government.

Peel lasted a hundred days. The problem for the opposition was not so much if but when they should turn him out. Melbourne and Palmerston favoured delay – the concept that the function of an opposition was to oppose was not yet taken for granted and both men deplored factious resistance to the King's ministers. Russell, the Irish and the radicals were for defeating Peel at the first opportunity. A chance arose when the time came to elect a Speaker for the House of Commons. The Tory incumbent, Manners-Sutton, would normally have been returned unopposed but the more energetic members of the opposition were bent on ousting him and Melbourne had to give way. Moore was dining that night at Brooks's, which was packed with peers and other members who were not in the House of Commons, waiting to hear the result of the debate:

'Post-hour at length approaching, and the letters still kept open for the chance of news arriving in time to be communicated to country friends – but no intelligence arrived and many sat down to seal their letters, when a young fellow (Dundas, I believe) came running breathless into the room, and cried out "Won it by ten! Won it by ten!" He was soon encircled, and questioned, and pulled about by one and another, while the whole party hurrahed and shook hands and were as uproarious as a party of schoolboys.' Someone pointed out that Dundas had not been in the House himself and that the news might be false, but soon 'a whole party from the House of Commons came trooping in . . . and no doubt was any longer left of the victory. Denison [who had moved the resolution unseating Manners-Sutton] himself was hurrahed and hugged and twisted about like a top, and the whole group gave one as little notion of a party of grave and mature legislators as can well be conceived. The cry was then "let's all dine here" – some scruples were stated by one or two as to not being dressed, but these were soon overruled, and frock coats were the order of the day . . . We sat down a party of more than thirty (the waiters having added what they could to the repast) and Denison was put in the Chair with the Duke of Argyle on one side of him and Lord Ducie on the other.'

Peel was out within a few weeks. Superficially things seemed to go on much as they had before. All but two of Melbourne's second administration belonged to Brooks's; the exceptions being the Lord Chancellor, Cottenham, whose son and grandson joined the club but who somehow remained outside it himself; and the Chancellor of the Duchy of Lancaster, George Grey, who by all the rules of family and Whig allegiance should also have been a member. But behind this traditional façade, power was shifting away from the closed world of the St. James's Street clubs. The first challenge to their hegemony came in 1834 when the Carlton Club was opened. 'The object is to have a counterbalancing meeting to Brooks's, which is now purely a Whig reunion,' explained Raikes, 'White's, which was formerly devoted to the other side, being now of no colour, and frequented indiscriminately by all.' The existence of this new club, larger than Brooks's, Boodle's or White's, more overtly political in nature and less exclusively limited to territorial grandees, their relations and hangers-on, inspired the Radicals to think that something similar could be done for the party of reform. The first plan was for an institution that would embrace Whigs and Radicals. 'The great object is to get the Reformers of the country to join it, so that it may be a place of meeting for them when they come to town,' wrote Sir William Molesworth, himself a member of Brooks's since 1832. 'It is much wanted. Brooks's is not liberal enough, too expensive, and not a dining club.' Other prominent members of Brooks's, like Durham and

Mulgrave, also supported the enterprise but the less progressive Whigs were notably unenthusiastic. Little progress was made, until the Radicals decided to go it alone, and set up their own club which the Whigs could join or not as they pleased. Enough members of Brooks's felt an important opportunity was being lost to ensure that Ellice and Stanley were despatched to negotiate terms. When the Reform Club opened in May 1836, with a thousand members, there were twenty Radicals and fifteen Whigs on the committee, most of the Cabinet were members, and even the more recalcitrant grandees like Lansdowne joined within a year or two.

With the famous *chef de cuisine*, Alexis Soyer, to lend lustre to its new premises, the Reform Club flourished. Some said that it contributed to the extinction of the Whigs as a political force, others that on the contrary it ensured that the Radicals were tamed and disciplined. What is certain is that the new club quickly replaced Brooks's as the unofficial headquarters of the reform movement. Even by 1839, at the time of the Bedchamber crisis, the two clubs were dealing with each other on more or less equal terms; Ward coming over from the Reform Club to Brooks's to hammer out the terms of a compromise which would allow Radicals and Whigs to act together. Twenty years later, when a new reform bill was introduced with provision for the equalization of town and country franchise, no one expressed any interest in the views of Brooks's – in so far as they existed at all, it was taken for granted that they would be in favour of restraint. The motive force for reform came from elsewhere.

In 1839 Greville was chatting with Lord Kensington and remarked how much the membership of the club had changed in recent years. 'But think what a change it must be since I first entered it, who remember Fox and Sheridan here!' exclaimed Kensington. In fact, the club in 1809, 1839, or for that matter 1859 was remarkably unchanged. Give or take a generation or two the same families – Spencer, Cavendish, Grey, Lambton, Howard – provided as significant a part of the membership as ever; the same great houses – Bowood, Althorp, Chatsworth, Petworth – received them when the season demanded that they adjourn to the more tranquil pleasures of the countryside. Fashions changed from decade to decade, but broadly speaking the same people were eating and drinking at the same time, talking about the same subjects, worshipping the same gods. Brooks's had stayed still, it was Britain that had changed. Socially Brooks's retained its lustre, politically it had been relegated, if not to the sidelines, then at least to a less central role. Whether that made it a worse or better club was a matter each member had to decide for himself.

Victorian Brooks's

Robert Blake

B ROOKS'S remained throughout Victoria's reign *the* grand Liberal
club, socially superior, because of its Whig flavour, to those other
centres of liberalism, the Reform and the Devonshire. Trollope
with his unerring eye for social and political nuances makes the point in
Phineas Finn. It is the morrow of a general election (in reality that of 1859)
and the government of Lord de Terrier – a pseudonym for Lord Derby –
has just lost a crucial division in the Commons by nineteen votes. This
was on a Thursday. On the Tuesday night before, Phineas has been at his
club, the Reform, listening to the gossip about the likely figure for the
Liberal majority. Some said seventeen, others twenty-two. The day after
the division, knowing that Lord de Terrier has resigned, Phineas walks up
St. James's with his slightly dubious friend Laurence Fitzgibbon MP,
youngest son of an Irish peer. Fitzgibbon turns into Brooks's.

'You should belong here', said Fitzgibbon as his friend entered the cab,
and Phineas immediately began to feel that he would have done
nothing till he could get into Brooks's. It might be very well to begin by
talking about politics at the Reform Club. Such talking had procured
him his seat at Loughshane. But that was done now . . . Nothing, as he
told himself, of political import was managed at the Reform Club. No
influence thence was ever brought upon . . . the arrangement of
cabinets. It might be very well to count votes at the Reform Club; but,
after the votes had been counted – had been counted successfully –
Brooks's was the place, as Phineas believed, to learn at the earliest
moment what would be the exact result of the success. He must get into

Brooks's, if it might be possible for him. Fitzgibbon was not exactly the man to propose him. Perhaps the Earl of Brentford would do it for him.

Certainly, if membership statistics are anything to go by, the predominance of Victorian Brooks's was formidable in terms of the cabinet ministers who belonged. The high point was Lord John Russell's ministry of 1846–52. It contained when first formed thirteen members of Brooks's out of a cabinet of fifteen. Palmerston's cabinet of 1855 had eleven out of fourteen. The real life, as opposed to Trollopian, Cabinet of 1859, Palmerston's second, had eight out of fifteen. But it was in a sense a coalition which included four or five ex-Conservative adherents who would never have been 'natural' members of the club. The most famous was Gladstone. There is no record of his having at any time belonged though he was a frequent guest. He presented his *Gleanings* in seven volumes to the library. Volume 1 is inscribed 'Presented in Brookes's [*sic*] Club by the author W.E. Gladstone June 1883'. Gladstone's first Cabinet in 1868 contained ten members of Brooks's out of fifteen, his second in 1880 nine out of fourteen and his third in 1886, despite the great split over Irish Home Rule, eight out of fourteen. It was not till his last government of 1892 that Brooks's was in a minority – just: eight out of seventeen.

By then there had occurred the most bitter battle in the Club's history since the days of Fox and Pitt. It stemmed from Gladstone's conversion to Home Rule for Ireland, i.e. a Dublin Parliament with devolved and limited powers over Irish affairs. Gladstone had privately reached this momentous decision as early as August 1885, but he did not announce it at the general election called by Lord Salisbury in the autumn, as he hoped that there might in due course be a Conservative-Liberal consensus on the matter and wished to avoid its becoming a party issue. The Liberals now had a majority of eighty-six over the Conservatives, but the Irish Nationalists led by Parnell had exactly that number of members; thus they could deny office to either party but only give it to the Liberals. At this juncture, just before Christmas, an indiscreet newspaper interview by Gladstone's son, Herbert, revealed his father's conversion.

Parnell, hitherto wavering as to which English party would give his cause support, at once plumped for the Liberals. The lines of battle were soon drawn. Salisbury met Parliament and was defeated on 27 January

1886, resigning next day. Gladstone became Prime Minister amidst general confusion, head of a party which had not been consulted, let alone united on one of the most controversial issues in Victorian political history. For Home Rule raised questions which had implications beyond Ireland. To Lord Salisbury and the Conservatives, Irish Home Rule was running against the course of history, which was flowing toward consolidation into larger units. The great states of Europe were at one time composed of numerous small states. Did not Germany once have four hundred, and France and Italy a very large number, if not as many as that? 'Rightly or wrongly' wrote Salisbury in 1890, 'I have not the slightest desire to satisfy the national aspirations of Ireland.' Gladstone was not an opponent of Empire though he dreaded its expansion. He wanted to preserve it as it was and put it on a basis of consent. 'Within this vast Empire,' he wrote, 'there is but one spot where the people are discontented with their relation to the central power. That spot is Ireland.'

But this raised other problems. What was 'Ireland'? 'Ulster will fight and Ulster will be right' declared Lord Randolph Churchill, and he later observed that the Orange card was the card to play. Gladstone never allowed for Ulster nationalism. There were atavistic Protestant sentiments to consider, embodied in the slogan 'Home Rule is Rome Rule'. Then there was the whole question of land. Would an Irish Parliament dispossess the Anglo-Irish landowning class, and what sort of precedent would this give to the agitators for land reform in England and Scotland? Gladstone with the best of motives was warming and stirring up a witches' cauldron of deadly fears and hatreds.

It became clear at once that the Liberal Party was deeply divided. The leading Whigs, Lords Hartington, Selborne, Northbrook, Carlingford and Derby, along with the Duke of Argyll, all members of Gladstone's previous cabinet and of Brooks's, refused to join the new government. So too did G.J. Goschen, another member of Brooks's who had been in Gladstone's Cabinet of 1868–74. G.O. Trevelyan, who also belonged to Brooks's and had been in the government of 1880–5, accepted office with great misgivings. He resigned in April along with Joseph Chamberlain who was emphatically *not* a member of Brooks's (he would certainly have been blackballed if anyone had dared to put him up). But Lords

Herschell, Spencer, Rosebery, Granville, Kimberley and Ripon, together with the Home Secretary, H.C.E. Childers, represented Brooks's in the new Cabinet.

The statistics of those members of Brooks's who declined or accepted office mask a much bigger change in allegiance of the Whig element in the Liberal Party. There is no question that Home Rule turned what had been a trickle away from Gladstone into a torrent. Although the Conservatives had long held a majority in the Lords it could still be said in 1885 that the Whig/Liberals at least matched them in territory, title and general grandeur, if not in numbers. The Dukes of Devonshire, Bedford, Westminster and Cleveland, the Marquess of Anglesey and Earl Fitzwilliam could hold their own with anyone. Home Rule changed all this – or, perhaps one should say, sparked off a latent change. Gladstone's second Home Rule Bill which, unlike the first, passed through the Commons, was to be defeated in the Lords by 419 to 41 in 1893. The vast majority of the landed aristocracy was now on the Conservative side. The line of cleavage which till 1880 had been largely vertical now became horizontal. There was no class conflict in the days of Gladstone's duel with Disraeli, but there was one when he fought against Lord Salisbury.

The eighteen months between June 1885 and early 1887 are among the most dramatic in British political history – two general elections, three changes of government, and the break up of what had been the dominant party ever since 1830. Gladstone's Home Rule Bill was introduced amidst immense public excitement on 8 April 1886 and amidst even greater excitement rejected on its second reading by 343 votes to 313. Some 93 Liberals voted against it. The ensuing general election resulted in a Liberal rout (316 Conservatives and 78 Liberal Unionists against 191 Liberal Home Rulers and 85 Parnellites). Nor had the drama ended. Salisbury took office dependent on the dissident Liberals, and within six months his government was shaken by one of the most sensational resignations in modern times, that of Lord Randolph Churchill from the Chancellorship of the Exchequer just before Christmas. Salisbury offered the premiership to Hartington as leader of the Liberal Unionists. He declined but used his influence to persuade Goschen to become Chancellor – 'I forgot Goschen,' Lord Randolph is alleged to have said.

The transactions of the last year and a half had left a train of ill will and bitterness in the Liberal Party and all its appendages. Charges of treachery and disloyalty were bandied about. The animosity felt by the Gladstonians for the 'betrayal' of their cause by the Liberal Unionists was only equalled by that of Hartington and his friends at having been presented out of the blue with Gladstone's unexpected change of course. The Devonshire and Reform Clubs were riven, the majority following Gladstone. Brooks's was deeply divided too but there the Liberal Unionists were probably in the majority.

Some accounts of what followed in the Club are exaggerated. R.C.K. Ensor in his history of England refers to 'an orgy of mutual blackballing only quelled in 1889 after it had gone to great lengths by a speech from Lord Granville'. He bases his account on A.D. Elliot's biography of Goschen. Elliot is wrong about the year of Granville's intervention. It was 1887 not 1889, and he does not use the expression 'orgy'. He simply says that 'recourse was had to the most detestable of all methods of political fighting – the blackballing of candidates'. Some colour is given to the word 'orgy' in the account by Lord Edmund Fitzmaurice in his life of Granville which is reproduced in *The Memorials of Brooks's*. He describes the process of mutual blackballing in picturesque language:

Then gradually the circle of carnage widened and widened until it came to be whispered that it would soon be impossible for anybody to get into Brooks's at all, and that the time might be more or less accurately calculated when the last member of the Club would in solitary glory be seen contemplating the declining sun of London Society from the large window which looks down St. James's Street. One member declared that the shade of Mr Fox had been observed flitting in the passages; and though another member surmised that it was only the solid figure of an ancient servitor of the Club with a bottle of port in his hand, which had been mistaken for the shade of the statesman, both agreed that the gravity of the situation was worthy of the appearance of one of the Whig saints.

It is an enjoyable picture but not entirely accurate. In fact there do not seem to have been more than four candidates who were victims of 'the most detestable of all methods of political fighting'. The great row stemmed from a dinner at Brooks's on 26 January 1887. The host was Sir Edward Hamilton, principal private secretary to Gladstone 1882–5, a civil servant who moved in and out of the Treasury. He was an indefatigable diarist and a brilliant, hard-working administrator. Like Gladstone he had been at Eton and Christ Church, though more than a generation later (he matriculated in 1866, Gladstone in 1828). He was deeply devoted to his chief and to the causes which he supported. He became a member of Brooks's in January 1881, proposed by Lord Rosebery. He was tactful, diplomatic and courteous, but possibly his tact somewhat deserted him in his choice of guests that evening, as the Brooks's dinner book shows.

One of them was Gladstone, but even the most embittered Liberal Unionist could hardly have regarded the creator of the Liberal Party as *persona non grata* in a club so deeply associated with the Liberal cause. The others were John Morley, a strong Home Rule supporter and biographer of Gladstone; Sir Reginald (later Lord) Welby, a Treasury expert on public finance; and Sir William Harcourt. Morley had been Chief Secretary for Ireland in the government of 1886 and Harcourt was Chancellor of the Exchequer. Welby was a passionate supporter of Treasury economy, the very issue on which Lord Randolph Churchill had resigned to be replaced by Goschen, a renegade Liberal. It was an article of faith among Gladstonians that Conservative – or Conservative-appointed – Chancellors of the Exchequer could not be trusted to apply the correct rules of Treasury finance as laid down in the great series of Gladstone's budgets from 1859 to 1866. In reality the budgets under Disraeli from 1874 to 1880 were very little different from those of the Liberals, and Goschen was to be as rigid an 'economist' as anyone before him. But that was not how it seemed to the displaced Gladstonian ministers or to Welby.

The most controversial guest was Harcourt. Sir William Vernon Harcourt was a younger son of a father connected with many noble houses both in England and France. He could lay claim to Plantagenet descent, and was proud of it. His elder brother inherited a large estate in Oxfordshire. William Harcourt made a substantial fortune at the Bar. In his Cambridge days he was an 'Apostle' and debated the Liberal cause against the Conservative exponent, Sir James Fitzjames Stephen. He

Left: Sir Francis Dashwood (Lord le Despencer), 1742. *Right*: The Earl of Bessborough, 1743

Left: Sir Bourchier Wray, 1744. *Right*: Mr Samuel Savage, 1744

All these portraits are by George Knapton and are in the possession of the Society of Dilettanti

A meeting of the Society of Dilettanti in 1777, by Sir Joshua Reynolds, PRA, a member
from 1785–92. In the possession of the Society of Dilettanti

became Solicitor General (hence the knighthood) in November 1873 for three months before the fall of the government. He was Home Secretary 1880–5. Harcourt was essentially a Whig figure and must have seemed an obvious candidate for Brooks's, but when his name came up in the ballot on 24 May 1854, proposed by the Duke of Bedford and seconded by the Earl of Bessborough (supporters as powerful as one could well imagine), he was blackballed. Many who suffered this rebuff were put up again and got in on a second or third attempt. Harcourt was not proposed again, but whether by his own volition or the decision of his proposer and seconder there is no way of knowing. One can assume that the fact of his having been 'pilled', as the slang of the day had it, would have been widely known in the Club.

The candidates' book naturally gives no reasons why a particular person was blackballed. The process is by its very nature anonymous and one can only guess. We do know, however, that Harcourt was a 'difficult' character. He had an acid tongue and made remarks to people which he forgot but they did not. As his notice in the *Dictionary of National Biography* puts it: 'Imbued with the spirit of the gladiator he possessed the gift of the advocate and could quickly concentrate his powers of picturesque invective, sarcasm and paradox . . . Unable to suffer fools gladly and impatient of mediocrity he earned the reputation of irascibility and haughtiness.' It may well have been the power of invective and sarcasm which caused him to be blackballed. It was certainly this that sparked off the great row in Brooks's. For 26 January 1887 was a notable day. Goschen, an arch-traitor in Gladstonian eyes, had lost his seat in East Edinburgh in the general election of July 1886. He was, thus, not in Parliament when he accepted the Chancellorship of the Exchequer on 5 January 1887, and had to get himself re-elected as soon as possible. The Conservative Party managers, with singular ineptitude, chose for him the Exchange Division of Liverpool, which had been won by 170 votes by a Home Ruler six months earlier. It was obviously a most marginal seat and Goschen lost it by seven votes on 26 January. The news came through to Brooks's that very evening, after Gladstone had left but while Hamilton's other guests were still at the dinner table. There were cries of triumph and glee, and while walking down the stairs, as they left, Harcourt said something highly disparaging about the Liberal Unionists, which was overheard by several members. Harcourt was not the man to speak *sotto voce*. The triumphalism of a person who had been blackballed from the Club over a man who was a member and whose views on the iniquity of Home Rule were shared by the majority of members was something that could not be borne.

There was an easy means of vengeance to hand. Harcourt's son, Lewis, known as 'Loulou', was up for election at the next ballot on 3 February, proposed by the Duke of St. Albans, Charles Cotes and the Earl of Northbrook, who had been First Lord of the Admiralty in Gladstone's second administration and Viceroy of Ireland 1872–6. Thirty seven members balloted and there were six blackballs. Loulou was not elected and he made no further attempt. Similar treatment was meted out next day to Lord Rosebery's cousin Henry Primrose, proposed by Rosebery and Hamilton. There were only two blackballs but this was enough in a ballot of sixteen to keep him out.

However, two could play at this game. The Liberals resolved to get their own back at the Liberal Unionists. One of the most prominent of Gladstone's ex-ministers was the Earl of Selborne, Lord Chancellor 1880–5, who refused to join Gladstone in 1886. His son, Viscount Wolmer MP, was up for election three days later on 7 February, proposed by the Hon. A.D. Elliot MP (Goschen's biographer) and seconded by Lord Carlingford. There were thirty five ballots and three blackballs. He was rejected. The Liberal Unionists resolved on revenge. Sir Horace Davy QC, who had been Gladstone's Solicitor General in 1886, was due for a ballot next day on 8 February. He was proposed by Lord Kensington and seconded by Charles Cotes. Forty-two members took part in the ballot and there were five blackballs. So he too was rejected.

So far the score was three against one to the Liberal Unionists. There were no further ballots due till 19 April, and one can well imagine the degree of wrath and recrimination pervading the Club's premises. It was all too clear that the process of blackballs and counter-blackballs would begin again with renewed venom unless something was done to stop it. The 2nd Earl Granville had been elected as Lord Leveson on the proposal of the Earl of Carlisle and Lord John Russell as long ago as 18 February 1838. He had been three times Foreign Secretary, twice under Gladstone, and was Leader of the Liberals in the House of Lords. He was a Knight of the Garter and Warden of the Cinque Ports. He could be described as the doyen of the Club. He was an intimate of Gladstone, though this, according to Walpurga, Lady Paget, did not stop him expressing the hope in November 1884 'that the G.O.M may die soon and that he may become Prime Minister'. In the event Gladstone outlived him by seven years.

Granville was not a great statesman, but he was a diplomat, popular, tactful and persuasive. He was just the man to stop the feuding if anyone could. He was persuaded to make the attempt. When the clock struck three on the afternoon of 19 April and the balloting was about to begin, he stood up with much trepidation and made a speech to the assembled members expressing, according to his biographer, the hope that he would be forgiven for turning the meeting into a discussion forum.

> In a few well chosen words he then alluded to the antiquity of the Club and the previous divisions in the party which it had survived, and expressed a hope – using almost the words which Burke had employed in a slightly different connection – which he believed all present in their hearts really shared, that there should be at least one place left in London where a truce might be allowed to the divisions and animosities of mankind, and friends might still be allowed to meet one another on the same terms as of old. A murmur of suppressed applause ran round the room. All felt that a true note had been struck and the better feelings of human nature had been vindicated.

The result was immediate. All candidates from whatever faction were elected unopposed, and members walked away relieved at the end of the row and happily united in cursing Sir William Harcourt as the cause of all the trouble. 'I never felt so nervous in my life,' Granville said as he walked home. It was a happy ending to an unhappy episode. The reign of Queen Victoria had another thirteen years to run, and the political gap between Liberals and Liberal Unionists widened. The latter joined in a coalition with Lord Salisbury in 1895 and, as the years went by, they became almost indistinguishable from the Conservatives till the two parties amalgamated in 1912. But Brooks's remained a club to which members of both sides could belong and it ended the century in a state of harmony which few people would have predicted in the early months of 1887.

Edwardian Brooks's

Roy Jenkins

THE Edwardian decade was the last in which a member of Brooks's became Prime Minister. Indeed, as a final political flourish the Club produced not one but two. Campbell-Bannerman, not a natural Brooks's figure, had been a member since 1889, and his Cabinet of 1905 contained twelve Brooks's members out of a total of twenty-five. This was not up to Melbourne's performance in 1834, but it was not bad going for a pawky Scots radical who came to power on a reforming electoral landslide. His successor, Asquith, was a more active club figure at least until he became Prime Minister in 1908, frequently proposing or seconding candidates and even, occasionally, resolutions at annual meetings.

Since Asquith fell in 1916, the 32 St. James's Street/10 Downing Street connection, which since the Reform Bill had sustained Grey, Melbourne, Russell, Palmerston and Rosebery, has never been reactivated. Lloyd George was the last Liberal to be Prime Minister, but he was no more of a Brooks's man than, for very different reasons mainly but not entirely stemming from his Tory provenance, Gladstone had been. And none of the subsequent ten Conservative or four Labour Prime Ministers have been Brooks's members, though Harold Macmillan was a member at an earlier point in his career. The club did not even contribute a candidate to the 1990 excitements. The two who came nearest to giving Brooks's a post-Asquithian premier to set against the long line of eighteenth- and nineteenth-century incumbents were Austen Chamberlain (elected 1895) and the first Earl of Halifax (elected 1914) who, as we know from Churchill's memoirs and other sources, came very near indeed.

This is not, however, by any means the same as saying that the first decade of this century was the key period for the depoliticization of Brooks's. That was most contributed to by three disparate events, the consequences of each of which took a little time to work themselves out, and none of which occurred during the reign of King Edward VII. The first was the establishment of the Reform Club in 1836, the second the Liberal Unionist Home Rule split of 1886, and the third the replacement as a party of government of the Liberals by the Labour Party in the 1920s.

This first meant that there was another and self-consciously different club which became much more the embodiment of nineteenth-century Liberalism than Brooks's, at any rate after the mid-century mark, had either the capacity or the desire to be. When a club for reformers was first mooted after 1832 the Whigs were in two minds about it. They did not want the Radicals in Brooks's where, apart from anything else, there was not room for them. On the other hand, they did not want to lose all control of a new institution. So some of them, like Ellice, Grey's brother-in-law, his chief whip and later his Secretary at War, took an active part in setting up the Reform Club and most of the politically committed grandees subsequently joined it. They did so rather as prominent figures in the University of Oxford were later to encourage the setting up of the red-brick universities, whilst firmly keeping their own spiritual home amongst the dreaming spires. So the Whig magnates kept theirs at the upper end of St. James's Street.

The new model club in Pall Mall, it must be said, did not wish to copy what some of its members regarded as the aristocratic rakishness of Brooks's. It was the age of improvement rather than of imitation. Most of those who commissioned Charles Barry's palace believed they were achieving something more splendid and more worthy of mid-Victorian England than a fashionable gambling den. They did not however treat themselves too puritanically, and apart from their architect the other most remembered figure from the early days of the Reform was their chef, Alexis Soyer. Progressive politics accompanied by solid, even lavish, bourgeois comfort was the keynote.

Whether or not this recipe gave it better food than Brooks's, it certainly made it more the home of late-Victorian Liberalism. When Campbell-Bannerman became leader of the party in 1899 he rather tactlessly wrote to Asquith, who at that time used Brooks's quite a lot and hardly ever entered the Reform, laying it down that the latter should be the place for the confirmatory meeting of the Liberal parliamentary party: 'As to its scene, my disposition is all for the Reform Club. Anything else would be a confession of weakness and decadence. Why should we lose our hold on so excellent a property? And as a matter of fact I believe more of our men (certainly the best of them) belong to it than any other. . . .'

It was a far cry from the events of *circa* seventy years before when Brooks's was the centre of activity for the advent of the Grey and Melbourne governments. Ironically, however, the tide of political commitment was in turn already ebbing away from the Reform Club when Campbell-Bannerman assured himself and Asquith that it was not. The National Liberal Club (the convenience of whose lavatories so attracted F.E. Smith on his Edwardian walks from the Temple to the House of Commons that he affected to believe they were open to the public, or any rate such few members of the public as had his own swashbuckling confidence) had been established in 1884. The magnificence of its plumbing was cocooned in a Waterhouse building which was almost as striking an example of the architecture of the 1880s as Barry's had been of the 1840s. And this gradually freed the Reform Club to follow Brooks's into nominal political neutrality and into the reality of having rather more right-wing ideologues amongst its members than Brooks's could manage.

The effect of the Home Rule split had not however, been nearly so great upon the Reform Club as upon Brooks's. While the anti-Gladstonian cave had embraced a few like Joseph Chamberlain and Goschen who were remote from Brooks's, it was more typically a revolt of Whig magnates and therefore produced a far more visceral upheaval in Brooks's. This is illustrated by the fact that the names of the families commemorated in the names of Brooks's rooms – Cavendish, Spencer, Lansdowne – were all in Gladstone's second (1880) government, but only one of them (Spencer) was in his fourth (1892) government. The 8th Duke of Devonshire, better known as Hartington, had led the Whig breakaway from Gladstone in 1886 and had joined a Conservative government in 1895, although resigning from it in 1903 because of his continued attachment to free trade.

The 5th Marquess of Lansdowne had resigned from Gladstone's 1880 government as early as 1880 in protest against its Irish policy. During the Edwardian decade he was the Foreign Secretary of the *entente cordiale* and the leader of the Opposition in the House of Lords for the People's Budget/Parliament Bill struggle. Towards the end of his life, however, rather like Hartington in 1903 he reasserted his reputation of Whiggish independence by writing the Lansdowne letter advocating a negotiated peace. He was an active member of Brooks's in the early years of this century, and in 1902 complained to the committee about being overcharged three shillings and ninepence on a dinner bill and got the sum refunded.

The 5th Earl Spencer, known as the 'red earl', although for his beard rather than his politics, may have been influenced in accepting Home Rule and remaining faithful to Gladstone by the fact that (unlike the other two) he was not a great Irish landlord but a former Irish Viceroy. Nor was Ireland his only radical issue. At the time of the Boer War he inclined much more to the Little Englander position of Campbell-Bannerman than to the Liberal imperialism of Rosebery, Asquith and Edward Grey. There was some thought that he might be prime minister of an incoming Liberal government, but by 1905 his health had cracked.

The list of trustees of the Club over the 1870–1914 period shows how politics complicated social harmony. In 1870 they were the 8th Duke of Bedford, the 5th Earl of Bessborough, the 7th Duke of Devonshire and the 6th Earl Fitzwilliam, as fine a quartet of Whig magnates as could be imagined, and one united in the same attachment to both rank and Liberalism as was exhibited by Trollope's Dukes of Omnium and St. Bungay. In 1872 Bedford died and was followed in 1880 by Bessborough and Fitzwilliam. Lansdowne was appointed and for eleven years he and Devonshire served alone, during which period both of them resiled from Liberalism. The outbreak of the so-called Irish land war in 1881, which led to the murder of Devonshire's younger son, was almost as decisive a factor as Gladstone's conversion to Home Rule.

At the advent of the Liberal government of 1905, Lansdowne was still there, Devonshire had been succeeded by his son, and Rosebery and Evelyn Baring, first Earl of Cromer, the returned Egyptian proconsul, had been recruited. Rosebery was still nominally a Liberal, the other three were Unionists rather than Conservatives but none of them supported the controversial measures of the Campbell-Bannerman and Asquith governments.

In these circumstances the Club had only two effective choices. The first was to split, the second to live together in more or less mutual tolerance, but without pretending that a Brooks's view or a Brooks's faction still had any collective political effect. Happily the second course was followed, although more by inertial acceptance than by any process of formal decision-taking, and not without some sporadic frontier warfare. There was a fine spate of mutual blackballing for a few years after 1886, which Robert Blake's chapter covers. By the time my period opened the frontier warfare had subsided into only occasional harrying incidents, mostly conducted by those under doubtful control of the commanders on either side, and the second state of depoliticization had been accomplished.

The third stage in the process, the replacement of Liberal by Labour as a governing party and the twenty inter-war years of Conservative hegemony which this caused, came equally outside my period at the other end. But it has to be mentioned to round off the account of the decline and fall of the Brooks's political tradition. It can be illustrated by saying that not merely was no inter-war Prime Minister a member but that it would have been very difficult, for differing reasons, to imagine any one of them – Lloyd George, Bonar Law, Baldwin, MacDonald or Neville Chamberlain – having been so. Baldwin was the nearest to an exception, although he was most at home in the Travellers' (despite rarely going further than Aix-les-Bains), buttressed by the Carlton for political form and the Athenaeum for *gravitas*.

The occasional harrying incidents mainly occurred in relation to what was called the Ballot Book until 1907 and then the Candidates' Book. At the beginning of the century this recorded who was accepted and who rejected for membership and gave the names of those participating in the election, together with the figures for and against, but did not reveal which way individuals had voted. All candidates were elected very slowly. It took about three and a half years in the first half of the decade and four years in the second half. This was despite the fact that the club, then much smaller than it has been since the St. James's merger, was none the less coasting gently up in size. There were 618 members in 1901 and 648 in 1911.

Quite a lot of those who were eventually allowed through the narrow gates were elected unanimously, although the likelihood of achieving this appears to be almost in inverse ratio to the fame (certainly if it was political) of the candidate. Ironically, in view of his subsequent disgrace and Lord Marchmain-like exile (although his peccadilloes were not quite the same as those of Waugh's character), Earl Beauchamp, proposed by Rosebery and seconded by Lord Burghclere, was one of the few politicians to get through unopposed; he was elected in 1910 when he was a Liberal cabinet minister.

Conversely, but not surprisingly, fame brought support as well as opposition, and the candidatures of a number of those without it simply died of inertia. Support, however, was not much use if the opposition was at all strong. The unwritten rules appeared to be that modest support could overcome one blackball, that strong support could overcome two, but that three or more were invariably fatal. Thus in the 'nineties Austen Chamberlain had got through with thirty-four supporters against two blackballs, but Augustine Birrell, great wit that he was, even though ineffective Irish Secretary that he became, went down with four blackballs, though proposed across the split by Lord James of Hereford, a very urbane Liberal Unionist lawyer who had remained on good terms with both parts of the split party.

In 1902 Reginald McKenna, who was to be both Home Secretary and Chancellor of the Exchequer under Asquith, was elected over two blackballs, but (Sir) A.F. Pease, a prominent Durham Liberal, went down with no less than five blackballs, despite being proposed by Victor Cavendish, soon to be 9th Duke of Devonshire, and seconded by Sir Edward Grey. So, in the same year, did Mr Beamish, a somewhat anonymous nominee of the reigning 8th Duke himself, a surprising slight for that grand and popular panjandrum of Whiggery close to the end of his life.

Even such a paragon as Raymond Asquith has, at least posthumously, become had to be elected over two blackballs. However, he had an exceptionally strong favourable vote of forty-two when, under the aegis of the club's prize nominator Lord James, seconded by his own father (by then just Chancellor of the Exchequer), he came up for election after a four-year wait in early 1906.

He was a considerably more successful nominee than the next man H.H. Asquith put forward. In 1906 Asquith proposed Edwin Montagu, then his parliamentary private secretary and later to be both the husband of Venetia Stanley, who had been Asquith's favourite correspondent, and Secretary of State for India. Montagu was seconded by Freeman-Thomas, a Liberal whip who was to become Viceroy and a marquess (of Willingdon) from scratch, which is a rare rate of ascent. The distinction of his sponsors did Montagu no good. After another four-year wait, during which his nominator had become Prime Minister, he was unceremoniously rejected.

Despite the long waiting-time for membership and the general ease of St. James's Street life at a time when food and drink and servants were cheap and the austerity of Victorian self-help had given way to the opulence of Edwardian display, the internal running of Brooks's does not seem to have been altogether smooth. There were constant losses on the coffee room, there were quite a lot of complaints about the food (there were frequent changes of butchers until it was decided to try dealing with the other end of the problem and sack the chef), there was a certain amount of neurosis that other clubs gave better value for money, and particularly in the first year or so of the century the minute books betray a querulous feeling about the general running of the club. Sir Henry Primrose was not, I think, a very successful turn of the century chairman of the Managers. His successor, Lord Sandhurst, seems to have done better. When he in turn gave way in 1904, a most fulsome vote of thanks was proposed by Lord Edmund Fitzmaurice, Lansdowne's younger brother who had remained faithful to Liberalism, and seconded by Asquith.

One thing the Managers could be depended upon to do was to pay most careful attention to the complaints and suggestions of members. The meticulously recorded objections of the Earl of Cork and Orrery to a shortage of baked potatoes at 9.40 p.m. on 28 April 1902 were taken very seriously. Perhaps a little less attention was given to a suggestion of Lord Ampthill's that dumb-bells and Indian clubs should be provided in the bedrooms. It was described as being 'not entertained'. This was perhaps a little hard on Ampthill, who was not only the son of the famous ambassador Lord Odo Russell and the grandfather (maybe) of the Russell baby in that most notorious case, but also the heaviest man who used the club's weight book during the decade. Perhaps he should not have been discouraged from exercise even in the bedrooms.

On the other hand the complaint of Lord Selborne, the son of one of Gladstone's early Lord Chancellors, may have been treated too seriously. The relevant 1903 minute of the Library Committee read: 'A French novel found on the library table having been strongly objected to by Lord Selborne, the Committee directed the Secretary to request Messrs. Rolandi to be more careful in the selection of books they supplied and to inform Lord Selborne accordingly.' This sounded more suited to the tradition of Lord Eldon than to that of C.J. Fox.

This however was probably an isolated incident (reminding us that the Club was then heavily dependent upon subscription libraries; the range and quality of its own stock was only built up in this century), and some part of the libertarian spirit of Fox, even if not quite so pervasively present as his likenesses, could still be considered to hover over Brooks's. But it was on a strictly all-party basis. Even though, as late as 1914, the astonishingly high proportion of a half of the members of the Club were at some stage of their lives members of one or other House of Parliament (it had been as high as sixty per cent in the Club's first century of existence), the Liberal governments of both Campbell-Bannerman and Asquith would have been in a pretty poor way had they had to depend upon Brooks's votes.

This was despite the fact that Asquith must count, on some scores at least, as a core member of the Club. He was elected in 1889, soon after he began to make his way as an MP and QC. During his marital interregnum after the death of his first wife in 1891 and before his marriage to Margot Tennant in 1894 he used the clubhouse a lot. He was indeed there on an 1892 August Sunday afternoon (a feat he would find doubly difficult today) when a messenger from Gladstone arrived with a letter offering him the Home Secretaryship. He replied immediately, gratefully, and upon Brooks's embossed paper, although that, according to Crewe, who was to become Asquith's Lord President, had only recently become available amidst some complaints that it was a vulgar innovation. (I suppose it was the equivalent of fish knives in my early days in Brooks's. A request for one from a guest produced a look of horror followed by the bringing of a second fork. I cannot remember when that citadel was abandoned.)

Then in ten years of opposition Asquith, as we have seen, was active in electing or trying to elect new members and at annual meetings. After he became Prime Minister he used Brooks's less, but did not become a stranger to clubland for he developed a habit, extraordinary as it would seem in a modern Prime Minister, of slipping out of Downing Street on his own, walking across to the Athenaeum and reading more or less haphazardly for a couple of pre-dinner hours in the library there. Maybe he chose it because of the shorter walk or because he felt more anonymous in that rather cavernous room. It is unlikely that he felt more politically cosseted there, for the bishops had voted with near-unanimity against the Liberal Government's first major measure, the Education Bill of 1906, Canterbury and seven other diocesans going into the non-content lobby against a solitary favourable vote from the right reverend prelate of Hereford. The Brooks's peers from old Whig families, while they would not have given Asquith a majority, would have given him a much better proportion than that.

Nor is there any indication that the bitterness of the Parliament Bill and the Ulster revolt struggles between 1911 and 1914 weakened Asquith's attachment to Brooks's. All five of his sons became members and at least three of his grandsons are members today. Indeed, great though were the political strains, spilling over into social disruption, Brooks's does not seem in this period to have been a particularly bloody battlefield in the way that it had been after 1886. There was one joust in 1914, with very emblazoned champions (or victims) on either side. Edward Wood, later Halifax, was blackballed on the curious ground that he was a member of the Carlton Club and that there was an archaic rule that no member of Brooks's should be a member of any other club except for White's. Wood's supporters retaliated by blackballing Lord Althorp, the nephew of the red earl, and about to be a seventh-generation member.

The knights were regarded as too illustrious to be left unhorsed and a truce was arranged. It also led to a recasting of the method of election which was described earlier, and presumably to a formal burying of the archaic rule. Indeed the Candidates' Book now makes it look as though membership of other clubs is a positive qualification. This whole storm, if not exactly in a teacup, at least in a double decanter, was an isolated incident which both sides wanted to forget, and certainly not to repeat. It was rather like one of the aircraft incidents which occurred accidentally and embarrassingly at stages in the Cold War when neither the Russians nor the Americans were looking for an escalation.

There were at least two reasons why the 1909–14 political disputes, bitter though they were, left fewer scars on Brooks's than the events of 1886 had done. The first was precisely because of 1886; the Club had been through it all before and had learnt something from the experience. Furthermore it was no longer surprised that there should be political enemies as well as friends within the portals. Second, the large clutch of Brooks's ministers in Asquith's Cabinet, while they represented a minority position within the Club, were none the less very well-respected members. Several of them were part of the warp and weft of the Club, more so indeed than the Prime Minister, despite his active membership.

Above all there were Lord Crewe and Sir Edward Grey. Robert Milnes, great-grandson of one of the founding fathers of Brooks's and son of Monckton Milnes, the notable mid-nineteenth-century wit and giver of breakfast parties who was created Lord Houghton, himself became the first and last Marquess of Crewe as well as Rosebery's son-in-law. He was elected to Brooks's in 1879 and in later life (he lived until 1945) was thought to be one of the greatest depositories of Brooks's lore, which was not surprising after sixty-six years of membership. His 'Recollections' were circulated to members in 1944 and formed one of the best chapters in the commemorative volume published for Brooks's bicentenary in 1964. But already by 1909 he was regarded as a guarantor of the respectability of Liberalism. Asquith was careful to take Crewe with him when he went to see the King for the most delicate of the Parliament Bill audiences. In 1922 Crewe became ambassador to Paris, with the experience of having been in pre-war days a very good ambassador from the Liberal government to St. James's Street.

Edward Grey was regarded as even more of a *chevalier sans peur et sans reproche*. His record as Foreign Secretary is in fact far from impeccable. He was insular, imprecise and slightly priggish. He watched birds and the lights going out over Europe. But he always gave a non-partisan impression and he was almost miraculously free from criticism or enemies. He had something of Alec Home's qualities. At the end of his life he was unanimously elected Chancellor of Oxford four years after Asquith, a much more considerable man, had been ignominiously defeated. He was certainly not a Fox-like figure, but he was very respectable and difficult to denounce.

In addition there were the old Marquess of Ripon, an ex-Viceroy, the 10th Earl of Elgin, and the 1st Earl of Loreburn, as well as R.B. Haldane, who succeeded Loreburn as Lord Chancellor and was powerful both in intellect and in personality, and at that stage regarded as a very right-wing Liberal. Neither Reginald McKenna nor Walter Runciman was a roisterous character, but they too were respected and moderate politicians. It was a formidable Brooks's ministerial array, buttressed by one or two other lesser Cabinet members.

Admittedly the list did not contain either of the two political geniuses of that government, Lloyd George and Churchill. But patriotic fame was then some way ahead of Lloyd George and much further ahead of Churchill. They were regarded as the dangerous firebrands of the government. In Brooks's they might have been red rags to the bulls of St. James's Street. But perhaps fortunately they were not there. Nor were the other (for Marconi scandal reasons) most criticized members of the government, Rufus Isaacs and Herbert Samuel. Nor, thanks to a few blackballs in 1894, was Augustine Birrell who attracted a lot of blame as Chief Secretary for Ireland, or Colonel Jack Seely, who at the War Office made a real dog's breakfast of the 'mutiny' at the Curragh, or John Burns, the South London 'working man' whose oratory had been incendiary but whose administration of the Local Government Board was rigidly right-wing, or John Morley, whose position on the frontier of literature and politics earned him an OM, but whose ministerial style was more querulous than constructive.

So that star-studded last Liberal government presented its most acceptable face to Brooks's. The radical revolution, old Whiggery, and an increasingly non-political but probably instinctively Tory new member-ship co-existed in some degree of mutual tolerance. The subscription was kept down and standards were kept up. Dining unchanged was not permitted, although this was less easy-going than eighteenth-century practice when it seemed permissible to spend thirty-six-hour sessions of eating, drinking, gambling and making speaking forays to the House of Commons without any change of coat or even linen.

Perhaps this is an illusion (though I doubt it) and Fox was as meticulously attired when he walked down St. James's Street as was the king who gave his name to the Edwardian decade and who liked to see his standards observed by his friends as well as himself. Meeting one of his ADCs, Lord Harris of Seringapatan (cricketer and descendant of the vanquisher of Tippoo Sahib), the King observed with distaste that he was wearing a brown suit in the heart of the West End and the height of the London season. 'Mornin', Harris,' he is said to have gutturally growled, 'going rattin' I presume.' Harris was a member of the Cavalry Club, not Brooks's, but Fox might none the less have been more on his side than on that of King Edward.

The Great War

Patrick O'Brian

MOST houses of some age have places with an aura entirely of their own; and at Brooks's this is perhaps most apparent in the hall. In spite of the glowing fire and the comfortable seats it is hardly a room in its own right but rather a shapeless means of reaching the stairs and of course the half-dozen real rooms that open off it; yet members often sit there, not only to receive their guests but also because they like it.

And there can scarcely be anyone who, sitting there with his back to the staircase, has not gazed respectfully at the marble tablet bearing the names of those members and servants of the club who were killed in the last two great wars.

Between 1914 and 1918 no less than forty gave their lives: and since the Imperial War Museum states that the wounded outnumbered the dead by 2.367 times, the club's full casualty-list was in the nature of a hundred and thirty-four. During this period the average number of members was about 609 and of these well under half were of an age for active service – three-fifths being over fifty-seven: 134, therefore, represents a loss hardly to be equalled by any body of men with so small a proportion of professional soldiers. These figures are not set down in any spirit of invidious comparison, but only to make this point: in the nature of things the members were rather better off than most of their contemporaries; they had rather better lives; and they took it entirely for granted that they should pay for these privileges.

τῶνδε δὲ οὔτε πλούτου τις τὴν ἔτι ἀπόλαυσιν προτιμήσας ἐμαλακίσθη οὔτε πενίας ἐλπίδι

Nearly all these forty were young men in the flower of their time, men whose family names are sometimes most tragically repeated in the Roll of Honour for 1939–1945. In some cases those names are well known to anyone concerned with the country's history, but the list is long enough to be a fair sample of the younger members of the club in 1914; and their backgrounds were as varied as the ships or regiments they served in.

Some belonged to families of great political consequence: the Hon. Neil Primrose was Lord Rosebery's second son, and since he had a strong inclination for politics he too might have formed a cabinet had he survived. He was born in 1882, and like his father he was educated at Eton and Oxford; he was elected to Brooks's in 1904 (his father had been a member since 1872) and to the House of Commons in 1909, where he represented the Wisbech division of Cambridgeshire until his death. Early in the war he went to France with the Bucks Yeomanry, but in 1915 he was recalled to serve first as Under-Secretary for Foreign Affairs, then as Joint Parliamentary Secretary to the Treasury; and it was at this time that he married Lady Victoria Stanley. In 1917, however, it appears that he became dissatisfied with Lloyd George: at any event he rejoined his regiment, which was then fighting in the Near East; and in November of that year, at the very end of a successful engagement with the Turks near Gaza, he was killed.

Then there was Raymond Asquith, promised to a brilliant future. He was born in 1878, and after Winchester went on to Balliol, also as a scholar. There he had a career even more spectacular than his father's, winning the Craven, Ireland, Derby and Eldon scholarships, becoming president of the Union, taking a first in Greats in 1901 and in Jurisprudence the next year and being chosen a fellow of All Souls. He was called to the bar in 1904 and in 1906 he was elected to Brooks's, where his father, proposed by Lord Rosebery and seconded by Lord Lymington, had been a member since 1889. In 1907 he married Katharine Horner, and he was doing well in his profession when the war broke out. He joined the Queen's Westminsters and a few months later transferred to the Grenadier Guards, where, as his close friend John Buchan says, 'he was perfectly happy'. After a short, distasteful spell with the Intelligence Staff at GHQ he managed to rejoin his battalion, and he was with it early in September 1916 when his father saw him just behind the front, looking 'radiantly strong and confident'. A few days later, in the first stages of the Battle of the Somme, he was killed, leading his men as they went over the top.

Others came from houses that differed architecturally as much as, say, Rockingham and Castle Howard but which had much the same kind of influence in their own county. The St. Aubyns, for example, have been leading men in Cornwall time out of mind, guiding the affairs of the Duchy and the Stannaries from various manors or from their splendid St. Michael's Mount. The Hon. Piers St. Aubyn, who was born in 1871, was the fourth son of Lord St. Levan, and like most of his brothers he was a soldier. He served with the KRRC in South Africa and in the first Great War; he died of his wounds in October 1914, while his brother, Colonel Edward, was drowned in HMS *Persia* at the end of the following year. Yet for most it is probable that home meant one of those comfortable, unambitious country houses scattered about the kingdoms whose presence has surely done more for civilization than all the statutes put together; and it is fair to assume that the majority of these men would have been content to live as their fathers had lived, without any struggle for predominance, political or professional.

At this length of time, with almost all their contemporaries gone, it is hard to distinguish those members who were more wholly given over to country pursuits than others and it may well be that Edward Horner and Lord Lucas were not as typical as others who have left less trace. Edward Horner was born heir to a very large but impoverished estate in Somerset; he was educated at Eton and Balliol and became a member of Brooks's in 1911. By dint of privileged string-pulling he contrived to join the 18th Hussars in 1914 and two years later was very badly wounded in France. His mother and sister, together with Lady Diana Manners, were allowed to go over and bring him back to convalesce; when he was fit enough he was appointed to the staff in Egypt, but he disliked it extremely and used all the influence at his command to rejoin his regiment in France: there he was killed in November 1917.

Auberon Herbert, Lord Lucas, seems a less obvious example, for although he too owned a great deal of land he was in fact President of the Board of Agriculture when the war broke out. He was born in 1876 and educated at Bedford School and Balliol, where he rowed in the university boat. After Oxford he went to report on the Boer War for *The Times*, and there he was wounded, eventually losing a leg below the knee; but this never interfered with his trout-fishing, stalking, fox-hunting or watching birds. In 1905 his maternal uncle, Earl Cowper, died without issue and Auberon Herbert inherited his estates (which included Panshanger and Wrest Park) and those of his titles which did not follow the direct father-to-son descent, becoming 8th Baron Lucas and 11th Baron Dingwall. As one of the few Liberal peers he was pressed into service – a politician more by circumstance than design – and he held a junior post before becoming a minister. But his heart was not in it; he was not a good speaker; and when the coalition government was formed in 1915 he threw up his appointment and in spite of his age and disability managed to join the Royal Flying Corps, serving first in Egypt and then in France. He was a particularly lovable man with a great many friends and to their grief he was killed in November 1916, shot down over the German lines. Maurice Baring was among his friends, and he wrote a long poem in which appear the lines *O liberal heart fast-rooted in the soil/ O lover of ancient freedom and proud toil*. It is said that if he had lived until the peace he would in all likelihood have returned not to politics nor to his other estates but to Picket Post, his small and primitive house in the New Forest, there to watch birds and tie trout flies.

Varied as their backgrounds were, they were all clubbable men and they all shared a liberal attitude towards the world: not so much Liberal in the party sense – indeed, many of them may scarcely have been politically-inclined at all – but liberal as one says the liberal arts or a liberal education, which surely encourages a certain openness and candour.

And they all used this same hall, sitting there and talking to their friends or waiting for the people they had invited, looking from time to time at the same clock on the mantelshelf. They all, coming through the front door from an Edwardian St. James's Street, stepped into another world: not so much an eighteenth- or early nineteenth-century world as a wholly traditional place untied to any of the set periods and surviving them all. For those young men of seventy-five years ago, accustomed to motor-cars, glaring advertisements and the gutter press, the change was already considerable; but for the older members of today it is immeasurably greater, since they step back to the world they were born in, into a timeless way of life, a material and spiritual civilization that has almost vanished. And the fact that they and their descendants can do so is owing in no small part to those whose names are carved upon the marble.

Brooks's between the Wars

James Neidpath

THE period between the two German wars is rightly regarded as one of the least satisfactory in British history – two decades during which the hard-won fruits of military victory were squandered through political irresolution and economic failure, and at the conclusion of which all for which Britain had stood faced utter destruction.

Brooks's Club, in a less dramatic fashion thank God, mirrored this *Zeitgeist*: the self-confidence in its own identity which it had enjoyed before the Great War was supplanted by doubt and some despair concerning its function in a changed world. Before 1914 Brooks's was perceived as a club for gentlemen – an elastic term – especially popular with Whigs or right-wing Liberals. But the Whig doctrine – always a source of amazement to its opponents – that by continuing concessions to radicalism a landed aristocracy could not only retain the maximum political influence, but actually increase its material prosperity, had been in retreat since the 1870s. The 5th Marquess of Lansdowne, who had been Under-Secretary of State for War for Gladstone in 1872–74, but left his administration in 1880 over Irish policy – the Compensation for Disturbance Bill stuck in his gizzard – is regarded as the harbinger of this change, accelerated by the Home Rule crisis of 1885–6, which left only one Whig grandee – the Marquess of Crewe in Asquith's 1914 Cabinet.

Right-wing liberalism – or liberalism of any kidney, for that matter – had been additionally threatened by the dramatic rise of the Labour party, which increased its seats in the Commons from 39 in 1918 to 191 in 1923, and by the rancorous split of the Liberal party between Squiffites (followers of Asquith) and Georgeites, (followers of Lloyd George), crystallized in the Maurice debate of 9 May 1918.

With the Whig-Liberal doctrine in a state of such dissolution, could Brooks's continue to represent it in clubland? Or must the club acquire some other ethos? Or must it fold altogether?

The manner in which the club responded to this crisis may be deduced from an analysis of the membership, its political activity and its occupations in 1920 and in 1940 respectively.

The centre of gravity of the Club in 1920 could be said to lie in the liberal landed classes, with an admixture of radically-minded business-men. It was this combination which characterized Whiggery's strangely selective brand of snobbery: when Archibald Sinclair stood as a Liberal candidate for Caithness & Sutherland in 1922, it was alleged that he was *too snobbish to stand as a Tory*. A notable feature of the period is the decline of the landed interest – members, that is to say, who if not owners of estates themselves, came from landed families. In 1920 259, or 36% of the total membership fell into such a category; by 1940 only 151, or 14% of the total of 636 members came from the same background – evidence, no doubt, of the difficulties confronted by landowners in a period of low rents and agricultural depression. The aristocracy – or, at least, the peerage – was another (over-lapping) group to dwindle. There were 319 peers or peers' sons who were members in 1920, by 1940 the figure was 204 – a decline of 12%.

Regular army officers fell away too. In 1920 the Club was surprisingly military, 18% of the members, including many politically active Liberals, holding regular commissions. By 1940 the proportion had dropped sharply, to 12%. Lawyers, bankers, members of the Foreign Office, civil servants and business men remained fairly constant or increased proportionately – 10% of members were bankers in 1920 and 1940, for instance. There were at these dates few academics, priests, artists, doctors, historians, authors or journalists – only one identified author, in 1940.

It was in the political field, however, that the centre of gravity shifted most dramatically. Between 1920 and 1940 the number of Liberal MPs (past, sitting, or future) fell from 95 to 25, and of Liberal peers (i.e. peers who had been Liberal MPs or who had been in Liberal governments) from 56 to 14. Over the same period the numbers of Conservative MPs and peers actually rose. Liberal MPs had out-numbered Conservatives by 95 to 31 in 1920. By 1940 the ratio was twenty-five to thirty-four. Brooks's still considered itself liberal, but it had lost its character as a Liberal political club.

In common with their compatriots, the members of the club hoped above all for a 'return to normalcy' after the privations and compromises of the late conflict. Thus on 3 January 1919, eight former menservants having been demobilized, it was resolved by the House Committee to give all the waitresses notice to leave. A campaign to improve the quality of the club food after the horrors of wartime was also in order. So on 12 December 1918 'A backed luncheon bill of Mr C.W. James complaining of the quality of an egg served to him was laid before the Meeting [of the House Committee]'. On 13 February 1919 the Committee considered a further complaint from Mr James about the butter, and from other members about cheese and a sole ('eatable but not fresh'); and on 16 January 1919 the Committee had resolved that 'Complaints having been received about the qualities of the celery, other tradespeople to be tried.'

While the House Committee laboured to improve the material condition of the club, the Literary Sub-committee, conscious that in its library the club possessed an asset which set it apart from, or above, its neighbours and rivals in St. James's Street, addressed itself to the members' intellectual and moral welfare. On the principle of 'know thine enemy', it resolved on 7 January 1920 to purchase (second-hand, of course) copies of von Tirpitz's, von Falkenhayn's and Ludendorff's memoirs. The Sub-committee's task was not assisted by the tendency of some members to purloin books from the Library. On 28 July 1920, for instance, the Sub-committee noted that *A Remedy against Sin* had gone missing; it was still missing on 9 May 1921, although *Night Haunts of London*, also missing, had by then been found. No doubt the Subcommittee's decision on 4 December 1924 not to purchase the *Life and Times of Nell Gwynne* sprang from a fear that it would only go the way of *A Remedy against Sin*.

In the great work of moral reconstruction there was, however, room for differences of opinion. Viscount Moore (later 11th Earl Drogheda), proposed that '*La Vie Parisienne* is a "bad" paper and should be discontinued.' But, 'bad' or not, this paper – of which a copy is being read by one of the members of the Bachelor's Club in the Batemanesque cartoon in the members' downstairs lavatory – was so popular that the Library Committee resolved on 6 April 1932 to reject Viscount Moore's advice.

The Library Committee was one forum in which the question of how far the less cerebral country sports should be allowed to invade the life of the club had to be decided. On 27 November 1933 it was resolved to send a suitable letter of thanks to Mr A.H. Pollen for his presentation of the volume *Trencher and Kennel* by Charles Simpson to the club, and the Managers on 26 April 1934 agreed to a suggestion that the publication *Game and Gun* should be taken – for a three month trial period. But there were limits, as the Managers affirmed on 10 February 1932 when they resolved that the 1920 ban on 'the posting of notices of Hunters and Polo Ponies, etc:, for sale' should be continued.

The struggle for the soul of the club was, however, best expressed in the Great Billiards Table Controversy. Brooks's had started in the eighteenth century as a club for heavy gamblers. With the triumph of the Non-conformist view of gambling, and the financial exhaustion of the membership, card games in the club had, by the 1920s, become pretty tame if judged by the standards of Charles James Fox. The 9th Duke of Devonshire thought that 'at present the Club after Dinner was a gloomy place for those who were not Card players', and that as 'Clubs ought to do all they can to attract the younger generation who would be the Candidates of the future', the Small Smoking Room should be turned into a billiards room. At the Extraordinary General Meeting [EGM] called to discuss the Duke's motion on 10 February 1925 there was brisk opposition, led by Sir George H. Murray (formerly Chairman of the Board of Inland Revenue, a functionary unlikely to have been popular with His Grace), who took the view that the Small Smoking Room 'was the only room in the Club where a Member who wished to slumber peacefully had any chance of doing so', and the motion only passed by the narrow margin of 36 votes to 31 against. A Billiard(s) Room Sub-Committee under the Rt. Hon. Harold John Tennant, brother-in-law of H.H. Asquith, was therefore constituted to resolve the vexed question of the size of the pockets, and 'to enquire as to the extra cost of fitting a railroad underneath the Table'.

The difficulty that the club found in recruiting enough members of the sort it wanted cannot be adduced from the numerical strength of the membership, which only fluctuated between 631 and 657 during this period, nor from the Candidates' Book, as the reasons for withdrawal of candidates are always obscure. But chairmen's reports to AGMs throughout the 1920s emphasized the necessity of, and difficulty in finding enough suitable members to bring the club up to its theoretical strength of 650.

The difficulty that some members found in funding the subscription – which rose from 12 guineas to 15 guineas during this period, is also evident from the decision of an EGM on 10 February 1932 to permit the 'Payment of Subscriptions in two instalments during the financial stringency.'

Absorbed as it was in its own problems, the club nonetheless found time to do its bit towards the solution of other problems in the wider world.

On 29 January 1931 the Managers accordingly agreed to pay the usual annual subscription of two guineas to the 'Bribery & Secret Commissions Prevention League' (sometimes more laconically named the 'Anti-Bribery League'). And during the 1933 World Economic Conference – graveyard of many hopes for freer world trade – the club liberally bestowed Honorary Membership on members of the German, French and Swedish Delegations. But, here again, there were limits, as when the Managers regretted that a 'proposal from the Prince of Wales that a percentage of the 1934 Derby Sweepstake may be allocated towards a fund for slum relief of dis-abled ex-servicemen . . . cannot be approved.' Royalty did better at the hands of the club on 20 February 1938 when Queen Mary, a keen student of architecture, paid a visit, causing near-apoplexy to one unforewarned member asleep under his newspaper in the Morning Room. The Managers had considered presenting to Her Majesty a set of eight old gaming counters to mark the occasion but, on further reflection, decided that a copy of *Memorials of Brooks's* would sufficiently embellish the Royal collection.

This was the heyday of 'the appeasement of Europe' conducted by Chamberlain and Lord Halifax, culminating in the Munich settlement of

29 September 1938, 'a triumph', in A.J.P. Taylor's words, 'for all that was best and most enlightened in British life.' Brooks's, of which Halifax as well as many others of the enlightened and high-minded were members, was one of the epicentres of the appeasing movement. But Herr Hitler, it turned out, was not so high-minded after all, and on 3 September 1939 the nation reluctantly went to war against him. Brooks's characteristically rose to the occasion, and this era in the Club's history may well close with the Managers minuting public-spiritedly on 2 November 1939, that 'The Members of the War Cabinet have been made Honorary Members for the duration of the War.'

The Second World War

James Lees-Milne

I RECALL the late Lord Crewe expatiating round a table in rather more
detail than in his written *Recollections of Brooks's* on the dreadful
row which rent the club in the early 1880s. A new secretary had dared
to have the club's address inscribed on the writing paper. Half the
members threatened to resign over this signal act of vulgarity. Now Lord
Crewe's great-grandfather (and many people have known their great-
grandfathers), John Crewe, was a founder member of the club before it
moved to its present premises in 1778, and a boon companion of its
presiding genius, Charles James Fox, who died in 1806. In that Lord
Crewe fathered a son after I was born, there could well be several dynastic
members of Brooks's with a mere four-generation gap between its
foundation in 1765 and 1990. Possibly they possess hitherto undisclosed
anecdotes of Brooks's in the eighteenth century.

When I was elected in 1937 there was very little evidence of that
raffishness associated with Mr Crewe, who was described by his
contemporaries as a macaroni. Brooks's was still a Whig preserve in fact
if not in name. It was singularly staid. If there were macaronis about they
kept quiet. Indeed, young members kept a low profile and minded their
betters. Geoffrey Madan, a brilliant but unfulfilled contemporary of the
pre-1914 *jeunesse dorée*, used to stalk, a sombre spectre, round the club,
pouncing on junior members and impressing upon them their lowly
status and required subservience. An alarming man. On the other hand
some older members, like John Christie, smiled upon the young. Christie
would even insist, if there was a coincidence at the desk, on paying for the
novice's meal, a kindly gesture strictly speaking contrary to club

etiquette. But he was a law unto himself. For one glorious half at Eton he was meant to teach me mathematics at early school. Since he invariably arrived in a chauffeur-driven Rolls Royce more than ten minutes late we were permitted a run back to bed. A very different breach of etiquette was that of the enigmatic adviser to Prime Ministers, Dr Tom Jones. He was not a member and when my guest would, on being served first at table, dump a meagre helping upon my plate and hog the greater part of the dish for himself.

I do not recall footmen in knee-breeches during the 'thirties. Certainly members always dined in black ties by candlelight. Possibly a Highlander about to take a sleeper to Inverness might wear a dark suit, for which he would give a rather self-conscious explanation. The silver on the tables and sideboard was very resplendent, and even famous, until it was stolen in 1959. A member claimed to have seen a stranger with a genial face and enormous sack over one shoulder emerge from the back regions, walk past the hall fireplace saying 'Lovely afternoon!' and disappear unruffled into the street. A very fine George 1 cup by Paul Lamerie given to the club by two Farrer brothers was not stolen, but, with the donors' consent, sold to raise funds for the club. In 1943, when most clubs had become somewhat tatty, Harold Nicolson purred with approval of the silver and the way it was cleaned. I do not remember the china being much to write home about. In 1935 cheese plates were replaced at 10s. 3d. (51p) a dozen and meat plates at 1s. 6d. (7½p) a dozen, which even for those days does not indicate high quality. In 1940 the portrait of Fox by Opie was presented by Lord Rosebery, and the picture of 'Edwin' by Reynolds by Sir Chartres Biron.

The club subscription was only fifteen guineas a year. Members certainly got value for their money. The club was open every weekend. This was a particular boon to bachelors, of whom there seemed a great number. Brooks's was a veritable home to some who existed on slender incomes in distant West Kensington bed-sitting-rooms. Those who could afford them had all their meals in the club. Others disappeared for half an hour to return for coffee which in those days was free. I knew one so poor that for luncheon he either went to a pub (a place gentlemen seldom entered) or ate sandwiches in the lavatory behind a locked door. For the exclusive members, *al fresco* meals were obtainable on demand at any time of the day and throughout most of the night. In 1935 one member complained that he was made to pay 9d. (3½p) table money for eggs and bacon.

Sundays were festive days for the bachelors, of whom I recall with esteem and affection regulars like Sir Orme (Moley) Sargent, Lord Stanmore, Gerry Villiers, Eddy Sackville-West (my seconder) and Eddie Marsh. They often ate together merrily and then retired to sleep in the library. This was a strictly silent room where never a sound was heard, if loud snoring from white pillows was discounted. The Victorian library was a holy sanctuary and like Mount Athos never desecrated by female foot – except once. In 1938 Queen Mary was escorted into it as a great privilege by her equerry, John Coke. To her consternation the late Duke of Devonshire, at full length on a sofa, opened a bleary eye and exclaimed, 'My God, a woman!', then jumped to his feet with 'Ma'am!'

On the whole Brooks's was less convivial before the war than today. Unless members were close friends they seldom spoke to one another. They might nod in casual salutation rather like the two explorer members who when passing on camels in the Sahara silently raised their caps. Eddie Marsh, naturally garrulous in company, would maintain an oyster-like taciturnity if sitting in the coffee room next to a member to whom he had not been introduced. In fact it was customary for the single eater to be reading from a book-rest automatically provided by the waiter for that purpose. Four or five might thus be seen in a row poring over, say, *Brideshead Revisited* and a cutlet.

Change in the club from peace to wartime conditions was gradual. As the rigours of everyday life broke down the Englishman-in-the-street's endemic reserve, so too within the portals of Brooks's formality gave way to a freer and easier manner. Hitherto topical events had been held of little account, or were strangely muted. Thus a minute of the annual meeting of 1937 reads: 'The Chairman made a few remarks regarding the Coronation and the question of a new kitchen range.'

The Secretary's correspondence reveals that when in 1938 the European situation worsened there was an unwonted number of resignations. In 1939 the trickle augmented and by 1940 turned into a spate. Amongst others Sir Edwin Lutyens deeply regretted that he could no longer afford to continue membership, being obliged to curtail all expenses that were not absolutely necessary.

On the outbreak of war the Managers immediately lowered the subscription of members serving in the armed forces to three guineas. Even so some serving members defaulted until brought to heel by a sharp reminder from the Secretary. He received some pitiable letters complaining of lack of funds. Indeed, having left their peacetime jobs many army, navy and air force members found themselves with no earned income at all beyond their exiguous service pay. I blush to be reminded that I was one of those subjected to the Secretary's quite proper admonishment for being behindhand with my subscription. On the other hand one over-age millionaire landowner was surprised that his plea to pay the serviceman's three guineas was politely rejected by the Secretary. Not until 1946 was the general subscription raised to eighteen guineas, in 1949 to twenty-two guineas, and in 1953 to twenty-five guineas, which many members thought portended the end of the world.

The instant war broke out, the club chairman wrote to the Prime Minister offering free hospitality to those members of the War Cabinet who did not already belong to Brooks's; and also to a number of accredited diplomatists among the Allies. Full use was made of this generous proposition.

Positive blackballing of candidates had been done away with after a devastating upheaval in the club over Gladstone's Home Rule for Ireland Bill of 1886. Henceforward the election of members was controlled by a special committee. The committee remained pretty autocratic, as I once experienced in seconding a distinguished friend of seemingly impeccable Whig lineage whose forebears had been successive members of Brooks's. To the proposer's and my amazement we were asked to withdraw his name. No reason was given. Later I discovered it. Within a few weeks of being divorced he had married a well-known film star. Ordinary members could be vilely exclusive. In 1943 a baronet protested to the committee against the admission of a candidate of Russo-Jewish extraction. 'I do not know this person,' he wrote, 'but I feel he is not the type the majority of the members of Brooks's want as their fellow-member.' The election committee evidently agreed with him.

Never in the recorded history of Brooks's had a member been expelled, but in 1941 great excitement was caused by the summons of an

A meeting of the Society of Dilettanti in 1779, by Sir Joshua Reynolds, PRA. In the possession of the Society of Dilettanti

Self-portrait, 1776, by Sir Joshua Reynolds, PRA. In the possession of the Society of Dilettanti

extraordinary general meeting for this purpose. Complaints had been lodged of the accused's general misconduct, bad language and, worst of all, rudeness to some of the club servants. Rightly, the last offence was considered unpardonable. The whole staff had threatened to leave unless he did. Invited to do so by the Chairman he truculently declined. However, at the meeting, heavily attended although it was wartime, the Chairman was able to announce that the miscreant had sent in his resignation and promised never to cross the threshold of the club again. At the time I sensed a faint ripple of disappointment over the assembled company for being deprived, as it were, of some lively *schadenfreude*.

Brooks's building was miraculously spared destruction. Far less damage was caused during the five years' bombardment of London than by an IRA bomb chucked through the coffee-room window in 1974. In April 1941 I got caught in one of the worst raids on London. I had been up from the country for the day and was unable to take a train back to where I was billeted. Emerging from a restaurant near Piccadilly Circus I dared not risk walking to Brooks's for a bed, and was obliged to take a room in the Piccadilly Hotel for the night in which 2,300 Londoners were killed and 3,000 injured. At 5 a.m. the all-clear siren sounded. I surfaced from the hotel cellars and roamed the streets. The fate of Brooks's was my chief anxiety. It took an hour to get to it through the debris which actually looked worse than it proved to be. Mysterious fires belched from gas pipes in the streets. The pavements were knee deep in broken glass, the wares from shop windows, smashed doors, fallen parapets, twisted motor cars and a bus or two. In King Street Christie's was a furnace, hurling furniture and pictures high into the air. Amidst the devastation on all sides Brooks's survived unscathed. At dawn the façade under a pall of black smoke twinkled in the flickering light from neighbouring furnaces. It is a fact that most of London's greatly-loved buildings, like Westminster Abbey and St. Paul's, came off comparatively lightly so long as they were spared a direct hit. I believe that volunteers watched on the roof of Brooks's, scooping up firebombs and shovelling them into the street.

Not surprisingly the decoration of the club grew shabbier. I fancy it had in any case been dreary for a long time. A document headed *Redecoration of the Club 1903–1933* discloses that distemper was sloshed annually on the bedroom walls. In 1913 the front rooms were indiscriminately painted an overall eau-de-Nil. In the 1920s a craze for pickling woodwork and chimneypieces ensued. In the 1930s Harvey Nichols were employed to carry out strictly utilitarian redecoration. The impression gained from the club accounts is that good taste was considered unmanly. The late Lord Spencer complained that members knocked out their pipes on the stair walls. Fortunately Professor A.E. Richardson was appointed the building's architect. What precisely he did is hard to ascertain, but it must have been for the good. The staircase ironwork balusters were his, he told me. He also complained bitterly of the Managers' philistinism. 'They' would not give him a free hand, and were suspicious of his love of the Georgian style. From Boodle's window he once showed me how after the war he would remove the roof balustrade put up by the Victorians. He would restore the first-floor balcony which featured much in Georgian prints and caricatures. These schemes were not adopted.

I had some experience of the Managers' philistinism. On leaving the club in a hurry one dark November morning of 1942 I saw workmen tearing down the William IV railings. I admired these stalwart railings for, although of later date than the building, they represented the peak of London club prosperity and popularity. At Waterloo station I had time to send telegrams of protest to the Secretary and Lord Ilchester, then Chairman, who reluctantly took the matter up with Lord Portal at the Ministry of Works. Apparently it was the result of a stupid mistake. I am not sure that the Secretary knew what was happening, or would have cared if he had known. The railings were spared, but not for long. Soon after the war they were replaced by neo-Georgian substitutes deemed more 'in keeping'. Whenever a house owner's back was turned his railings might be taken for scrap willy-nilly, as indeed the contemporary gates of Spencer House went while Lord Spencer was in the country for a week.

From 1939 to 1945 Brooks's, hitherto apparently indifferent to world events, became a sort of secondary War Cabinet assembly place, or so it seemed. Ministers were constantly in a huddle, either confabulating together at luncheon and dinner, or hunched on sofas in the morning-room. I sometimes wondered whether highly secret deliberations were not overheard by the hidden enemy. Free French resistance fighters, having just crossed the Channel, would be gesticulating and narrating adventures to their embassy officials. The American Ambassador, John Winant, who resembled Abraham Lincoln with his limpid black eyes under beetling brows, would be sketching plans on the tablecloth with Lord Reith. This nervous man kept passing a fountain pen through his lanky hair as though it were a pen-wiper. I remember Lord Trenchard, Marshal of the RAF, booming at the top of his voice to General Lord Mottistone in front of the hall fire one January day of 1942. 'Believe me, the Japs can't hold out much longer now,' he shouted, somewhat prematurely. 'Well, you ought to know,' said the other. How wrong the great could be. Lord Trenchard, when Commissioner of Metropolitan Police in the 1930s, confided to my friend Robert Byron after dinner, 'I have it on authority that there are quite twenty-five homosexuals' (only he didn't use that word) 'in the London district alone.' To him they were synonymous with spies.

I do not remember seeing either Neville Chamberlain or Winston Churchill eating in Brooks's. Sir Austen Chamberlain, on the other hand, was a frequenter. Spruce, monocled, buttonholed, starch and upright, he wore a bland mask which revealed nothing going on behind it. Lord Halifax, dark, Jesuitical, pillar of rectitude, Foreign Secretary and Ambassador to Washington, was constantly in and out. 'Wasn't it awkward, sir,' Newman the hall porter once said to me, 'there was Mr John [Fox-Strangways] using the most dreadful swear words while I was helping his lordship with his overcoat.' Lord Woolton, Minister of Food, beaming, friendly, protested that food in the British Restaurants which he had invented was better than at Brooks's. And, at the risk of repeating myself, I conjure up the memorable vision, which somehow epitomizes Brooks's conjunction of past with present, of the octogenarian Bertram Godfray Falle, 1st and last Baron Portsea, spreading the tails of his immaculate frock-coat, his back to the hall fire in which a few embers glowed, and waiting for his jingling carriage and pair to drive him through the snow and blackout, home to Carlton House Terrace.

The truth is that my memories of Brooks's over the years are so multifarious and the building is so haunted by ghosts of the eminent and the ordinary, including many old friends, that to view them in their proper context is an effort. Time does not so much stand still as work itself into an inextricable muddle. Against a familiar and more or less unchanging background the ghosts are as real, sometimes more so, than the living, their presence just as unpredictable and their conduct often mystifying. Was it yesterday or half a century ago that I saw in the lavatory an ancient peer of the realm, false teeth in hand, scrubbing them with one of the hairbrushes? And saw and heard Sir Edward Elgar talking on the telephone to his dogs in Worcestershire?

I see again those who during the war reappeared at the club on leave, having flown from the East, North Africa, Lisbon or the United States; those due to sail the next morning for, say, the second front or Burma, like Tom Mitford of the Queen's Westminsters who did not return. He was shot by a Japanese sniper. And I rejoin an eager throng in the entrance hall, looking over shoulders at the tape as it rattles out the first good news of the war, the unconditional surrender of Italy on 8 September 1943. My first reaction was one of relief; my second of anxiety lest worse fighting than ever against the Germans might take place in that wonderful and vulnerable country.

The Roll of Honour in the hall is a reminder of the toll taken in the two world wars of members and staff of Brooks's, mostly very young men. Whereas those of the 1914–1918 war number forty, those of the 1939–1945 war number thirty-four. It might be supposed that the discrepancy would be greater, because casualties amongst servicemen generally in the first war were infinitely worse. But in the second the Brigade of Guards and the Royal Air Force suffered extremely heavy losses. John Piggott-Brown was a Coldstream casualty in Tunisia in 1942. Meysey G.D. Clive and twenty-one-year-old Hugh Trenchard, both Grenadiers, were killed in 1943. The next year, was a deadly one. Mark Howard was killed by a stray bullet after the invasion of Normandy and Billy Hartington in Belgium just five weeks after his marriage. Both were in the Coldstream. In August Edward Fitzmaurice (Irish Guards) fell in Normandy, aged twenty-two, nine days before his elder brother Lansdowne was wounded in Italy. Christopher Howard, Mark's youngest brother in the RAF was brought down over Germany, aged twenty-two. Nigel Richards, an extraordinarily gifted and courageous man, was another RAF victim.

Victor Cazalet MP likewise lost his life in an air crash in 1943 while serving as political liaison officer to the Polish leader General Sikorsky. Cazalet had fought in the trenches in the first war. An Oxford blue for tennis and racquets, he became amateur squash champion of Great Britain between 1925 and 1930. He was much travelled, a connoisseur and patron of the arts who commissioned for himself a country house, Great Swifts, in Kent from the architect Geddes Hyslop.

The only member serving in the Marines that I am aware of was Christopher Hobhouse. With an extremely sharp intellect and great self-assurance he was in civilian life a barrister whose ambition it was to become Lord Chancellor. Who knows whether, had he survived, he might not have attained that ambition? As it was, on reaching his majority he stood, unsuccessfully, for Parliament, being dubbed by the press to his chagrin 'the children's candidate'; and in 1934 he published while only twenty-four a first-rate biography of Charles James Fox. He was bombed while on duty at Plymouth in 1940.

These were tragically wasted lives of promise, whose names may now mean little except to a dwindling few who still hold them in respect and admiration. Their places at Brooks's were soon taken by a younger generation for when the war was over the waiting list of candidates filled up apace. Brooks's was either luckier, or more prudently managed, or more popular than several long-established clubs doomed to disappear in the lean years which followed the return to peace. It has never yet had to comb the highways and hedges for entrants, and let us hope it never will be reduced to doing so.

Brooks's since the War

Christopher Wood

'There is nothing which has yet been contrived by man by which so much happiness is produced, as by a good club.'

I found this quotation, unattributed, among the papers of the late Esmond Warner, a member of Brooks's from 1954 until his death in 1984, and for many years Honorary Librarian. It is equally axiomatic that there are few institutions contrived by man which are more conservative, or more resistant to change, than a man's club. The story of Brooks's since the war is the story of its evolution from an old-fashioned, rather sedate, Victorian establishment, into a modern club. As the 1990s dawn, and the twenty-first century approaches, Brooks's has at last adapted itself, reluctantly, to the twentieth.

Like all London clubs, Brooks's has been forced to change with the times, and it has succeeded in doing so, without losing too much of its distinctive style and atmosphere. It is now one of the liveliest, most interesting, and most successful of London clubs. Its finances are healthy, its membership strong, its candidates' book full of applicants. It has a total membership of over fourteen hundred, of whom fifty-two have been members for over fifty years, which argues that the changes have been successful and have not interrupted the essential continuity of the club. No longer can Brooks's be described as like a Duke's town house, with the Duke lying dead upstairs. A new Duke has succeeded, who drinks at the bar, plays backgammon and snooker, and even entertains ladies to dinner.

The two most fundamental changes to Brooks's since the war have been the amalgamation with the St. James' and the admission of ladies. Equally important, although less visible, has been the putting of the club's finances in good order. This has only really happened in the last ten years. Looking through the minutes of the Managers' meetings from 1945 up to about 1980, one gets the impression of a more or less continuous financial crisis. One also gets the impression that financial extremity was usually the motive force behind any change. In other words, the Managers only changed things when forced to. Perhaps this is true of all clubs. Thus, with every crisis, the subscription was increased, to twenty-five guineas in 1953 and the membership to seven hundred and fifty. In 1974, a notoriously difficult year, the subscription had to be increased twice, first to £70, then to £80, and two hundred more members were admitted. So it went on, through the 1970s and 80s, and now the subscription for an ordinary member over thirty stands at £525.

The profitability of any club is largely dependent on the amount its members drink. During the 1950s and 60s the average Brooks's member ate little, and drank less. Francis Sitwell, who joined in 1958, described the older members as the 'bowler hat and barley water brigade', who usually ate frugally and drank at the most one glass of dry sherry. One member, C.W. Buckingham, made an agreement with the Managers to lunch for £1 a day. His meal consisted of a plate of beef, pickled walnuts, and one and a half glasses of sherry. Mr Buckingham would also hiss like a snake at anyone he found sitting in his usual chair. The club in those days was said to be so quiet that upstairs the only sounds to be heard were clocks ticking and cards hitting the table.

The best way to induce the members of a club to drink more is to have a bar. This was for many years an extremely thorny question. It was discussed by the Managers throughout the 1940s and 50s, but nothing was done. Clearly both the Managers and the majority of members regarded the whole idea of a bar with aversion. They preferred the proper, old-fashioned method of ringing a bell, and having drinks brought on a tray. Bars would do for hotels or golf clubs, but not for Brooks's. Only in the 1960s, after another particularly bad financial crisis, was a bar first introduced into the club. It was small, poky, apologetic, and situated in a corner of the old Strangers Room, now the Backgammon Room, just inside the front door. This remained the location of the bar until 1975, when the arrival of the St. James' led to the bar moving to its present location, in the old back morning room. After some teething troubles over decoration and the precise size of the bar itself, it has proved a very popular and successful room, and greatly contributes to the financial prosperity of the club.

Next to the bar, the greatest problem to agitate the minds of the Managers since the war has been the admission of ladies. It first appears in the Managers' Minutes about 1960 and from the start met with fanatical resistance. Before this, the only ladies to enter the club at all had been Queen Mary, whose secret visit has been described elsewhere, and the Queen Mother, who attended the Rout held after the Coronation in 1953. During the 1960s, nothing further was done about ladies. Alastair Wedderburn, one of the Managers during this period and a die-hard reactionary, even by Brooks's standards, described Queen Mary's visit as 'the thin end of the wedge'. His prediction proved correct. During the 1970s ladies began to be admitted to private parties, in the evenings. At the same time, a ladies' wing was proposed but this foundered, partly through apathy, but also because of the severe practical problems of adapting the building. Finally, ladies were allowed in every evening after 6 p.m. although not into certain rooms, such as the bar and the Members Room. This has proved a successful compromise, and ladies are now a regular feature of the dining-room every evening. It is all a far cry from the old dining-room, where elderly gentlemen would sit at separate tables, each with his stand for a book or magazine, the food being served in dishes on the table, so that he could help himself. Now the dining-room is both lively and popular, and often fully booked during the summer months. As with schools, so it is with clubs – the ladies have had a civilizing and beneficial influence, as well as helping the all-important finances.

Another vital contribution to the club's financial well-being has been the renting out of the first-floor rooms for private parties. In 1978 two semicircular bedrooms and a bathroom at the top of the stairs became once more a small circular dining-room together with an ante-room, and were renamed the Cavendish and Lansdowne Rooms. These and the other rooms used for parties have proved extraordinarily popular and successful. It is now quite common to find two or three parties taking place in the club on the same night. This has inevitably led to staff and catering problems, and to complaints from grumpy members, but it has helped more than anything else to put the club on a sound financial footing. Any club occupying a large eighteenth-century building in the centre of London containing such fine rooms as Brooks's does have to make the maximum use of them. Since 1987, Pavilion Opera has given regular performances in the Subscription Room. Another innovation has been the introduction of a buffet lunch for members on the first floor. This began in the 1970s in the Library in emulation of the St. James', and was successful in providing a cheaper and quicker lunch than the dining-room below. It was felt, however, that it altered the atmosphere of the library too drastically, so in 1982 it was moved to the Card Room next door, which was then renamed the Spencer Room. This has proved one of the most successful institutions in the club. Many members use it in preference to the dining room. It is usually crowded, lively and conversational. Charles James Fox would surely approve. It must also be one of the few places in central London where a man can eat a good lunch, and enjoy congenial company, for under £10.

Wars and revolutions cannot be compared with the upheaval caused by the amalgamation of one club with another. It is no exaggeration to say that nothing in the entire history of Brooks's compared with the decision taken in 1975, to merge with the St. James'. The core of the problem was the different characters of the two clubs. Brooks's was old-fashioned, aloof, Whiggish – the St. James' was cosmopolitan, artistic, occasionally boisterous. The arrival of so many new faces at Brooks's, all at once, was bound to cause discontent. The late Lord Gage expressed the rather extreme view that the new members 'reminded him of Al Capone's bodyguard', though a more tight-lipped Michael Beaumont described them as 'rather a mixed hand of cards': for their part, they found their hosts a little dull. But in the end things settled down, and the marriage has proved an extremely happy one. The St. James' members may make more noise, drink more, and play backgammon, but they have contributed greatly to the present character of the club, and to its success. The amalgamation has really given birth to a new club, combining the best of both their traditions.

It is not easy for me to write about the spirit of the old Brooks's, as I only joined in 1979, after the amalgamation. Nor is it easy to describe some of the personalities of those days. The two most often recalled by the present members are Newman, the head porter, and the late Lord Spencer. In their different ways, these two men seem to have dominated the club during the 1950s and 60s. Newman was the very model of an old-fashioned club porter: immaculate, courteous, amazingly knowledgeable about the club, its members, and their families; rather daunting to younger members. When Francis Sitwell joined Brooks's as a young man, his father, Sir Sacheverell Sitwell, said to him, 'Newman will look after you'. Newman finally retired in 1969, after fifty-one years' service. Lord Spencer, known as 'Jolly Jack' Spencer to his friends, was an autocratic figure, and the virtual ruler of the club during the post-war years. He was a Trustee, and a Manager, and in 1952 began the Decoration Subcommittee. Virtually no decision about the club, even where to put a picture or a chair, was made without reference to him. Although famed for his outbursts of rage, Lord Spencer is remembered by many in the club as an affable, loyal and highly knowledgeable man. He was absolutely devoted to the club and its welfare, and in 1964 wrote what is still its only modern history. Typically, there was little love lost between him and Newman. James Lees-Milne remembers that whenever he had forgotten an umbrella, Newman would say, maliciously, 'Take *his*,' pointing to Lord Spencer's.

Lord Portsea, so vividly described by James Lees-Milne, died soon after the war, in the club, still wearing his top hat: the last of Brooks's Edwardians. During the 1950s and 60s the club was still much dominated by older men, many of them rather alarming to the younger members. There was Alastair Wedderburn, who still addressed everyone by their surnames, and employed rather archaic language with the staff; in the dining-room he would ask for a wench to bring him 'the bill of fare'. John Christie, the founder of Glyndebourne, Albert Richardson, architect and President of the Royal Academy, and John Wheeler-Bennett, the historian, were all members during this period. As always in a club, the members remembered the longest are those who create the most mayhem. Chief hell-raiser of those days was undoubtedly John Fox-Strangways. On finding his favourite bedroom already reserved, he went upstairs and threw all the bedclothes and a good deal more, out of the bedroom and down the stairs. His most famous or notorious exploit was to kick Aneurin Bevan down the stairs of his other club, White's. Another member of the same ilk was Lord Revelstoke, who after one of the Routs was found fast asleep in the chef's bed. Lord Hesketh is chiefly remembered for his habit of escaping by the side door, while importunate ladies were kept at bay by Newman in the front hall.

The Secretary during the 1950s was Major Harold Lucas, formerly a Quartermaster in the Grenadiers. His usual reply to any order or suggestion from the Managers was to answer 'Sir!' in a loud military manner. At that time the Secretary of Brooks's was also the Secretary of Pratt's, the dining club around the corner in Park Place. Now the two clubs have their own Secretaries.

During the 1970s and 80s, the person to exert the greatest influence over the life of the club was undoubtedly Geoffrey Agnew, Chairman of the famous art-dealing firm in Bond Street. His greatest interest was on the decoration and appearance of the interior of the club, and it was thanks largely to him that the whole of Brooks's was gradually redecorated and modernized between 1975 and 1990. Most importantly, he was the founder of the Fine Arts Committee, of which the present chairman is Martyn Beckett. This committee was formed largely in response to the rumpus over the decoration of the new bar in 1975. Sir Geoffrey objected strongly to a large glass structure proposed for the back of the bar, and demanded that this unfortunate 'reredos', as he described it, be removed. Thanks to his influence, and that of his new committee, it was, and the bar was eventually decorated again. Lord Clark, a former St. James' member, was also briefly a member of this committee. It fell to Sir Geoffrey to hang the magnificent collection of Dilettanti Society portraits, part of the legacy of the St. James', and now such an outstanding feature of Brooks's. A less happy task was the eradication of dry rot, which was discovered in the Great Subscription Room in 1980. Under the guidance of Claud Phillimore, this was successfully dealt with, at a cost of over £60,000. It was also Sir Geoffrey who supervised the conversion of the Cavendish and Lansdowne Rooms for use as private party rooms. Like Lord Spencer before him, Geoffrey Agnew could be autocratic both with the staff and his fellow members. His appearance, tall, angular and bespectacled, inspired both respect and awe; any servant or member who displeased him was likely to receive the full force of his wrath. But he could also be genial and fascinating company, particularly when talking about his early days as an art dealer before the war. For all his high-handed ways, he was devoted to Brooks's and its welfare. However busy he was, he found time to visit the club almost every day.

One of Sir Geoffrey's closest cronies, and someone still remembered with great affection at the club, was Esmond Warner. Esmond was the son of Pelham Warner, the famous cricketer and England captain, and like him, known as 'Plum'. With Geoffrey Agnew he was closely involved in the club's affairs during the 1970s, particularly the redecoration. He was also the club's honorary librarian from 1973 to 1981. Thanks to his experience as a bookseller, the library was completely overhauled, and new books were acquired on a regular basis. The previous librarian had been Philip Magnus, who either for reasons of economy or excessively high literary standards rarely bought anything. The librarian before him was a military man who only bought thrillers. It is thanks, therefore, to Esmond Warner that Brooks's has such a good library, from which books can be borrowed. Many authors and historians belonging to the club, some of whom have contributed to this book, have also donated their own books to the library. It might also be mentioned here that neither White's nor Boodle's possesses a library, although I would naturally hesitate to draw any conclusions from this. Plum Warner was a natural clubman, with a tremendously fruity laugh, and a limitless fund of anecdotes for those not in too much of a hurry to listen to them. He gave a number of splendid dinners in the Subscription Room at which the principal after-dinner speaker was invariably himself. The library continues to flourish, under the chairmanship of John Ogden, with the highly professional assistance of John Saumarez-Smith of Heywood Hill. The library is now the only old-fashioned distinctively 'clubby' room left in the building, and it is the earnest wish of this writer that it may remain so. On the sofas at the far end pillows are placed for the convenience of those members who wish to sleep after lunch, something which never fails to cause astonishment, and disbelief among lady visitors in the evenings. Some members' wives seem convinced that the pillows betoken some darker, less moral, purpose.

It is perhaps typical of Brooks's that it should have a library rather than a billiard room. For many years, the location of a possible billiard room was discussed by the Managers, ranging literally from the attic to the basement. Now at last, the billiard room has found a home in the basement, although it is not much used. Also in the basement is a rarely watched television set. Another feature of the modern club is reciprocal arrangements with other clubs overseas. This was first begun in 1955, with the Knickerbocker Club in New York. Now the club has reciprocal arrangements with clubs all over the world, including the Travellers' in Paris, and the Caccia in Rome. During the summer closure Brooks's members always traditionally exchanged facilities with Boodle's, but in 1982 this arrangement was unfortunately abandoned, after a number of rows. It is to be hoped that the arrangement may one day be revived.

One or two other events of the 1970s and 80s need to be mentioned. In 1974, a bomb was thrown through the window of the breakfast room, next to the dining-room. Considerable damage was done, and two club servants badly injured. It was discovered later that the bomb was probably intended for Edward Heath (not a member), who was in fact dining in Pratt's, the entrance to which is on the opposite side of Park Place. In 1979 it was discovered that the cashier in the dining-room, a Thai lady who was the wife of a minor diplomat, had been systematically defrauding the club, to the tune of over £45,000. Thanks to an insurance claim, and the bringing of an action against the club's auditors, most of the money was recovered. Nothing was ever recovered from the lady herself, who fled back to Thailand. This, and the dry rot outbreak in 1980, placed a considerable strain on the club's finances. In 1981 came the celebrated Cockroach incident. A somewhat over-zealous Health Inspector from the Westminster Council descended on the club, while lunch was in progress, and demanded to inspect the kitchens. One cockroach was discovered, and the Council then instigated a case against the club. The case aroused extraordinary publicity. Journalists badgered members on the steps of the club, and Brooks's cockroaches were the subject of numerous cartoons. When the case finally came to court, the publicity had already died down, and the club was fined a small amount and ordered to make a few changes to the kitchen. Cockroaches are nothing new to Brooks's. In the nineteenth century the club kept a kind of game book, recording exactly where each cockroach had been found, and eliminated. Eventually the problem got so bad that the American Black Beetle and Cockroach Company, ancestor of Rentokil, had to be called in.

Every club is dependent on its servants, and in this respect Brooks's has been very fortunate. Many of the staff have been both loyal and long-serving, and in 1987 a separate Staff Hostel was purchased for them. Like the members many of the staff are remembered for their personalities as much as their abilities. Newman has already been mentioned. In 1978 Johnny Macrae, formerly barman at the St. James', retired after thirty-two years' service. All who knew him described him as the best barman in London. In the dining-room, the steward for many years was Gibbons: the wine steward was Potter, a good wine waiter, although often bad-tempered and sometimes drunk. Upstairs the coffee waiter was the rather wobbly-handed Frank MacKinnon, whose rolling gait was perhaps acquired from working on transatlantic liners in the summer holidays. The post of head porter has been occupied in recent years by Joe Murphy, a very popular figure, now regrettably retired. In 1989 a new porter's lodge was erected on the left of the entrance hall, replacing the old, cramped position just inside the front door. This has been done so discreetly that it looks as if it had always been there.

My advice to anyone writing about a club is to read the Suggestions Book. Here one will find the members engaged in their favourite occupation – grumbling. Here too the club wits can have free rein. The Suggestions Book is the small change of club life, and nothing gives a better feeling of the true flavour of Brooks's. Studying the books from 1970 to the present day, the vast majority of complaints concern food, drink, newspapers, and noise. But beyond this, the sheer variety of things that Brooks's members find to complain about is astonishing. Ink, pens, envelopes, paper, snuff-boxes, fires, coffee cups, clocks, telephones, waste-paper baskets, coat hooks, shoe polish, pumice-stones, towels, hairbrushes, combs, wallpaper, wobbly tables, curtains, pepper mills, porridge, cigars – there is no aspect of club life that is not mentioned. In 1971 James Lees-Milne requests footstools for gout sufferers. Lord Sudeley, writing in 1975, suggests that the club should 'consult Monsignor Gilbey of the Travellers' Club, a very wise Catholic priest, who says that the presence of women in men's clubs should be fought tooth and nail'. Those who complained about ladies received a sharp rebuke from Cyril Ray, suggesting that they 'would be happier in White's, where they could luxuriate in the company of their fellow-reactionary misogynists, and obliterate from their minds any consciousness of the existence of half the human race'. More seriously, Richard Wallis complains in 1978 that 'the club is being swiftly taken over by an utter mafia of pompous young idiots'. In 1980 these complaints even led to an attempted *coup d'état*. A vote of no confidence in the Managers was proposed, but defeated at an Extraordinary General Meeting. Much more frequent were complaints about food, though Mr A. Low complained that the 'excellent treacle pudding' was finished before he could get to it. F.B. Lillis campaigns ceaselessly for better service at the bar; Giles Eyre conducts a running battle with the chef over several pages; Miles Jebb calls for more fresh fruit. Lord Jellicoe apologizes for giving one of the servants 'a nasty biff on the head', but only by accidentally going through one of the kitchen doors in the wrong direction. Ludovic Kennedy bemoans the absence of newspapers and magazines, although another member protests 'Surely we can live without the *Guardian*?' Lord Falkland requests more tabloids, particularly the *Sun*, and claims 'we are all old enough to cope with page three'. The absence of the *Sporting Chronicle* and *Sporting Times* drives some members to fury; another suggests that the member who has removed *Private Eye* should receive a public spanking. Complaints about members bringing business papers into the club crop up from time to time, prompting T.B. Barlow to recall that in the 1920s there was a business room, known as the Cads' Room, mainly used by party whips. One irate member complains of hearing 'jazz music' in the Subscription Room. This later proved to be the singing of 'For he's a jolly good fellow' at a dinner given for elderly clergymen.

But the subject to arouse the greatest furore was the Saga of the Club Cat. The club cat, Mr White, was black, liked watching backgammon, and was given a tartan collar by Alan Clark, MP. During the 1970s, Mr White began to develop a number of bad habits, particularly that of misbehaving on chairs and sofas in the Morning Room. Eventually, a member was brave enough to enter in the Suggestions Book, in early 1980, that 'the club cat is an unwelcome member'. The extraordinary storm of protest that this unleashed must have surprised its author. The first response was categoric – 'No!! Powis'. Members vied with each other in singing Mr White's praises. 'Mr White is doubtless cleaner than many members,' claimed William Armstrong. Alan Clark went further: 'Not only is he cleaner than those calling for his dismissal – he is better company.' 'Mr White has elegance and charm,' wrote Maurice Lancaster, 'and it would be madness to think of destroying a *black* cat.' A course of cat training was suggested. Another member was moved to threaten, 'If Mr White goes so will I. . . .' An entire eighteenth-century poem about cats entitled 'Jubilate Agno' was entered into the book. The Managers, however, were not be moved. Mr White's fate was pronounced on 26 March 1980. 'The Suggestion Book was seen and it was noted that the main topic was the cat. After much discussion, it was agreed that another home should be found for the cat, and another black cat, who was house trained, should take its place.' And so Mr White departed, much lamented, but not forgotten. In June 1982, Mr John Gillum wrote that 'Whilst dining in the club this evening, we were joined by a mouse in the dining-room. Such an occurrence would not have been allowed by Mr White during his regime.' This brought renewed calls for Mr White's return, but it was not to be, and to this day no replacement has been found.

But even without Mr White, Brooks's goes from strength to strength. Its success has confounded all those who predicted in the 1970s that clubs were an anachronism, and would die out. The need for a good club seems now to be stronger than ever. The secret of Brooks's success seems to lie in the great diversity of its membership. Less aristocratic than White's, more intellectual than Boodle's, Brooks's has a distinct flavour of its own. A member once said to me that if you need information on any subject, you can find it in Brooks's Club. This is perhaps one of the clues to the success of Brooks's, and what makes it such a stimulating club to belong to. For this writer, and I hope for all its members, it is simply the best club in London. It can no longer be described as a political club, although a few MPs are members and occasionally a Cabinet minister. Roy Jenkins is a long-time member, and now a trustee, together with the Duke of Devonshire, Lord Spencer, and Edward Adeane. Politically Brooks's could be described as liberal, with a small l. In today's terms, its members are more likely to be Conservatives of the 'wet' variety. Perhaps it is still in a sense a Whig club, although I would hesitate to try and define Whiggery in the august company of this volume. Looking through the membership lists of the 1940s and 50s, and those of today, certain names do seem to recur – Adeane, Anstruther, Asquith, Astor, Balfour, Baring, Bonham-Carter, Buxton, Clive, Dugdale, Eden, Guinness, Gurney, Herbert, Hoare, Hood, Russell, St. Aubyn, Scrope, Strutt, Wake, Whitbread – are these the Whigs of today?

PART II

The St. James' Club

Desmond Seward

'THIS Club resembles Rome after the arrival of the Ostrogoths,' a voice was heard crying in Brooks's in 1975. The speaker was lamenting the recent amalgamation with the St. James'. Yet it had been a club with a good deal in common with Brooks's. Since the union its former members have had a distinct influence on their new home, importing something of the St. James' liveliness and cosmopolitan quality.

The founder of the St. James' was that pillar of Brooks's, Earl Granville. One of nature's clubmen – by the end of his life he belonged to seven major London clubs – and a former Foreign Secretary, 'Pussy' Granville had many friends among what were then known as diplomatists. A meeting place for such people had come into being in 1857 after some 'friction' at the Travellers', when most of the *corps diplomatique* there resigned. Led by Marchese d'Azeglio, the Sardinian minister, they set up a club in two rooms in Charles Street, Berkeley Square, and then in a small house in Albemarle Street; its other leading lights were Count Corti, d'Azeglio's first secretary, and the Marquis de Jaucourt, second secretary at the French embassy. Among the few Englishmen to frequent it was the young Sir Horace Rumbold, who years later recalled how the little circle had been ruled by d'Azeglio, much liked despite his vanity. Luigi Corti, a small, snub-nosed man who resembled Socrates, was to be Italian foreign minister at the Congress of Berlin.

Seeing a potential alternative to the Travellers', which had a twenty-year waiting-list, Lord Granville canvassed the entire diplomatic corps in London, British as well as foreign. In April 1859 a Mr F.W. Cavendish sent out a circular from the Foreign Office to every British embassy and legation. The response was enthusiastic, and on 24 May an inaugural meeting was held, chaired by the Earl of St. Germans. The first membership-list, printed that autumn, contained 300 'permanent members' who paid the full subscription of six guineas, ninety-one 'members of the English Diplomatic Body' and sixty-one 'members of the Foreign Diplomatic Body'. The committee included Granville, d'Azeglio, St. Germans, Count von Kielmansegge (the Hanoverian minister), Lord de Tabley and the Marquess of Ailesbury. Three other committee members besides Granville belonged to Brooks's.

Among ambassadors and heads of legation who joined were those of Austria, France, Russia, Turkey, the Two Sicilies and the United States. There were also five 'royal personages': the Duke of Cambridge, the Comte de Paris (Pretender to the throne of France), the Duc d'Aumale, Prince Edward of Saxe-Weimar and Prince Friedrich of Schleswig-Holstein.

While the club had been created by Granville and d'Azeglio, the members who did most to establish it were Francis Cavendish and Lords de Tabley and St. Germans. Cavendish had been private secretary to two successive Foreign Secretaries, Lord John Russell and the Earl of Clarendon; he once declared that every Foreign Office clerk must be 'considered a gentleman, and therefore fit to be entrusted with any confidential correspondence'. De Tabley was a Conservative peer from Cheshire, a lord-in-waiting, rich, but somewhat dull. Edward Granville Eliot, Earl of St. Germans and a former Lord Lieutenant of Ireland, was red-haired and formidable; an American described him a few years later as 'looking with his blazing head of hair and whiskers as if he had just come through hell with his hat off'.

The first clubhouse was at the top of St. James's Street, opposite White's, in a wing of the old Crockford's, the rest of the building being taken up by the Wellington Restaurant. (The house still stands and until a few years ago was occupied by Hoopers, the carriage builders.) The entrance was in Bennet Street. Accommodation, leased from Mr Crockford, consisted of a morning room on the first floor; a coffee room on the second; and a smoking room and a room for cards and billiards on the third; there were also four dressing-rooms and a bathroom. At de

Tabley's suggestion the bill of fare was modelled on that at the Travellers', the best in clubland, by an excellent French chef, Blot.

The new club flourished and there was talk of building a bow window in emulation of White's. Although the subscription soon rose to eight guineas, the number of permanent members grew to 500. Among them were the Dukes of St. Albans and Hamilton, together with the future Dukes of Atholl, Buccleuch, Marlborough and Devonshire ('Harty Tarty'). There were a number of soldiers, notably from the Scots Fusilier Guards and the 60th, and some very young men indeed, such as the future Lord Rosebery (one day to be Prime Minister) and Lord Randolph Churchill. Foreigners started to become permanent members – Count Edmond Batthyany, Maharaja Duleep Singh, and Baron Ferdinand de Rothschild who began a family connection which would last the club's lifetime.

A great deal of whist, piquet, and écarté was played, amounts as large as £150 being won or lost; on at least one occasion the committee posted a notice expressing alarm at the considerable sums staked. Sometimes there was trouble with members who did not pay their card debts. Other nuisances included sitting at the card-tables till dawn or noisy singing in the smoking room on Sunday evenings, but the main worry concerned those who would not pay their subscriptions.

There were quieter members. Rumbold remembered 'many a delightful hour' there in the 1860s with John Warren (de Tabley's son) and Lord Strangford. The former, a now forgotten poet, was author of the lines:

In the garden of life a most exquisite flower
Is growing and blowing for me.

Strangford was an awe-inspiring linguist who could 'quote the Tartar classics as well as any mollah in Khiva or Bokhara'.

Success brought more problems. The clubhouse was too small but Crockford refused to let it take over any more rooms from the Wellington Restaurant. In spring 1867 the club moved to 4 Grafton Street, 'a good house with two large drawing rooms', formerly Lord Brougham's residence. (Edward Malet's mother had been Brougham's stepdaughter; he recalled 'after the reverence, not unmixed with fear, with which I had always regarded the place in my childhood, it was a strange sensation to find myself, as a member of the club, playing whist in my grandmother's bedroom.') Everything was done to make the house cheerful, a piano being installed in the smoking-room, but the committee never intended to stay in Grafton Street. After toying with the idea of building a new clubhouse on a vacant site in St. James's Street, negotiations began in November 1867 for Coventry House at 106 Piccadilly. A twenty-one-year lease was bought, the St. James' moving in the following spring.

Small but exquisite, Coventry House had been built for Sir Hugh Hunloke in the style of William Kent about 1764. It was then the only mansion in Piccadilly west of Devonshire House. Hunloke never lived there, selling it to the seventh Earl of Coventry, lord of the bedchamber to George III, for £10,000 and a ground rent of £75. Lord Coventry gave the rooms their Adam decoration, engaging Angelica Kauffmann to paint a ceiling, while his wife had a passage dug beneath Piccadilly to the Ranger's Lodge in Green Park. In the 1840s it became a high-class gaming hell, admitting 'lady' members, but regained respectability on being bought by the Comte de Flahaut – the French ambassador, once an ADC to Napoleon and a member of Brooks's – for use as a private residence. The interior was swiftly converted to club use; male guests were allowed, in a strangers' smoking room and a strangers' coffee room. The walls remained without pictures until 1889 when embassies began to present prints.

Henry, 15th Duke of Norfolk, joined in 1870. The club list already contained such Catholic names as Throckmorton, Stourton, Langdale, Tichborne, Townley, Hornyold and Dormer (General the Hon. Sir James Charlemagne Dormer, a member since 1861 – popularly known as 'Cesspit' Dormer on account of an exploit during the Crimean War – was to suffer the melancholy fate of being eaten by a tiger when Commander-in-Chief, Madras.) Some of these families continued to be represented until the very end.

The Russian ambassador known as 'The Fascinating Schou' often made use of the St. James' during the mid '70s. *Spy* said of Count Schouvaloff in February 1875, 'Painfully polite, extremely handsome, and a good talker, he has easily achieved popularity in Society; and when he has fully learnt that it is better to shoot woodcock than foxes, he will

be thoroughly adapted as a desirable furniture for any country house.'
No one trusted him. In the House of Lords Granville accused Schouvaloff
of giving 'false and deceptive' assurances over his government's policy in
central Asia. During the Balkan crisis of 1878 and the ensuing Jingo
frenzy, Russian candidates were blackballed.

Several members played an important part in public life. Lord
Frederick Cavendish became Secretary of State for Ireland in 1881 – to be
murdered on the evening he arrived in Dublin. Lord Lytton was Viceroy
of India, dying as ambassador to Paris. Bartle Frere's governorship of the
Cape coincided with the Zulu War of 1879. Lord Odo Russell was
ambassador to Berlin, Augustus Paget to Rome. There were younger men
who would also become ambassadors, such as Horace Rumbold
(Vienna), Edward Malet (Berlin) and Henry Drummond Wolff (Madrid,
after a spell as a Conservative MP). They seem to have been refreshingly
free from pomposity. *Spy* describes Malet in 1881 as 'fond of lawn-tennis,
pleasant company and good living' – during his time at Berlin he gave an
annual luncheon for chimney-sweeps – while Drummond Wolff was long
remembered as a 'witty, kindly, *rusé, raconteur*'.

Henry James used the St. James' in the late 1870s to study 'English
colloquialisms', introduced as a visiting member by the American
historian Henry Brooks Adams. (He claimed that he never heard more 'I
say's' in his life.) The composer of the Savoy Operas, Arthur Sullivan,
belonged for some years; an inveterate gambler, he must have been
attracted by the high card stakes. A less agreeable figure was Colonel
Baring, formerly of the 19th Hussars and a brother of Lord Revelstoke,
who during the '80s and '90s dominated the club, even buying the food
and wine, going to Bordeaux to see Messrs Barton. 'Go away, you know
nothing about wine,' he snarled when someone asked if the club might
stock another champagne. In the row which followed Arthur Labouchere
called Bob Baring 'a damnably cantankerous old man' whereupon he
resigned and went to the Turf.

In February 1898 the committee disclaimed responsibility for the loss
of a diamond locket which had been sent to the club for redirection to
Italy. The member who complained was 'G. Norman Douglas', the
future author of *South Wind* and *Old Calabria*, who had recently
resigned from the Diplomatic Service but was still in his respectable

period; apparently the locket was intended for the unfortunate lady about to become Mrs Douglas.

The thief was almost certainly the hall porter, White, a former coffee-room waiter, who bolted with the petty cash a year after; Mrs White revealed that he had not been home and that she had had to pawn her furniture, which the committee redeemed for £3. 10s. 0d. Several weeks later White was arrested in Dover Street, working as porter for a club called the Sandringham, to be given three months' hard labour.

The St. James' behaved well to staff in those pre-welfare-state days, paying for a servant's funeral on more than one occasion. When Ackhurst, steward of the club, butler and head waiter, retired in 1896 after twenty-nine years' service, he was given a pension of £60 per annum, his wages having been £130. The founder of the Rowton House hostels, Lord Rowton, was on the committee and no doubt exercised a benevolent influence. Formerly Monty Lowry Corry, Disraeli's indispensable secretary, he was known by the Press during the '90s as 'the Queen's emergency man'.

Amenities were excellent at the turn of the century. An attempt to engage the head chef at the Savoy failed but a gifted cook was found for £175 a year. There were four bedrooms, one being let to a member at £140 – horse traffic over the wooden blocks with which Piccadilly was then paved must have made sleep almost impossible – and a bathroom. A telephone was installed in 1896. At the Diamond Jubilee of 1897 stands seating 400 were set up in front of the club; ladies were invited, a set luncheon at 5s. being served, with champagne at 4s. 6d. a bottle and claret cup at 1s. 6d. In 1899 it was agreed that members might use Boodle's during the summer closure. The subscription was now eleven guineas, the entrance fee twenty-five guineas, and there were 650 members.

Links with the Foreign Office remained close. Between 1882 and 1906 all three permanent under-secretaries belonged (Lords Pauncefote, Currie and Sanderson), as did numerous ambassadors and heads of legation. Envoys continued to join, notably the Portuguese minister, the Marquez de Soveral, who was often seen in the club. Known as 'The Blue Monkey' because of his simian features and dark jowls, Luis de Soveral was one of the Prince of Wales's closest companions, reputedly the funniest member of the Marlborough House set; it was said that he made

love to the most beautiful women in England, while all the nicest
Englishmen were his friends. The French ambassador, Baron Alphonse
de Courcel, was not so popular, though it was scarcely his fault.

For the St. James' attitude towards Frenchmen in general had been
sorely tried by Louis-Philippe, Duke of Orleans and Pretender to the
throne of France. In 1899 the Paris magazine *Le Rire* published a cartoon
by Willette, entitled '*V'la les Anglais*': it showed Queen Victoria
stretched over the knee of a grinning President Kruger, her enormous
bare buttocks being soundly spanked. During the ensuing uproar the
Duke wrote to the *Morning Post* in defence of Willette, saying that he
found the cartoon most amusing. The committee summoned an
extraordinary general meeting in May 1900, to expel him after passing
the resolution 'That the conduct of HRH the Duc d'Orleans has been
such as to endanger the character, good order and welfare of the St.
James' Club.'

The Club was at the height of its prosperity during the years before the
Great War. Ralph Nevill, a member, tells us in his *London Clubs* (1911):

> The St. James' Club is the special home of diplomatists, and cordially
> welcomes foreigners of distinction . . . Certain Continental customs
> flourish, such as the second breakfast, or *déjeuner à la fourchette*:
> billiards are permitted on Sundays, and the card tables are kept open. A
> music room is maintained, and the piano may sometimes be heard on
> the Sabbath afternoon. A good deal of high play is common . . .

Lord Poltimore, a member from 1911 to 1975, remembered that when he
joined one was lucky to hear English spoken in the coffee rooms.

Nineteen British members lost their lives during the war, with two of
the staff. Sacheverell Sitwell used to recall a Finnish baron, a fine bridge
player, who gave dinner to all those on leave from the trenches and threw
lavish parties at nearby hotels, with beautiful unattached girls but no
wives. The baron fled the night before he was to be arrested as a German
agent, his last act in the club being unprintable even today.

The St. James' would not readmit German members until 1926. In
contrast seven members of the old Imperial Russian embassy were elected
en bloc in 1923, including M. Sabine, the first secretary, and Admiral

Wolkoff, the naval attaché. However, the most interesting White Russian to join was probably Sir Peter Bark, the Tsar's finance minister from 1914 to 1917, who had become a British subject and a director of the Bank of England.

Lockhart was made head porter during the '20s. The St. James' equivalent of Newman at Brooks's, originally a steward with the Great Western Railway on board the *Cheltenham Flyer*, he was a kindly, bespectacled little man with an iron will, who practically ran the club. For a small charge he would place bets with a bookmaker and in consequence received – and gave – excellent racing tips.

Osbert Lancaster joined the St. James' in 1933. He remained a member till the end, immaculately turned out and with a fund of anecdotes, delivered in a resonant, slightly hoarse voice. In his memoirs he describes the club in the '30s:

> The membership at that period was divided into the card-room set, dominated by such eye-catching personalities as Lord Castlerosse and 'Crinks' Johnstone; the diplomats, British and foreign, active and retired – including such fascinating figures as an immensely aged Russian prince in a skull-cap whose Continental method of throat-clearing was clearly audible at Hyde Park Corner, and Mr Zirkis, formerly first secretary at the Imperial Ottoman Embassy, so appreciated a bridge player that he had been prevailed upon to remain a member, uninterned and unmolested, throughout the First War; and a rather younger group, several of whom had been my contemporaries at Oxford.

Valentine Browne, Viscount Castlerosse and later last Earl of Kenmare, was certainly eye-catching. Half Irish, half Jewish, he weighed over twenty stone in consequence of a truly staggering appetite and, while dressing more or less formally, tended to wear bright blue tweed suits with spats over carpet slippers. A compulsive gambler, he survived by writing a column in the *Evening Standard* for his friend Lord Beaverbrook. Harcourt Johnstone – 'Crinks' – was a raffish Liberal MP, named '*Le Misanthrope*' by Lady Cunard. Cards and gluttony formed his bond with Castlerosse. 'He was a Regency figure,' wrote Chips Channon, 'immense, noisy and an intelligent bore.' When Crinks died of a stroke in 1945 Channon recorded, 'He was only 49, and can really be described as having dug his grave with his teeth, for all his life he over-ate and drank.'

There was also Lord Tenterden, turned out of the house with five shillings by his wife every morning and told not to come back till lunchtime. By noon the money was spent. 'All those entering the bar received a mournful and thirsty look from his lordship to which most responded,' Lancaster recalls. He describes him as having 'a purple face surmounting a wing-collar several sizes too small, a waxed moustache and a strong resemblance to a popular music-hall artist of the period called Billy Bennet ("almost a gentleman").' There were others stricken by poverty, one old member living on a bag of bananas a week, which he ate in the library.

Lancaster thought that the St. James' greatest cultural asset was Dr Tancred Borenius, the Finnish art expert, who assembled a collection of old masters for another member, Lord Harewood, and ran a weekly luncheon club for kindred spirits. There were a surprising number of aesthetes, such as Willy King, an expert on ceramics at the British Museum; Peter Wilson, a future chairman of Sotheby's; and Villiers David whose father had founded the Percival David Foundation of Chinese Art. On Sundays Osbert and Sacheverell Sitwell would sometimes entertain their sister Edith, members sitting within earshot to overhear their conversation. (Ladies had been let in as guests for tea on Sundays since before 1914.) There were few other writers, apart from Terence Rattigan, but two painters, Augustus John and Wogan Philipps. The former was lionized on his rare appearances, generally in the bar at about 6 p.m. Philipps sat in the Upper House as a Communist when he became Lord Milford.

The atmosphere of the St. James' is recaptured as it must have been about 1937 in Anthony Powell's novel *At Lady Molly's*. 'The name of the club surprised me a little,' says the hero, who is invited to lunch by Widmerpool. 'There was no reason at all why he should not belong there, yet its mild suggestion of cosmopolitan life and high card stakes evoked an environment seemingly unsuited to his nature.' In the background a fat man (Lord Castlerosse) consumes a vast meal while two Balkan diplomatists discuss Hitler in stilted French. The model for the young

Widmerpool, Denis Cuthbert Capel-Dunn, really was a member, a loud-voiced, opinionated figure, prominent in the bar and known as 'Mr Bloody'. The son of a consular clerk at Leipzig called Dunn and regarded as a super-ambitious have-not, he was an impecunious barrister who became a colonel in the Intelligence Corps during the war, to be killed in an air-crash in 1945.

The German embassy was much in evidence. Most of its staff were charming, such as the ambassador, Herr von Hoesch, who was remembered by Osbert Lancaster as an 'amiable and cultivated Anglophile'; or the fat, lazy, councillor, Albrecht Bernstorff, a Rhodes scholar. But they changed when the Nazis came to power. Hoesch died suddenly in 1936. There were rumours that he had been murdered by one of his own staff, also a member of the St. James'; the night before his death he had dined, seemingly in good health and spirits, with English friends who always remained convinced that he had been poisoned. One curious circumstance was Hoesch's dog being found dead outside the embassy, before the discovery of his body.

Among '*Members of the Corps Diplomatique*' to join the club in 1937 was Joachim von Ribbentrop, Hitler's adviser on foreign affairs and the new German ambassador. 'Rose to fame on foam of champagne' was how Sir Robert Bruce Lockhart (who also joined in 1937) epitomized his career. 'For some years sold French champagne to German Jews. Married Fräulein Henckell, etc. Went in early with Hitler.' He soon made himself the most unpopular envoy in London, being loathed at the club; in 1938 Crinks Johnstone publicly proposed the toast 'Death to Ribbentrop', while after the war he was referred to fondly as 'Our member who was hanged'. Yet until the 1970s the butler, appropriately named John Butler, recalled 'Mr von Ribbentrop' in a surprisingly amiable light. 'Such a nice gentleman. I know they say dreadful things about him but he was always very polite to me. He used to send Prince von Bismarck to arrange his parties, another very nice gentleman.'

During the Munich crisis the St. James' became the headquarters of the non-appeasers in the Foreign Office, led by the permanent under-secretary, Robert Vansittart. They included Van's brother-in-law, Eric Phipps, ambassador to Paris; Berlin still spoke of his embassy there with awe – when Goering had arrived for dinner two hours late, saying 'I have been shooting,' Sir Eric inquired, 'Animals, I hope?' Winston Churchill was often seen in the club. On the other hand, with some embarrassment Osbert Lancaster heard a former ambassador to Prague tell a guest in the coffee room – within earshot of the Czech military attaché – that the crisis was due to the Czechs' lack of an officer class.

Evelyn Waugh joined in the last months of 1939, reputedly to have a bolt-hole when Randolph Churchill was at White's. He records dining off 'half a dozen oysters, a grouse, a whole partridge and a peach, half a bottle of white wine, half a bottle of Pontet Canet 1929'. (The claret was one of the finest ever produced.) During the war, however, clubs had to serve extremely frugal meals to comply with rationing. Those wise enough to belong to two could supplement their diet – thus Lord Castlerosse would lunch first at the St. James' and then at White's.

In the summer of 1940 the Bachelors' Club in South Audley Street was bombed out and the St. James' took in its members, together with Mansfield the barman who had been there since 1902 and served Edward VII. As with every amalgamation – it was not finally implemented until 1946 – there were teething problems; an area in the Inner Hall (next to the fireplace by the staircase) which was appropriated by the newcomers became known as 'Cads' Corner'. Yet the Bachelors', founded in 1881, had been a most distinguished club; as its name implied, those who joined had had to be bachelors and, should they marry, submit themselves for re-election. The union transformed the St. James', making it younger and livelier. Backgammon replaced the bezique beloved by Van and Eric Phipps, the St. James' becoming the first club to have a backgammon room, the strangers' smoking room being taken over.

M. Maisky, the Soviet ambassador, was invited to join on presenting credentials in 1941, just as Count Benckendorff had been thirty years before when representing the Tsar. After all, it *was* a diplomatic club. Probably Maisky never dared go inside, since there were so many White Russians.

The Earl of Harewood, the Princess Royal's husband, was chairman for most of the hostilities. Early in 1942 it was announced that King Haakon of Norway had accepted an invitation to lunch. The day came, chairman and committee waiting in the Inner Hall. Just as the royal car drew up, Willy King (the ceramics expert) passed out at the foot of the staircase leading to the coffee room. 'Remove that member, Lockhart,' ordered Lord Harewood. 'Can't do that, m'Lord, nothing about it in the rules,' came the reply. The club watched the committee and King Haakon step stony-faced over Willy's slumbering form as they went up to luncheon.

The St. James' settled down after the war in a Socialist Britain antipathetic to clubland. Some members had been killed, others came back maimed; a substantial proportion of the old *corps diplomatique* disappeared into the gulags. Fortunately a large number of exiles joined. Among them were the Rumanian Ion Ratiu, now leader of his country's Peasant Party, and the Yugoslav Vane Ivanovic, the shipowner and consul for Monte Carlo. There were numerous Poles and Hungarians, besides a few second generation White Russians, such as Ivan Terestchenko, son of Kerensky's foreign minister. Those who still had a country included Spaniards and many Greeks – usually Athenians who spoke beautiful French. But English and non-diplomatic members predominated far more than hitherto – Van was no longer in a position to recruit Foreign Office members as he had done so enthusiastically when permanent under-secretary.

Lord Harewood died in 1947, to be succeeded as a trustee by Van. However, the club's leading light at that date was Oliver Lyttelton, afterwards Viscount Chandos, the colonial secretary in Churchill's 1951 government. ('Secretary of State, something rather awkward has happened in Blankland' was how he recalled his own private ministerial nightmare. 'The police have disembowelled the Crown witnesses and there is a Private Notice Question.') Oddly enough, he had been a boon companion of the Liberal Crinks Johnstone. He loved the St. James' and after being Chairman was elected President.

A colourful and extremely popular chairman of the 1950s was Sherman Stonor, of Stonor, later Lord Camoys, who once rebuked Harrod's pet department for failing to stock baby elephants when he wanted one for his wife's birthday. (He had an amazingly wide range of friends, from Harold Wilson to the black *chanteuse*, Eartha Kitt.) He was not the only member to belong to an ancient Catholic family. Another was Sir Anthony Doughty-Tichborne, of Tichborne, last of his line; a noble trencherman – a favourite meal was *cold* grouse and claret

Lord Melbourne when Prime Minister. From a mezzotint at Brooks's

Earl Granville (1815–91), the saviour of Brooks's and founder of the St James' Club. From a drawing by Richmond at the National Portrait Gallery

followed by a chocolate soufflé with *yellow* chartreuse – Tony Tich was enormously stout and bore an uncanny likeness to the 'Tichborne Claimant', who in the previous century had impersonated the missing heir to the baronetcy. There was also Nicholas Throckmorton who, when asked if his people had been in the Gunpowder Plot, replied laconically, 'No, we had our own.'

Sherman Camoys was a great friend of Evelyn Waugh. Both suffered from depression, sharing their gloom in lengthy drinking sessions at the St. James', which generally ended up at the Hyde Park Hotel after a brief walk through the Park; they acted out 'Pinfold' fantasies together, long before *The Ordeal of Gilbert Pinfold*. There were other writers, such as Alfred Duggan, Lord Curzon's stepson, a reformed alcoholic who in the final fifteen years of his life wrote a dozen historical novels, in prose which even Waugh admired. (Waugh contributed a preface to the last, *Count Bohemond*.) There were also Kenneth Clark, the art historian, and Dennis Wheatley – the latter, who looked just like Humpty-Dumpty, being a regular in the bar.

Consumption of alcohol was thought by some to be even more impressive than at White's. The barman, Johnny Macrae, mixed delicious Martinis, as good as any in New York. (They inspired one member, himself a modest drinker, to have jugs of iced Martini served at his wedding, with horrific consequences.) Bridge was often played for a pound a hundred, very high in those days. An elaborate All Fools' Day hoax took place in the card room on 1 April 1959:

> The Duke of Marlborough, Dr R. L. Rolleston, Captain Minto Wilson and Mr Peter Thursby, when playing the first hand at bridge after luncheon, found that each of them had 13 cards of one suit, with the Duke of Marlborough having 13 spades and therefore able to outbid the others in a grand slam.

(The bridge-players had moved upstairs into what had been the library, the old card room having become the bar.) In the backgammon room a game was often played by five or more in a chouette, large sums being won or lost. The Marquess of Milford Haven, Lord Pender ('Josh') and Rupert Bellville were among the leading players. Then, in the early '60s, lured away by Lord Lucan, many began to play instead at the Claremont Club in Berkeley Square, where the stakes were far higher and lavish credit was given. However, backgammon continued to be played at the St. James' if for more modest sums, a member, Charles Jerdein, winning the world championship in 1968.

The club contained a number of horsy figures. The Earl of St. Germans, referred to by the Press as 'the bookmaker peer', listed his recreations in *Who's Who* as 'hunting the slipper, shooting a line and fishing for compliments', while at one period Sir Hugo Sebright – a worthy descendant of his ancestor, Squire Mytton – was the oldest stable-lad on Epsom Downs. During the '60s two members rode in the National.

The atmosphere was undoubtedly less staid than at Brooks's. There were many practical jokes, while singing was not unknown; occasionally, at night over the port in Cads' Corner, a Welsh member would give a soulful rendering of *David of the White Rock*. Someone wagered in the betting book that wearing white tie and white gloves he could catch a duck with his hands in St. James's Park in broad daylight. Another would hide, lying on a sofa and covering himself with newspapers, if his wife and gamekeeper called to take him home. After a maid became pregnant the committee decreed that no more pretty girls be engaged; they forgot about the page boy, who had a nasty experience with a Turkish member.

At the top of the social pyramid were the dukes – Argyll, St. Albans, Wellington and Marlborough. The last ('Bert') could be heard grumbling about the servant problem – 'Half my footmen are Filipinos.' On a few rare occasions Osbert Sitwell was still to be seen in the club, a tragic spectacle, ravaged by Parkinson's disease and unable to escape from the bores who waylaid him; his valet would collect the frail old man, wrapping him in a vast fur-lined overcoat.

At the other end was 'Eaters', a strange, sad figure of legendary gluttony, if one who could seldom afford a square meal. He lived in Dolphin Square on National Assistance in a flat piled high with stolen magazines, a life membership having been purchased for him in his youth. He was prone to daze the unwary with tales of the theft of his stamp collection from Tregunter Road in 1923. 'Eaters died today,' said a member when he passed on. 'Inconsiderate to the last – had a heart attack on the morning-room carpet.' Then there was a gaunt man who paced up and down, speaking to no one, never buying a drink, never eating. The committee discovered that an old aunt paid his subscription but otherwise he was penniless. It was decided that he should lunch and dine at the club's expense. He died three days later; the inquest found the cause to have been malnutrition.

There was a robust attitude towards death; when announcements of the demise of two members who had shot themselves were posted on the notice-board, someone remarked, 'I see we've got a right-and-a-left'.

It was a small house, which gave the club a sense of intimacy. Through the front hall one stepped into the 'Inner Hall', used as the main drawing-room, from which a graceful double staircase led up to the coffee rooms; the chairs on each side of the staircase were much sought after. On the left of the front hall, looking out on to Piccadilly, was the morning room. Going further in, the bar and quick luncheon room was on the right, the backgammon room on the left. The walls were dark green or dark red, with Turkey carpets and mahogany doors. (The dark colours were Osbert Lancaster's suggestion, on the advice of John Piper.) At the back were the billiard room and a vast, domed lavatory with allegedly the noisiest plugs in London. Climbing the staircase, with a copy of the Venus de Milo in a niche on the landing half-way up, one came to the coffee rooms, members' and guests', the latter with an Angelica Kauffmann ceiling; they looked out over Green Park, walls covered in thick, faded green silk and bell-pulls of bronze and ivory. Here hung the Dilettanti Society pictures. Behind were the back dining-room and the card room, once the library. There were seven bedrooms on the second floor, furnished like those in a Victorian vicarage; in 1960 they cost 30s. a night. Being in Piccadilly they were noisy, while it was impossible to go to sleep in No. 6 where a member had shot himself – with somebody else's gun which he took from the hall – in the early '50s, covering the wall with blood and brains. But a fitful night was soothed by breakfast in one of those heavenly coffee rooms.

The most coveted table was in a corner of the members', decorated with a silver-mounted coconut. Known by the younger as the 'Herren-volk Table', it was monopolized by such august figures as Bert Marlborough and Scatters Wilson. Anyone rash enough to try to sit with them (like Loopy Whitbread or the Acrobatic Crab) would suffer a lethal freeze-out or worse, but in their absence there was a rush to occupy it. Food and wine remained excellent in 1960; the French chef's specialities were trout Cleopatra (with oysters) and fillet of beef London House (in pastry with a truffle sauce), while the cellars contained a magnificent Richebourg '47. Some of this excellence was due to the presence on the house committee of Nubar Gulbenkian, certainly the most picturesque member with his forked beard, eyeglass and orchid, huge eyebrows brushed down during the Armenian Lent. Inevitably there were grumblers – 'The people who like the food in this club, they're coarse feeders, that's all I can say' is one comment which echoes down the years.

Several times a year the guests' coffee room was used by the Dilettanti for their dinners. Rumours circulated about what took place, such as a reputed exchange between the Duke of Wellington and Earl Spencer, their secretary. It was said that when 'Gerry' complained at sardines on toast being served as a savoury at dinner – 'more suited to a third-class boarding-house' – 'Jolly Jack' replied that he had never been in a third-class boarding-house but sardines on toast were frequently served at Althorp 'and jolly good they are too'.

For the last two decades of its existence the St. James' highly efficient secretary was Peter Hiller, brother of the actress Wendy Hiller and formerly manager of the Marine Hotel, North Berwick. He had a superlative staff. Lockhart died in 1961 (leaving £16,000) but O'Donnell was a worthy successor as head porter, charming and well-read, with a taste for the novels of Evelyn Waugh and Anthony Powell. The butler, the valet and the two floor stewards, who had all begun in house service as footmen, were unshaken by the vagaries of members or guests. (One evening a distinctly odd visitor fled from the coffee room in tears when his host was outside telephoning. 'Was my guest upset, O'Donnell'? inquired the host. 'Yes, sir, *very* upset,' was the reply. 'He left wearing His Grace the Duke of Marlborough's hat and carrying Lord Spencer's umbrella.') But such men were irreplaceable when they retired. Eventually only the superb barman Johnny Macrae would remain, among a new and less dedicated team.

During the '60s and early '70s the St. James' seemed to thrive. No one sensed that its days were numbered, if aware that the lease would expire in 1994. Yet it was dangerously small, a mere 900 members; there was insufficient income from subscriptions, which had to be raised from twenty-seven to forty guineas in 1960, making it the most expensive club in London. Nor could the public rooms be used easily to provide supplementary revenue. Admitting ladies for dinner did little to help. There were bad omens. In 1960 White's ended an arrangement of many years by which each club had taken in each other's members during the staff holidays; the reasons given being overcrowding and playing backgammon all night. In 1961 there took place what some called the 'Catholic exodus', when the Marquess of Bute moved to the Turf with his brothers and his friends. Without realizing, the club was going out of fashion.

The St. James' original inspiration, the world of *haute diplomatie* which provided the club's nucleus, had been mortally wounded in 1914, vanishing entirely in 1939. Fewer foreign envoys cared to join since they came from a different background than in the old days, as did many of the new British Foreign Service who preferred the Travellers', nearer Whitehall; in 1962 there were only twenty-seven members from it, as opposed to ninety-one in 1859. The last permanent under-secretaries to belong were Alexander Cadogan and Ivone Kirkpatrick, and unlike Van they did not bother to recruit. (Even so, as late as 1964 Anthony Sampson could write, in *Anatomy of Britain*, that 'grander diplomats go further on [than the Travellers'], to the St. James', with its backgammon and port.') At the same time non-diplomatic members were beginning to feel the lure of White's or the Turf. And in any case the club habit would decline sharply during the next few years.

Whatever the future, the St. James' always retained its cosmopolitan character. In 1962 a writer on London clubs illustrated this by citing the following names from the list of members:

The Duke of Accerenza, Count Anton Apponyi Jnr, Count Alexis Bobrinskoy, Count Dominic de Hemricourt de Grunne, El Duque de Primo Rivera, Constantin Goulandris, Count Henry Haugwitz-Rewentlow,, Raimund von Hofmannsthal, Prince Michael Obolensky, Arpad Plesch, Prince Stanislaw Radziwill, Count Charles Seilern-Aspang, Baron C.S. Stackelberg, Prince C. Wittgenstein and finally the Marquis de Jaucourt, MC, DCM, the doyen of the club, who joined in 1905.

In fact the doyen at that date was William Seeds, once ambassador to Moscow, who had joined in 1904. Very occasionally there was friction between foreigner and native. At the Herrenvolk Table, Baron Hatvany grew testy when Bert Marlborough spoke of the charms of his Blenheim estate. 'The few acres of bog and marsh owned by you little English dukes are as nothing to the lands which once I had in Hungary,' he told him.

There were some interesting new British members. They included the brothers Jimmy and Teddy Goldsmith (whose father had belonged for many years) and Algy Cluff, the future oil-magnate and proprietor of the *Spectator*, then a very young ensign in the Grenadiers. That bulwark of Brooks's, Lord Spencer, joined in 1963.

Someone who joined the same year as Jolly Jack and who is now notorious, was the Earl of Lucan, a committee member from 1970–3. Tall and handsome, he looked as though he ought to have been killed at Mons in 1914. The film producer Vittorio de Sica was so impressed that he invited him to Paris for a screen-test; there was much amusement in the bar when it was learnt that 'Johnny Luc' had failed it. Occasionally he gave dinner parties in the members' coffee room, bringing his family silver. Some people thought Lucan a surly brute but his friends seemed fond of him, while he was liked by the staff.

Outwardly the St. James' appeared viable until well into the '70s. George Labouchere, a former ambassador to Madrid whose family had belonged since the foundation and who embodied its traditions, enjoyed three terms as Chairman. Among foreign diplomatists who joined were the Japanese ambassador Shigenobu Shima and the Austrian trade commissioner Karl Eibenschütz (formerly of Prince Eugen of Savoy's Dragoons). Honorary members included René Massigli, Baron Ivo Rubido-Zichy and Count Edward Raczynski, head of the Polish government in exile. Among the royal personages were Archduke Robert of Austria and Prince Bertil, Duke of Halland. There were such links with the past as the sons of two attachés to Count Benckendorff at the Imperial Russian embassy, one Russian, the other Polish: Alexander Wolcough and Andrew Ciechanowiecki. Yet the connection with diplomacy was increasingly tenuous. There was no serving British ambassador by the end of 1974 when even fewer members of the Foreign Service belonged, their number having dwindled to sixteen.

In 1973 George Labouchere had been succeeded as Chairman by Lord Salmon. A law lord, he was perhaps a surprising choice but his delightful personality made him universally popular; many wondered how someone quite so kind-hearted ever managed to pass sentence on anybody. He soon found himself in a most unenviable position, the trustees warning that unless revenue was increased the club would no longer be viable. Heroic efforts were made. New chefs improved the food dramatically; at Osbert Lancaster's advice the great lavatory was turned into a handsome card room, enabling the old room to be let out for parties; admission was made much easier and there were attempts to recruit more members from the Foreign Service. But in the early summer of 1975 the committee went into a meeting in the belief that the club was saved, to emerge with the knowledge that it was doomed. 'I never thought that I would preside over the dissolution of the St. James' club,' said the poor chairman.

Amalgamation was the only course. At least one of the committee favoured the Turf, because of the exodus there in the early '60s. However, a much liked committee member, Julian Cotterell, belonged to Brooks's, so that it was not entirely a surprise when Cyril Salmon revealed the name of the 'most respectable club' which he had approached.

The St. James' closed its doors in October 1975 after a last party. It had never looked more beautiful. Then the members departed for ever, over 400 going to Brooks's with Johnny the barman, as did the Dilettanti and their pictures. The bulk of the furniture was sold, the remainder of the lease being bought by a language school. The secretary and his assistant stayed on in their basement office for a few weeks – the latter said that every day she heard footsteps overhead.

The amalgamation has undoubtedly altered Brooks's. A larger bar, a room for backgammon, an informal luncheon upstairs, women at dinner and the Dilettanti Society portraits are the more obvious changes. Less apparent is the presence of a substantial number of foreign members (and as many more of foreign extraction). There was some bickering to begin with, largely because of the St. James' livelier habits. But the newcomers,

British or foreign, have now been absorbed by the lovely old house, with its traditions and its ghosts. Among the latter is the amiable shade of Lord Granville. The founder of the St. James' must surely rejoice that its last members have taken refuge in what always remained his first club.

The Society of Dilettanti

Brinsley Ford

THE Society of Dilettanti was founded in 1732 by a group of young men who had visited Italy on the Grand Tour. Horace Walpole's gibe that the nominal qualification for belonging to the Dilettanti Society was to have been in Italy, 'the real one, being drunk for most of the time during their stay there', was unjust. Although originally the members may only have intended to form a convivial dining-society at which they could discuss their experiences abroad, they soon assumed a responsibility for promoting an interest in the Arts. Under the influence of Lord Middlesex, later Duke of Dorset, the Society made a somewhat ineffectual attempt to sponsor Italian opera in this country.

The Society's attempt to found an Academy of Arts in London was undertaken far more seriously. As early as 1749 the Society supported a scheme put forward by one of its members for founding an Academy similar to those existing in Rome, Bologna and other cities on the Continent. With this object in view negotiations took place in 1755 between the Dilettanti and a group of artists headed by Hayman, but the negotiations seem to have broken down because the Dilettanti claimed a greater share over the control of the proposed Academy than the artists were prepared to allow them. When, however, the Royal Academy was founded in 1768, its relations with the Society of Dilettanti were always very cordial, and starting with Reynolds no less than seven PRAs have been appointed Painters to the Society.

The most important role that the Society has played in the cultural life of this country has been the contribution it has made to the neoclassical movement by fostering an interest in the remains of classical antiquity. Between 1764 and 1914 the Society spent about £30,000 on equipping expeditions to Greece and Asia Minor and publishing the results in magnificent folio volumes dealing with such subjects as the *Antiquities of Ionia* and the *Principles of Athenian Architecture*.

The Dilettanti Society, which is limited to sixty members and six honorary members, is no longer in a position to sponsor archaeological expeditions. It was felt, however, that the Society ought to do something to emulate the example of our predecessors. In 1978 a Charitable Trust was set up with the object of contributing to causes which commanded the sympathy of the Society. Since 1978 over thirty small grants have been made. The appeals that we have assisted have included the restoration of the Doric Temple at Hagley, the Temple of the Winds at Shugborough, and church monuments at Ashburnham and Wimpole.

The Society holds five dinners a year at Brooks's, at which the Society's toasts are always drunk:

Viva la Virtu!
Esto praeclara, esto perpetua!
Grecian Taste and Roman Spirit
Seria Ludo!
Absent Members

The earliest recorded meeting of the Dilettanti Society took place on 6 March 1736 at the Bedford Head Tavern in Covent Garden. During the next twenty years meetings were held at a number of other taverns. From about 1757 until the end of the century the Society held its meetings at the Star and Garter Tavern in Pall Mall.

The members of the Society clearly felt the disadvantage of not having premises of their own, and from 1742 until the end of the century there were various projects for a permanent home. The nearest they got to achieving this was to buy a site on the north side of Cavendish Square on which they proposed to build as their headquarters an exact replica of the Temple of Augustus at Pola in Istria. Unfortunately the plan collapsed and the site was sold, but the idea was revived in 1761, when the Society unsuccessfully petitioned the King for permission 'to build an exact copy of an antique temple' in the Green Park.

In 1800 the Society moved to St. James's Street, first to a tavern owned by a Mr Parslow, and then, after his death in 1810, to the Thatched House Tavern. It was while they were there that T.H. Shepherd painted the charming water-colour of a meeting of the Society. This probably dates from 1841, when Shepherd was at work on his illustrations for *London Interiors, with their Costumes and Ceremonies*. The Society was forced to move again in 1861, when it went to Willis's Rooms in King Street. There it remained until 1890, when it changed its quarters to the Grafton Galleries in Grafton Street. When, in 1922, these premises were taken over by a dancing club, the Society was given short notice to quit, and from then onwards until 1975 it enjoyed the hospitality of the St. James' Club, Piccadilly. On the closure of the St. James' Club, the Society accepted the invitation to transfer its pictures and to hold its dinners at Brooks's in St. James's Street, which is only a stone's throw from some of its former meeting places. It would be impossible to find a more appropriate home for the Society than Brooks's: since its foundation in 1764 it has been more closely linked with the Dilettanti than any other club. In the first decade of its existence no less than forty members of Brooks's were to be elected members of the Dilettanti Society, (today nearly a third of its members also belong to Brooks's). They included statesmen such as Charles James Fox and Lord Carlisle; diplomats of the distinction of the Duke of Richmond and Lord Rochford; Topham Beauclerk and Bennet Langton, who were friends of Dr Johnson; the well-known wit, George Selwyn; Lord Grosvenor, a great figure on the Turf, and gamblers like Lord Stavordale who lost £11,660 in one night.

Its Pictures

The Society's collection of portraits originates with a rule passed on the 4th January 1741:

> That every member of the Society do make a present of his Picture in Oil Colours done by Mr. Geo. Knapton, a member, to be hung in the Room where the said Society meets.

Four years later it was decreed that every member of the Society who had not had his portrait painted by Knapton should pay one guinea a year until his picture was delivered to the Society. This annual payment, known as 'face-money', became a lucrative source of revenue for the Society, and was not discontinued until 1809. It was quite a hefty fine when one remembers that at the same period, in 1744, the young Joshua Reynolds, at the outset of his career, charged three and a half guineas for the portraits he painted in Devonshire.

George Knapton (1698–1778), a pupil of Richardson, studied in Italy from 1725 until 1732. While he was at Naples Knapton wrote an interesting account of the discoveries at Herculaneum. By 1736 he had been elected a member of the Dilettanti Society, with the official title of 'Painter to the Society'. He resigned from this post in 1763, and appears to have given up painting.

The Society owns twenty-three portraits by Knapton, and they were all painted between 1741 and 1749. Most of the members chose to be painted in fancy dress. Four of them are depicted in Roman costume; two, Lords Bessborough and Sandwich, who had travelled in the Near East, are portrayed as Turks. Lord Galway is attired as a Cardinal, and Lord Holdernesse, who had been Ambassador at Venice, as a gondolier. The most famous, or rather infamous, portrait in the series is that of Francis Dashwood, later Lord le Despencer, wearing the habit of a Franciscan monk [facing page 64]. He is shown holding a silver chalice and gazing fixedly at the pudenda of the Medici Venus. Around his head is a halo on the edge of which is the inscription, faintly indicated, SAN:FRANCESCO DI WYCOMBO, an allusion to the sham Franciscan brotherhood of Medmenham Abbey, with which Dashwood was closely associated.

Hogarth painted a rather similar picture, *Sir Francis Dashwood at his Mock Devotions*, in which he is shown in a monk's robe, holding in an attitude of devotion not a crucifix but a naked Venus.

In 1763 James ('Athenian') Stuart, better known as an archaeologist than a painter, succeeded Knapton as Painter to the Society. On its proving impossible to get Stuart to paint any portraits for the Society, he was superseded in 1769 by Reynolds. Reynolds had been elected a member of the Society in May 1766, and as he does not appear to have paid 'face-money', he probably presented his self-portrait on becoming a member [facing page 97]. Reynolds painted his two large portrait groups of members of the Society between 1777 and 1779 [facing pages 65 and 96]. The pictures represent a meeting of the Society held on 2 March 1777, at which William Hamilton was introduced as a new member. Sir William is seated, pointing to one of the magnificent volumes entitled *Antiquités, Etrusques, Grecques et Romaines* (1766–7), which D'Hancarville had produced on Hamilton's first collection of Greek vases. It was the second collection, illustrated in line engravings by W. Tischbein, which was lost when the *Colossus* was wrecked off the Scilly Isles in 1798. An unexpected detail in this group is the lady's garter, which is being held by a member with a sly look, and to which the Arch-Master is pointing. If the left-hand group represents the enthusiasm for ancient vases promoted by Sir William Hamilton, the right-hand group shows the passion for ancient gems.

On the death of Reynolds in 1792, Lawrence was elected to succeed him as Painter to the Society. Lawrence seems to have agreed to paint a large portrait group of members of the Society, but on reflection he decided that it was too formidable a task. Instead he offered to paint a historical composition for the Society. Mercifully nothing further was heard of this proposal. The Society is, however, fortunate in possessing three fine portraits of members of the Society by Lawrence: those of the famous antiquary, Richard Payne Knight, of Henry Englefield, Secretary of the Society 1808–22, and of Lord Dundas, the 'venerable father' of the Society. Lord Dundas also appears as a young man in the second of the groups by Reynolds. The fourth Lawrence portrait, the full-length of Lord Frederick Campbell, was presented to the Society in 1918, although the sitter had never been a member.

The Society had tried in vain to persuade Lawrence to present a portrait of himself to the Society. No such difficulty was experienced with Benjamin West. He was elected to the Dilettanti with Lawrence in 1792, and in the same year succeeded Reynolds as PRA. West presented his portrait to the Society in 1818, and it has been mistakenly thought that the picture was painted in that year. In fact the paper under his left hand in the portrait is inscribed 'Benjamin West, Esq / Painted this picture in 1793'. West is shown seated beside a bust of his patron, George III. The two volumes on the table, the Bible and the 'History of England', represent the sources from which the artist took most of the subjects which he painted for the King.

Thomas Lawrence died in 1830, and was succeeded as PRA by Martin Archer Shee, who also succeeded him as Painter to the Society of Dilettanti, of which he was elected a member in July 1830. In the following year Sir Martin was commanded by the Society to paint the portrait of John Morritt of Rokeby, wearing the robes of the Arch-Master of the Society. Archer Shee duly executed this commission, which resulted in one of the finest portraits he ever painted.

The Society has maintained the tradition of having some of its members painted, and it owns, for instance, fine portraits of the Secretaries of the Society by Lord Leighton, Sir E. Poynter, and John Sargent. In this century the Society has reverted to the precedent set by Reynolds of having portrait groups painted of its members. In 1954 James Gunn started a conversation piece of fifteen members of the Society, a picture which he had completed by 1959. In Gunn's picture the Dilettanti are shown in the dining-room of the St. James' Club, Piccadilly. Behind them on the walls are Reynolds's self-portrait and his two famous groups in the glass of which are reflected the upper parts of the windows shown in John Ward's two paintings.

In 1973 John Ward, RA, was commissioned to paint a conversation piece of the members of the Society. This he did in the form of two portrait groups which were completed in 1976 and exhibited at the Royal Academy's Summer Exhibition of that year. Thirty-five members of the Society are portrayed in the two groups. The setting is the dining-room of the St. James' Club on a summer evening with the windows opening on to the balcony overlooking the Green Park. In the left-hand group Lord Bessborough and Victor Montagu are shown standing beneath Knapton's portraits of their ancestors dressed as Turks. In the right-hand group the late Thomas Monnington, who was then President of the Royal Academy, is appropriately placed in front of Reynolds's self-portrait. Some people have been puzzled by his gesture; he is rolling a cigarette. In the foreground Lord Gowrie is shown studying an engraving of the Temple of Augustus at Pola in Istria, which was chosen in the eighteenth century as the model to be copied for the Society's premises in Cavendish Square.

As the then Secretary of the Dilettanti Society, it fell to me in 1975 to arrange for the move of our pictures from the St. James' Club to Brooks's, where Geoffrey Agnew and I hung them together. After much criticism that the Reynolds groups would have looked much better on either side of the door leading into the card room, I discovered that those walls would not have been strong enough to support the weight of the pictures. Shortly after this had been achieved, I received an indignant letter from a peer, now deceased, who accused me of being the greatest vandal in London for having hung pictures in the Subscription Room. Henry Holland, he assured me, would never have allowed the introduction of pictures to detract from the austere beauty of his room. I defended myself by pointing out that the rooms Holland designed at Althorp were studded with pictures; that the reason that there were no pictures in the Subscription Room was that Brooks's did not possess any worthy of it; and then I produced my trump card. Brooks's was built to the designs of Holland between 1776 and 1778: the Reynolds groups were painted between 1777 and 1779, so that it would have been quite impossible to find two such splendid paintings more exactly contemporary with such a splendid room.

Its Officers

The affairs of the Society are managed by the Secretary, who is a member of the Society. He is the only permanent officer and is present at all the meetings. Since 1837 he has been assisted by a Receiver, who deals with the routine business.

On 7 March 1742 it was decreed 'That the dress of the Secretary be according to the dress of Machiavelli the celebrated Florentine Secretary'. This was conceived to be a black robe, and broad lawn bands hanging in front from the collar. The first Secretary of the Society, Colonel George Gray, who held office from 1738 and 1771, is shown wearing the black robe over his red coat and broad white bands in his portrait by Knapton, and no one could conceivably look less Machiavellian.

The Society owns portraits of three of its Secretaries wearing the prescribed dress – Edward Ryan by Lord Leighton, Mr E.H. Pember by Poynter, and George Macmillan by John Sargent. The Secretaries can also be picked out in the different groups by the dress they are wearing. J. Crowle, wearing very broad white bands, appears in the second of the two Reynolds groups; Lord Ilchester, in black robe and bands, is seated on the left of the President in James Gunn's Conversation Piece; and Brinsley Ford in the Secretary's robe, with the minute-book under his arm, is shown standing in the centre of John Ward's left-hand group.

The President is nominated by the Secretary at each dinner from among the members who happen to be present; while there is no prescribed rule, an endeavour is made to secure that the office is undertaken by as many members as possible (excepting the most recently elected).

On 1 February 1741, it was resolved 'That a Roman dress is thought necessary for the President of the Society'. A month later the Society 'agreed with the Committee as to the model of the Roman dress, disagreed with them as to the Colour being crimson. Resolved that it should be scarlet.' The President only dons his scarlet toga when a new member is being introduced.

Watkin Williams-Wynn is shown wearing the toga in the left-hand of Reynolds's two groups, which represent the occasion when William Hamilton was introduced. A much less voluminous garment, but with the same clasp, is being worn by Dougal Malcolm, who is presiding over the meeting painted by James Gunn. In John Ward's painting the late Lord Spencer is represented as President, which is indicated by the colour of the garment he is wearing.

The Arch-Master only has duties to perform when a new member is introduced. He is nominated by the President on the advice of the Secretary and can be chosen from any of those present at the meeting.

On 2 May 1742, it was ordered 'That for the more decent Introduction of new members and for other ceremonious purposes it is very necessary there should be appointed an Arch-Master of the Ceremonies', and it was moved that Lord Sandwich should be appointed. Much thought was given to his attire and insignia. Finally, on 5 February 1743, it was resolved 'That a long Crimson Taffeta Robe full pleated with a rich Hungarian cap and a long Spanish Toledo to be the properest dress to dignify the Arch-Master'. The Arch-Master's appearance was further enriched in 1764, when the Society thanked Lord Sandwich 'for his magnificent benevolence in presenting to the Society a Baudrier embossed and embroidered with Gold for the Decoration of the Person of the Archmaster'. The original robe is still in use, though now faded to the colour of *'vieux rose'*. The Toledo and the Baudrier have also survived the hazards of many introductory ceremonies. The Hungarian cap is a modern replacement, and what presumably was once sable is now cat.

In Reynolds's left-hand group R. Thompson is shown wearing the Arch-Master's robe and Baudrier. But the Arch-Master's attire can best be seen in Archer Shee's splendid portrait of J.B.S. Morrit of Rokeby who is shown holding the Toledo. In his portrait of Sir Edward Ryan it will be noticed that Lord Leighton has introduced, as part of his still life on the table behind the decanter of port, the Toledo, the Baudrier, and the President's toga. In James Gunn's conversation piece the artist has depicted himself assisting the late Duke of Wellington to put on the Arch-Master's robe, while the Duke appears to be holding the hilt of the Toledo in his left hand. And finally the late Lord Plunket is portrayed wearing the Arch-Master's robe and 'rich Hungarian cap' on the extreme right of John Ward's right-hand group.

Like the Arch-Master, the Imp only functions when a new member is introduced. It has been suggested that as in the hierarchy of the underworld the leading figure is designated as 'Arch', the combination of Arch-Master with an Imp may reflect some reference to the Hell-Fire Club. The prescribed dress for the Imp is a red cape and two lighted tapers. It is by no means certain when this office was constituted. The first mention of the Imp occurs in the Minutes of January 1771, when he was paid five shillings for his services, and again in February of the same year and in April 1777 he is recorded as receiving the same fee. It does not seem likely that a regular member of the Society would have been so rewarded. As Cecil Harcourt-Smith has pointed out, the Imp's Satanic origin is still further hinted at by a Minute of April 1774, when it was 'ordered that a Tail be provided for the Imp by the Lord Despencer'. It does not appear that this order was duly carried out; at any rate it is, in Sir Cecil's words, 'only a Manx Imp who functions today'.

Lord Norwich holds the distinction of being the only member of the Society to be portrayed as the Imp. He is seen to be wearing the red cape and holding a lighted taper on the left in John Ward's left-hand group.

Its Regalia

A casket, known as the 'Tomb of Bacchus', was ordered in 1736 as a receptacle for the papers and dinner money of the Society. It was completed in various stages. In May 1737, Mr Thomas Adye, who was subsequently appointed *Scultore* to the Society, was paid fifteen guineas 'for carving and ornamenting the Box'. The design seems to have been taken from an engraving in Desgodetz' *Edifices Antiques de Rome*, 1682 of the celebrated so-called sarcophagus of Constantia, an engraving which is inscribed '*Tombeau vulgairement dit de Bacchus*'. The sarcophagus was removed from the Church of S. Costanza to the Vatican in 1788.

In 1744 it was decided that the 'Tomb of Bacchus' needed a Bacchus, and in the following year Mr Adye was paid ten guineas for 'having gott executed' the ivory statuette on the top of the casket. This figure may have been inspired by one of the many recumbent statues of fauns. It resembles most closely, perhaps, the one which was formerly in the Museo Borbonico, now in the Naples Museum. At this stage the casket had been decorated on the lid, on the front, and on the two sides. Finally it was decided in 1767 'that as Bacchus's backside appear'd bare, there should be some covering provided for it.' Nicholas Revett was asked to provide a design to be executed by Mr Moser. Nothing came of this proposal and it was not until 1780 that the ivory relief of 'Perseus and Andromeda' was added to the back of the casket. The ivory, which was presented to the Society by Sir John Taylor, is a copy of a large relief in the Capitoline Museum, which was greatly admired in the eighteenth century. When the ivory relief was fitted to the back of the box, some additional ornament was required to set it off. This was given the form of scrollwork adapted from that already existing on the other sides. It has recently been discovered that this work was done by the distinguished Anglo-Swedish cabinet-maker, Christopher Fuhrlohg, who was entrusted with other minor commissions for the Society.

By a minute of 4 March 1739, it was ordered 'That a Chaire be made for the use and Dignity of the Presd^t.' The bills are preserved, which show that in 1739 the cabinet-maker, Elka Haddock, was paid for 'a mahogany compass seat elboe chair, covering do. with crimson velvet, and a mahog pedestal to do, with castors £4 10 0.' This cost less than the velvet used for covering it, '4⅜ yds, richest crimson Genoa velvet, 26s. £5. 13. 9.' The original velvet has had to be replaced on a number of occasions and has recently been recovered with the finest velvet presented by one of the members.

In the eighteenth century the chair was sometimes referred to as the *sella curulis*, and since its form was clearly intended to suggest, at any rate in the lower part of the chair, a classical prototype, this makes it one of the earliest documented examples of neoclassical taste in furniture in this country, which is, perhaps, the only excuse that can be advanced for its ugliness.

The Balloting-Box, which is no longer used, was ordered at a meeting of the Society on 1 May 1737, and appears to have been completed some time before 7 May 1738, when a case (presumably the oak one which still exists) was ordered for it. It was arranged that George Knapton should provide the design and that Mr Adye, 'the Scultore to this Society', should execute it. The case cost £1. 11s. 6d; for the box itself £7. 10s. was paid in May, 1738, to Mr Adye on account of money laid out by him for the said box; and the additional sum of £25 was given to him for his trouble in carving and finishing it. The Balloting-Box, like the Presidential throne and the 'Tomb of Bacchus', illustrates the classical taste of the early members of the Society.

The 'long Spanish Toledo' was supplied by Tanner in March 1746, and cost, with 'gilding etc.', £2. 17s. 6d. The description must not be taken literally, for the inscription on the blade shows that it is the work of a German artist. It reads CORNELUS IHN SOLINGEN. Cornelius Wundes was probably a descendant of the Solingen swordsmith, Johann Wundes (1560–1610). The Dilettanti rapier dates from the latter part of the seventeenth century. The scabbard is modern. J.B.S. Morritt is shown holding the Toledo in his portrait by Archer Shee.

There have been occasions on the introduction of a new member when the Arch-Master has wielded the Toledo with so much panache that he has endangered his fellow members. As the result of this a motion was introduced in 1929 to the effect that in future only members over seventy, if available, should be called upon to perform the duties of the Arch-Master.

The Fox Club

Francis Sitwell

L ITTLE is known of the origins of the Fox Club, the inner dining club of Brooks's. Its traditions, as remembered in the early years of this century, are set down in that large, gloomy and, in my opinion, most aptly named volume *Memorials of Brooks's*, which traces the history of Brooks's from its foundation to the close of the nineteenth century. The *Memorials'* frontispiece is a reproduction of the portrait by William Russell RA hanging over the fireplace in the front hall, as if to emphasize Charles James Fox's importance both to Brooks's and to the dining club which commemorates him.

While Fox was alive a 'Whig Club' existed and it is almost certain that the Fox Club was a continuation. Account books and ledgers indicate that its first proper meeting took place in London in 1829, though there is some evidence of a dinner in Fox's honour being held in 1813. Most of the information which survives comes from notes left by Sir Augustus Stephenson, its Secretary for thirty-seven years. His father, one of the 1829 members – a member of Brooks's since 1818 who had been a Manager – had succeeded Lord Holland and Sir Ronald Ferguson as Secretary.

It seems that the Fox Club was also successor to a series of large dinners held in Edinburgh from 1821 to 1825 on Fox's birthday, 24 January. Of the final dinner held in 1825 Lord Cockburn remarked

This I think was the last of these festivals. They were never intended to be perpetual; but were only resorted to for political union, and excitement during the stage that we have now passed through. These

Fox dinners did incalculable good. They animated and instructed and consolidated the Whig party with less trouble than anything which could have been devised.

From 1829 until 1843 dinners appear to have been held at the Clarendon Hotel in New Bond Street but in the latter year, after an application signed by sixteen Fox Club members, permission was given to hold them in the 'Great Room' at Brooks's – i.e., in the Subscription Room. However, one of the four annual dinners continued to be held at Greenwich in the Ship Hotel, a well-known local hostelry whose proprietor, Mr Bale, arranged for members to be collected by boat from Westminster Pier. During the late 1880s the club met either at the Café Royal or the Hotel Metropole in Northumberland Avenue; I suspect that this may have been because of the disruption caused by the reconstruction of the additional club premises for Brooks's in Park Place next door.

At the time of the *Memorials'* publication in 1907 the dinners were already being held at Brooks's three or four times a year, always when Parliament was sitting. It seems that they were often on Saturdays – which would be unheard of today – and that menus were far more extensive and elaborate than could now be attempted. After oysters there would be two or three choices of soup, then half a dozen different entrées and fish dishes, two or three choices of game, followed by a sorbet and then a large selection of sweets and puddings and of course some savouries, and even a cold buffet. On the other hand the wines offered were rather limited by today's standards.

Membership is still restricted to fifty and we meet twice a year, in the spring and autumn, in the Great Subscription Room. No guests are allowed and the only time, to my knowledge, that women have been invited was when my predecessor as secretary, Simon Birch, invited Lady Charlotte Monckton, Fox's direct descendant, to dine with us. It was a most delightful occasion, but times had not changed in this instance, two or three members resigning in protest at the presence of a female guest.

No speeches are ever given at the dinners, the only formality consisting of the 'member highest in rank present' being invited to propose the four traditional toasts, one after another, which are taken seated. These are: 'In the memory of Charles James Fox', 'to the memory of Earl Grey and the Reform Bill' and 'to the memory of Lord Holland'. The fourth toast, 'to the memory of Lord John Russell', was added by general consent in June 1878.

The Fox Club is the proud possessor of a set of ten very fine George III candlesticks – four dated 1774, two dated 1787 and four 1817 – and a candlestick and snuffer mounted in a small glass case. The latter appears to have been made by the great silversmith Paul de Lamarie and is dated 1740. The regalia are always brought out and displayed in the Great Subscription Room, together with a seal and gavel which must have belonged to Fox.

Members are proposed and seconded with their names entered in an old Candidates' Book which dates from about 1845. Traditionally membership has almost always been drawn exclusively from Brooks's members, but the rules state that two members may be elected from outside Brooks's, a rule which still exists today. Down the years the members of the Fox Club have to some extent continued to represent the old Whig tradition.

Fox was a unique product of the eighteenth century, greatly loved and admired by his many friends. It is wholly appropriate that the club set up to venerate and perpetuate his name and what he stood for should continue to flourish nearly two hundred years later.

The Clubhouse

J. Mordaunt Crook

The quaint old dress, the grand old style,
The *mots*, the racy stories;
The wine, the dice – the wit, the bile,
The hate of Whigs and Tories.

(Frederick Locker)

I

It is 1799, and Beau Brummell has just been elected to Brooks's. A sedan chair bobs its way down St. James's Street and comes to rest before the portico of Mr Brooks's new clubhouse. The chairmen clamber down the area steps. Brummell sweeps into the entrance hall. Shrugging off a creditor lurking in the Strangers' Room on the right – no wonder Charles Fox calls it 'the Jerusalem Chamber' – he mounts the staircase, turning to the right, towards a hubbub of voices. At the head of the stairs he enters the Ante Room, and there – through open double doors – is one of the finest interiors in London, Henry Holland's Great Subscription Room. It is twenty-one years since 'Liberal' Brooks declared his clubhouse open – since Holland's 'Anglo-Graeco-Roman style' first took London by storm. The walls are greenish grey, the curtains crimson damask; painted allegories illuminate each overdoor – Venus, Bacchus, Minerva, Cupid; and all along the sweeping wagon-vault, gilded mouldings glitter in the candlelight. This is early Holland: cool, understated, patrician, Whig-gish; still English rather than French – less Gabriel and Rousseau than Sir William Chambers, 'Palmyra' Wood and 'Athenian' Stuart. After all, Mr Holland is Capability Brown's son-in-law.

Brummell strolls nonchalantly between the gamblers, and then turns right at the Venetian window, to find a table in the Eating Room. Here the colour scheme is paler, mostly fawn and gold, with gilded wreaths and classical medallions in bas-relief. Refreshments appear eventually from the kitchens in the basement; up the spiral stone staircase at the rear of the entrance hall, past the round Coffee Room upstairs and across the back landing. Conversation complete, Brummell returns via a side door to the staircase landing. Then down the stairs again and away, stopping only in the front Morning Room to leave a note for Prinnie. As he emerges into St. James's Street, he glances disdainfully at Boodle's. Horace Walpole's comments on Carlton House are on his lips: 'How sick we shall be after this chaste palace of Mr Adam's gingerbread and sippets of embroidery!'

II

Now it is 1858, and 'Poodle' Byng is on his way to luncheon. The hackney carriage deposits him at the door. There is no portico now – it did darken the Morning Room. Instead a balcony protrudes from the windows of the Subscription Room, supported by metal cantilevers. These windows now sport Palladian pediments, and the front door itself – with semicircular fanlight – has been shifted one bay to the right.

Greeting the liveried porter, 'Poodle' veers leftwards into the Morning Room to scan the daily papers. That room is lighter now, and longer, with a dove grey chimney-piece, two Ionic columns imitating scagliola porphyry (with a writing table shaped to accommodate one of them), and a shallow bay window facing into Park Street. Then out he goes, into the entrance lobby; he warms himself at the stove, then passes through a pair of red baize doors into the main hall and up the Grand Staircase. The new stone stairs climb upwards – in double flights with bowed iron balusters –

and open on to a spacious new landing lobby with three pairs of double doors. This Waiting Room (the old Strangers' Room downstairs has become a dressing-room) looms out above the hallway like a veritable Noah's Ark. Its weight rests on a single cast-iron girder, and that beam itself depends on a pair of cast-iron columns cased in wood and painted to resemble Siena marble. Lantern and cupola are coloured French grey. Holland's fine rooms on the *piano nobile* are glorious as ever; the round Coffee Room at the back has even been enlarged and turned into a Smoking Room. But everything is quieter now: serious gamblers have moved elsewhere. There is an air of comfort and sobriety, even an atmosphere of study. In the back Morning Room downstairs there is a rather useful collection of maps. There are busts of Milton and Fox, a gasolier in Holland's Ante Room, and Brussels carpets everywhere. And behind the grand Eating Room, burrowed into the adjacent property at No. 2, Park Place – along with dressing-rooms, pantries and billiard room – there are even the beginnings of a library.

III

1914, and Sir Edward Grey has just left his desk in the Foreign Office. Most of his Cabinet colleagues seem to be members of Brooks's, but at least in St. James's Street they wear their politics lightly.

Past the new railings he goes – no balcony now: it was rather precarious; at least there is a grand balustrade, and urns, and the window pediments are stone rather than cement. Through the entrance vestibule he stalks, and into a spacious new staircase hall. That curious landing lobby has gone: it certainly darkened the hallway. The Coffee Room is on the ground floor now (older members disapprove), filling the site of No. 2 Park Place. Here there are gilded brackets in the style of Louis XV, and curtains and chairs of dark maroon. Out in the hall there is a blazing fire in a massive new chimney-piece, marbled and mirrored. On the second floor there is a new billiard room, and bedrooms for members too – not just for servants – grandly approached by a new bedroom staircase.

Holland's three great chambers on the first floor are still there, but all Smoking Rooms now, and rather sombre. In the Subscription Room there are draped box pelmets; the Venetian windows have Tuscan colonnettes. There are three more medallions in the Eating Room and everywhere quantities of Turkey carpet, mahogany and plate glass.

Above the Coffee Room is the new Library: Persian carpeting, crimson velour curtains with Turkish tassels, bookcases in treacly mahogany, mottled marble columns, inlaid marble chimney-pieces and no less than five padded chesterfields in green morocco leather. How sensible to choose John MacVicar Anderson, an architect who was also a gentleman. Members still dine in white tie and tails; the waiters wear knee-breeches; change is given in washed silver; and all the rooms are kept at an equable 60°–65°F. The books on the shelves are mostly political. So is the conversation; muted now and apprehensive. But how comfortable it is here. When the lights do go out in Brooks's at least they will be electric, and in the style of Louis XV.

IV

Now it is 1938, and Professor A.E. Richardson has invited Queen Mary to view the improvements. For years Brooks's 'mid-Victorian appearance' has offended 'delicate taste'. There have been one or two changes for the better: in 1929 the club architect Paul Phipps even replaced plate glass with glazing bars. Now the Professor has gone much further. Outside, Her Majesty admires the removal of nearly all the nineteenth-century accretions, particularly the pediments. Only the balustrade and urns remain from Anderson's time. Brickwork is black, masonry white: Richardson solemnly explains the preservative qualities of boot polish and milk. Inside, the black and white paving in the hall catches her eye. There is a new brass lantern, and elaborately carved wall lights on the landing. Anderson's stair-rail has been simplified, Richardson assures her; so have the mouldings of the lantern spandrels. In Library and hall the heavy overmantel mirrors have been replaced by suitable portraits. In

Holland's Eating Room two Edwardian medallions have been removed, and two nineteenth-century chimney-pieces replaced with eighteenth-century ones supplied by Lenygon and Morant. Inside the Great Subscription Room Richardson assures his guest that the gilded pelmets are his; so are the pier-glasses over chimney-piece and consoles. Queen Mary seems more interested in the chocolate cake which the Professor has cunningly provided.

For an architectural historian, the lack of documentation for Brooks's is tantalizing. The club seems to have treated its records as carelessly as Fox treated guineas. The Managers kept no minutes before 1841. And not a single architectural drawing for the clubhouse, by Holland, Anderson or Richardson, has survived. Holland, 'the darling of the *cognoscenti*', is in general a shadowy figure. At Brooks's, he is almost invisible: no building accounts, no correspondence, no elevations and – apart from the famous Rowlandson sketch of 1808 – not a single interior view. All we have are a preliminary perspective and two preliminary first-floor plans. Only one of these is dated; none bears title or signature; and none shows the building as executed. To add to the confusion, all three seem to be from the hand of John Soane. As it happens, young Soane was indeed in Holland's office at the time. And key elements from all three drawings clearly found their way into the final scheme.

Documentation for the alterations of 1815 and 1835 is almost entirely lacking. The name of the architect who replaced the portico with the balcony in 1835 – adding a set of stucco pediments for good measure – is unknown. And who was the architect who enlarged the Drawing Room in 1815, erecting at the same time the second (and oddest) of the club's three great staircases? No building accounts, no correspondence, no drawings. All we have are inventories from which details of furnishing and fittings must be laboriously pieced together. Where is the scheme proposed in 1857 by Henry Faulkner? Where, above all, is the plan of that year supposedly proposed by 'Poodle' Byng?

With John MacVicar Anderson we are on safer ground. Anderson was the nephew of Scotland's most successful country-house architect, William Burn. Inheriting that practice, he worked at Althorp, Bowhill,

Knowsley and many other seats before 'gradually drifting into a commercial class of building' – with Christie's, Coutts's and a whole cluster of City banks and insurance offices. Anderson was the ideal Establishment architect: predictable, dignified, well-connected, well-mannered. When it came to clubs he had few rivals. The Conservative, the Carlton, the Junior Carlton, the Naval and Military, the Union – all these expanded in his hands. Curiously, he began his career with a 'Design for a Club House', exhibited at the Royal Academy in 1856 – the very moment when Brooks's was negotiating the purchase of No. 2 Park Place. Forty years later came the chance to rebuild. It was a commission which stretched all his skills as a diplomat. Right from the start there was a dispute between two groups of members: should the Coffee Room be on the ground floor, and the Library at first-floor level – or vice versa? Anderson deftly produced alternative schemes, then waited to see which way the membership was swinging before revising his original preference: Georgian tradition was abandoned, and Brooks's plumped for a ground-floor Coffee Room with Library on the *piano nobile*.

Each generation has remodelled Brooks's according to its own taste: first Neo-Classical (1786; 1815), then Neo-Palladian (1835; 1889), then Neo-Georgian (1935; 1952) – but always maintaining the continuity of classical forms. 'Progressively perfected and adorned', as T.H.S. Escott put it in 1914, through three staircases and four façades: that, after all, is the way of the Whigs. Neo-Classicism was a rationalist aesthetic rather than a structurally functional system: hence Holland's false doors and windows. Neo-Palladianism was an expressive system couched in visual conventions: hence Anderson's battery of pediments, balustrades and urns. As for Neo-Georgian, it was an aesthetic code based on a reverence for associational form: hence Richardson's meticulous archaeology. Never was rebuilding seriously considered, except perhaps in 1876 when at least one member – the Archbishop of Canterbury's son – suggested total demolition. There was probably only one missed opportunity. In 1926 Sir Edwin Lutyens was elected a member: would that the Managers had commissioned him to design a suitable entrance porch.

Over the years, continuity has been disguised by changes of

nomenclature. Holland's Eating Room has been subsequently known as the House Dining Room, the Coffee Room, the Drawing Room, the Strangers' Smoking Room and the Card Room: it is now the Spencer Room. The round room on the first floor has been in turn a coffee room, a smoking room and a bedroom; as the Cavendish Room it is now reserved for private parties. Holland's antechamber to the Great Subscription Room has in its time been called Card Room, North Smoking Room, Small Strangers' Drawing Room, Billiard Room, Writing Room and now, once again, Card Room. The old back Morning Room, later used for breakfast and lunch, is now the Bar. The present Backgammon Room was first a Strangers' Room, then a Dressing Room, then a Visitors' Room, then a Small Smoking Room, then a Cocktail Bar. Even the Subscription Room – carefully restored in 1966 – was known for much of its life as the Large Smoking Room. Only the front Morning Room – redecorated at last in 1989 – has never changed its name.

Much today is not what it seems. A lead cistern in front of the clubhouse is appropriately dated 1776, the year of Holland's design. Alas, it was supplied by Crowther in 1952. The exterior balustrade dates from 1889; the black and white pavement in the hall from 1936; the entrance railings and lampstands from 1953; the inner doors from 1948; the staircase handrail mostly from 1890, partly from 1934; the porter's box and telephone booth from 1989. Most important of all, the Dilettanti Society pictures arrived only with the St. James' Club in 1975. But the atmosphere is not all that different. 'There is something of the old-fashioned air of the past about the Brooks's of today,' noted Joseph Hatton in 1885. 'The house is more like a private establishment than a club. Collectively, the members affect Whiggism (if such a thing exists nowadays) in politics; individually they keep their principles pretty well to themselves. . . . The leading ideas of Brooks's are centred in comfort, good dinners, old wines, and a quiet rubber.' Perhaps it is still, as the Editor of *Punch* called it in 1867, 'the most aristocratic club in London'. There is no silent room now. There are even ladies in the Library. But the outward symbols remain the same. High up in the pediment, through traffic fumes and smog, young Bacchus and his friends still girdle the globe with laughter.

Brooks's, as re-fitted in stone in 1889 by J MacVicar Anderson, with
urns, balustrades and railings

Brooks's as re-furbished in 1935 by Professor Sir Albert Richardson:
black brickwork and white masonry

H H Asquith, later Earl of Oxford and Asquith (1852–1928). From a
mezzotint at Brooks's

The Pictures

Oliver Millar

THE visitor to Brooks's is greeted appropriately by two likenesses of Charles James Fox. Over the fireplace in the hall hangs a contemporary copy in pastel of the head and shoulders of Reynolds's celebrated three-quarter-length which was shown at the Royal Academy in 1784 (the original is at Holkham); and above, on the first floor, stands a version, signed and dated 1810, of the marble bust by Joseph Nollekens. The version made for the family in 1793 is in the possession of Fox's descendants at Melbury. A prime replica, of a work justly described as the sculptor's 'masterpiece in the Baroque manner', was made in 1791 and is at Holkham. The prototype, said to have been made for Catherine the Great, was shown that year at the Royal Academy. Nollekens's '*stock* pieces' were his busts of Fox and William Pitt. He is said to have made at least seventy replicas of the latter and at least fifty of his second bust of Fox. Of his bust of Pitt a version, signed and dated 1807, stands near Fox on the landing. Pitt, in fact, had refused to sit to the sculptor, but Nollekens took a death-mask in 1806 and used it as the source on which the busts, and the statue in the Senate House at Cambridge, were based. The difference between the personalities of the two statesmen could not have been better illustrated than they are in the busts: Fox, relaxed, open and friendly; Pitt, lean and formidably austere. Next to William Pitt stands a signed version of Nollekens's bust of William Windham of which the prototype, made in 1793, is also at Holkham.

The age of Fox and Pitt is brilliantly evoked in a notable series of Gillray's caricatures, dispersed throughout the Club, and in a fine series of portraits, engraved in mezzotint, hanging chiefly on, or near, the principal staircase. The caricature tradition is kept alive in works by such masters as Dighton, Cruikshank, 'Spy', Pellegrini, Beerbohm and Osbert Lancaster. Over two attractive works from the period of the Regency there hangs a certain doubt. The spirited chalk drawing by David Wilkie, signed and dated 1817 and hanging at the moment in the Bar, is claimed to be a portrait of Beau Brummell, but this is impossible; and I very much doubt whether specialists would support the attribution to Turner of the attractive large water-colour, in monochrome grey wash, of Cully near Lausanne. Mr Andrew Wilton has kindly informed me that it should be attributed to Edward Dayes.

The Club's own pictures are inevitably overshadowed by the splendid portraits on loan from various sources, notably from the Dilettanti Society. Our own pictures include a decorative piece by Peter Casteels – pheasants, partridges and domestic fowl in a landscape – signed and dated 1734; a characteristically dashing piece of drawing in pastel by Daniel Gardner in the portrait of Mrs Holland and her children; and Jacob More's tranquil, classical view of the Lake of Nemi and Genzano with country folk dancing in the foreground. More's view of the famous site can be compared with those, for example, by J.R. Cozens or Thomas Jones; and the scene had been drawn and painted, from a higher point of view, by Richard Wilson. More had left his native Edinburgh for Rome, where he settled in 1773 and where he remained for the rest of his life. Goethe visited him there in July 1787: 'an English [*sic*] landscape painter, most of whose works are admirably thought out.' One of the most successful landscape painters in Rome, he sent pictures back to London for showing at the annual exhibitions at the Royal Academy. Soft and rather pallid, the picture in our Backgammon Room is a characteristic example of the intensely nostalgic and undemanding nature – the 'empty grandeur' – of More's work. It is easy to understand why he was known as 'the British Claude'.

Members of the Club, and their guests, will be interested by drawings of such notable figures from our recent past as Johnny Macrae and Martin Newman, by Dufort and Daly respectively, and by the pleasing views of the Club, in the Front Morning Room, by F.C. Lodge, G.S. Fletcher and Hanslip Fletcher, arranged appropriately near Rowlandson's famous water-colour of the Great Subscription Room. This was the source for the plate, dated 1 October 1808, in Vol. II of Ackermann's *Microcosm of London*; and it illustrates the chapter entitled 'Gaming-House' – a well-known account of the Club and of the indulgence of its members in 'this destructive propensity'.

The pictures, prints and drawings in the Club were, for the most part, arranged by the late Sir Geoffrey Agnew, and it is nice to be able to point to the water-colour by Thomas Lound, in the Front Morning Room, which was given to the Club in his memory: a view of Castle Acre Priory, a landmark in the county to which Geoffrey was so devoted.

Table talk

Cyril Ray

'THE eternal joints, or beef-steaks, the boiled fowl with oyster sauce, and an apple tart – this is what we have, sir, at our clubs, and very monotonous fare it is.'

Captain Gronow, recalling a dinner the Prince Regent gave in 1814 to members of White's and Brooks's, quoted Sir Thomas Stepney's reply to the Prince's asking what sort of dinners they got at their clubs. Sir Thomas was a member of White's, described by 'Dandy' Raikes as 'the epicurean Croesus'. He was no doubt delighted by the royal reaction: the Prince asked his cook, Wattier, 'whether he would take a house and organize a dinner club. Wattier assented and named . . . Labourie, the cook from the Royal kitchen . . . the dinners were exquisite; the best Parisian cooks could not beat Labourie . . .'

But delicious though its cuisine and distinguished its membership, Watier's (so spelt as a club) lasted a mere five years – according to Gronow because of high play there, but according to Raikes 'from the paralysed state of its members', with a long obituary list in his diary (tactfully omitted from his published memoirs) and the note, 'none of the dead reached the average age of man'.

Half-way between his time and ours, Ralph Nevill (Beefsteak and the St. James') observed in his *London Clubs* that Watier's lasted long enough 'to set a pattern that has persisted in St. James's and thereabouts to our own day of great chefs trained in great kitchens being sought after – and captured – by those of the great clubs who are so minded . . .' Indeed, Crockford's arose in 1828 from the ashes of Watier's and appointed first Louis Eustache Ude, sometime (perhaps) of the kitchen of

Letitia Bonaparte, Napoleon's mother, and then, certainly, those of the Duke of York and of the acknowledged greatest gourmet of the day, the second Earl of Sefton.

Ude was succeeded by Francatelli, pupil of Carême (who had been Talleyrand's *chef patissier*, and chef to the Prince Regent) and himself formerly *maître d'hôtel* to Queen Victoria. After Crockford's he eventually succeeded Alexis Soyer, greatest of all club chefs, at the Reform Club.

Brooks's went its own way. The one name in its archives to ring a bell of the same sort is that of Nicolas Soyer, supposedly the famous Alexis's grandson (his father, also Alexis, claimed to be Alexis's son by an early liaison in Paris, and was belatedly acknowledged.) But young Soyer did not last long: engaged in December 1910, he was given, in May 1911, a month's pay in lieu of notice – the archives do not say why – at about the time his book on paper-bag cookery appeared, followed by *Soyer's Standard Cookery*, usurping the name of the greatest of all Soyers and proclaiming on the title-page, 'By Nicolas Soyer, late chef to Brooks's Club.' It should have read: 'late, and very briefly . . .'

Gronow must have been wrong, Raikes right in their reasons for the demise of Watier's – high stakes and deep drinking, respectively. Stakes were at least as high at Brooks's: the epicurean Stepney turned his back on Labourie's elaborations at Watier's to become one of the four who set up what Raikes recalled as 'that celebrated Faro bank at Brooks's which ruined half of the town'. This was the bank at which Lord Cholmondeley and Mr Thompson of Grosvenor Square each realized between £300,000 and £400,000.

All this on the five-shilling supper put out at 11 p.m. for the dedicated gamesters ('no gaming in the eating-room except tossing-up for reckoning' was the rule at the 4.30 p.m. dinner) at which there were neither fancy dishes nor potent potables, but sandwiches*, pulled chicken (cold chicken 'pulled' into shreds), cold fowl, fruit and bisquits (*sic*) with, to drink, tea, coffee, cyder (*sic*) and spruce beer (a dark beer made without barley but with spruce twigs, bark or cones, molasses and yeast).

---

*A fairly early use of the word: first OED reference is from Gibbon's *Journal* for 24 November 1762.

The wines, in order of preference, were champagne – sweeter in those days than in ours – claret, burgundy, madeira and port, with ice, cucumber, oranges, lemons, seltzer, Bristol water and Spa water, all of which suggests much precautionary dilution, and the rigour of the game: 'Don't drink and dice . . .'

Dinner was served only when Parliament was sitting, and was no more elaborate save, perhaps, for presentation. Sometimes claret, negus (a spiced wine-cup) and strong beer were the only drinks, and it could be that it was the boiled fowl with oyster sauce for dinner which Tom Stepney so grumbled about that provided the sandwiches, cold fowl and pulled chicken for supper. Not much evidence there of the heavy port-drinking that is generally supposed to characterize the period.

Indeed, it could be that this Regency period – although far more port was still drunk than in our own time – saw the beginning of the long, very gradual overtaking in importance of port by claret. We must be wary of taking as a guide to members' taste Christie's sale, on 18 and 19 July 1815, of 'part of the capital, extensive and very valuable stock of choice old wines, of the proprietors of Brooks's Club House, sold in consequence of a dissolution of partnership, consisting of about eleven thousand bottles of the very finest old port, a considerable part of which is warranted to have been from four to nearly eight years in bottle: three thousand bottles of genuine and high-flavoured East India and West India Madeira, and one thousand bottles of old sherry of the best quality.'

This was the year in which Griffith (or 'Griffin') who had succeeded Brooks on the latter's death in 1792, disappears as 'Master' of the club. As Anthony Lejeune has surmised, the sale must have been part of a deal between Griffith and his successor. Almack, founder of the club, had been a wine-merchant, and the early 'Masters' seemed to have run the club and their wine businesses almost as one. Brooks's membership in 1815 was a mere four hundred, for whom eleven thousand bottles of port even for maturing would have been a monstrous cellar – they were the property of 'the proprietors of Brooks's Club House', that is to say 'Griffin and Co', as the management of Brooks's was recorded until 1815.

Once the management of the club came into the hands of a committee of members, in 1795, and until the early 1900s, it was the custom for two members to choose wines from two respected wine-merchants, who would stock the cellars, retaining ownership and billing the club every quarter for the stock consumed.

Perhaps the most percipient bon vivant to take part in these exercises was Richard Burdon (later Lord) Haldane, elected to Brooks's in 1882, who took on the responsibility in 1897. According to Dudley Sommer's *Haldane of Cloan*, the future Labour Lord Chancellor owed his first brief to the knowledgeability he had shown when a mere twenty-five, at the table of a rich solicitor, about the Margaux 1864, and by his ability to polish off unaided a bottle of the Lafite 1858. (In the 1890s he was also more or less sole member of a short-lived cigar subcommittee.)

The wine-drinkers of Brooks's seemed to have been forward-looking and to have had forward-looking Managers to guard their interests. There are early requests for 'light' claret, at a time when there was plenty of so-called Bordeaux wine about – and enjoyed – that had been '*Hermitagé*', (some listed as such); laced, that is, with the heavier Rhône wine to give body.

The political significance of port and claret had long declined since the days of the early Georges, when Scottish Jacobites and Tory squires drank to the King over the Water in the wine of the country that had given him asylum, and Whigs pointedly chose the non-French port – all the more readily since the Methuen treaty of 1703 reduced the duty on Portuguese wines to two-thirds that of French. But the government relented in the 1780s, and the gap narrowed: by the time we were at war with Revolutionary France there were substantial stocks of claret in Britain – augmented by highly organized smuggling on a vast scale – to keep claret-lovers well supplied until after Waterloo, when young ensigns and cornets of Wellington's Peninsular army, now occupying Paris, indulged a taste for claret, acquired when they had stayed for a while in Bordeaux, enjoying wines more delicate than the rougher stuff of Spain – a taste that many brought back to St. James's.

By the time another war loomed, not with France but with Germany, provident Managers had arranged in 1914 for a reserve of a hundred cases of claret, fifty château-bottled, fifty London, to be laid down as a reserve – still supplied by merchants on a pay-as-you-drink quarterly basis: in 1890 the wine subcommittee had considered a suggestion that Brooks's should lay down its own cellar but decided that 'the consumption of wine by members of Brooks's is not sufficient to warrant the risks that attend such a course.' It was only after that war that the club did begin to lay down its own cellar, and we get a somewhat clearer view of its taste in wine: from 1920 to 1939 consumption of champagne declined; that of claret and of red burgundy more than doubled; white burgundy made its first appearance; and port went up from 350 bottles a year only to 502, whereas claret rose from 218 to 457, red burgundy from 70 to 162.

True, there was a lustrum following those two decades during which the trend was reversed, and it is difficult to explain the heavier consumption of sherry and port during the war and the immediate post-war years – 1072 bottles of port in 1943, for instance – unless it is that younger members, drinkers of light table wines, were away at the war, leaving their elders to sit longer over their old-fashioned pre-prandial sherries and post-prandial port, wines, as the Italians say, 'of meditation'.

Clarets and burgundies were up, too, but nothing like so steeply, and hocks and moselles understandably went down – by no means, though, to vanishing point. South African 'sherry' made what seems to be its first appearance. But port-drinking soon began to drop again and throughout the 1950s and the 1960s it declined so steadily, and eventually so steeply, that in the early 1970s the club sold off its Taylor, Fonseca and Quinta do Noval to members for some £26,000, and in 1980 another 285 dozen vintage ports were sold, along with other fine wines – primarily, this time, to fund the restoration of the Great Subscription and other rooms. The port fetched almost £14,000. A mere seven years later it would have been more like £100,000 in the sale-room: there are still devoted lovers of vintage port in Brooks's and elsewhere, but their numbers dwindle and the prices rise, thanks partly, at any rate, to moneyed investors.

Still, as will have been seen, the Managers and their Wine Committee have had a smooth passage, reflecting – sometimes perhaps helping to fashion – members' tastes, and to a great extent selling port to buy claret as those tastes changed.

Cellars are quiet places, kitchens aren't.

In its earlier days Brooks's kitchen was especially *mouvementé*: chefs and cooks came and went frequently (the styles for the job 'chef' and 'cook' – seem to have been interchangeable). As late as 1889, a (or is it 'the'?) cook, three waiters and three kitchen-maids went in the same purge and, in our own century, in 1903, two kitchen-maids had hysterics and were sacked immediately; the chef being carpeted and ordered to fire the rest unless things improved, 'and use young foreigners in their place'. A year later, a waiter shot himself in the Club. The verdict was 'temporary insanity', but it could well be that a psychiatrist, had such sages existed then, might have traced traumas to the kitchen.

From the beginning there have been two major schools of thought about the Club's catering – not, that is, about wines, on which a succession of subcommittees has found members biddable and even appreciative, but about the food. There have been and are those, like Tom Stepney, who would like a nice change, or those who echo the old axiom, 'all change is to be deplored, especially change for the better.' Skirmishing around the fringes of this more or less amicable confrontation have been the minorities.

There were those who sighed for the glories not so much of Brooks's past as of Watier's: in the 1850s or thereabouts the Master complained to the Managers that he didn't mind so much that 'Mr. H.B.' owed him £800 – he trusted him completely – were it not that he insisted on ortolans for dinner every night.

There were those who were faithful, as some are still, to the traditions not so much of clubland as of country-house cooking. One member, a century later, went to the length of penning in French for the benefit of the benighted chef the English way of preparing woodcock, snipe and golden plover – let the innards stay innard – and another went into still greater detail about still more game birds, ending with a comment, surely by now purely academic, on the relative merits of gulls' and gannets' eggs.

In 1866, a Mr Lamont enlisted himself among what we might call the Stepneyites by begging leave to suggest that as the Club now had a new chef 'could there be an occasional variation of the bill of fare, it being almost invariably the same every day for over seven years.' To a member of like mind it is courteously pointed out, years later, that if he ordered Sole Walewska at five o'clock the chef would not have time to find the ingredients.

On the other hand, a majority, not so voluble, accepted and accepts things as they are, only so long as they do not fail to include things as they used to be. There are wistful reminiscences in suggestion books about Brooks's apple pie (the chef, in return, asked for the recipe – there never was one: there used to be a deep *individual* apple pie, served hot or cold, which may have been, too, flavoured with cloves or with cinnamon, on request) and about spotted dog (or was it spotted dick?), the chef's reply to which was to produce it, masquerading on the bill of fare as 'Polka-dot Pudding'. It was about the same time that *crème brûlée*, most traditional, despite its name, of English puddings, began to wear a strawberry, no doubt frozen, atop.

For the kitchen feels obliged to make its own gestures of independence. As recently as 1982 the management discussed the difficulty of keeping chefs: 'They become disillusioned. They want to create different and unusual dishes. . . . opportunity for individual flair [is] limited as the types of dishes never vary greatly. Chefs lose interest in their work . . .'

Perhaps because so much is done for them. There seems to be no record of when the club first bought a deep-freeze machine and a microwave oven, but complaints about frozen and tinned foods began at least forty years ago. A complaint about tinned crab soup was countered by the information that it was one of the club's favourite soups – but followed by the placatory concession that vichyssoise would in future be made in the club kitchens.

Not so much, perhaps, a gesture of independence as an imp of kitchen mischief was the '*Fromage de Ville de Stilton*' so described on a menu, stinging an outraged member to comment, 'Here-today-gone-tomorrow King's Road Flash-Alfery!'

Some battles have long been lost and won: there are no more complaints about frozen peas – where nowadays in London does one find eatable fresh peas on a club or restaurant menu? The die-hards simply don't order them – or (frozen) potted shrimps, about which grumbles were thunderous, and upon which some members now dote. (Top of a 'popularity' index drawn up for the Managers in 1982.)

If the choice of cheeses is now a matter of pride it may be the result of one of the cruellest blows ever dealt by a member to the management: 'not so good as the Athenaeum's'. (To be fair to that much – unfairly – mocked institution, it was known within living memory to all club cheese-fanciers, and perhaps still is, as always having the best Blue Cheshire in London.)

Differences such as these between member and member, member and management, management and kitchen will never be resolved; Brooks's would be a saintly – and a boring – sodality if they were. The compiler of these random notes cherishes the fanciful notion of a conciliatory annual dinner of all interested parties, composed around the traditional for the traditionalist, yet new to all of us: Tom Stepney's despised boiled fowl (fat, free-range and unfrozen, as in Regency times) with oyster sauce (the relaid Portuguese, now available all the year round, would do admirably and should be used liberally), accompanied by that benign amalgam of Guinness and champagne once known as 'Bismarck' after the Iron Chancellor, who loved it, now as Black Velvet. It is reputed to have originated at Brooks's when, on the death of the Prince Consort, the barman laced a member's glass of bubbly with the black stuff saying, 'Your drink too, sir, should be in mourning!' A likely story, but a good excuse . . .

The Betting Book

Max Hastings

THE gambling mania which dominated London club life in the later eighteenth century provoked the creation of books to record wagers, which survive to this day in Brooks's, White's and Boodle's. Their justification is obvious, when more than a few bets must have been made in circumstances in which one or both parties were in no condition to be likely to recall the terms in the morning. Their fruits, for the great St. James's clubs two centuries on, are droll miscellanies of politics, personality and whimsy.

'Brookes's Betting Book' (*sic*) survives today as a cased leather-bound volume, inscribed on the opening page: 'Bett Book 1778'. But the first entry is dated 26 March 1771, the record of a ten guinea wager between Lord Bateman and Mr Conway, that Lord Bolingbroke's colt will beat Shafto when they run in October, and 'if they do not the Bett is off'. Horses were an obvious inspiration for members. Yet for most of the succeeding 180 years, the book has been dominated by political and military wagers, that provide diverting footnotes to the history of the period.

Most of the early entries are scrawled in black ink, untidily cancelled, heavily landmarked with ink blots. In December 1774, 'Ld. Bolingbroke betts Mr. Fox 150 to 50 that the Tea Act is not repealed this Session'. On 20 November 1775, 'Col. St. John bets 10 Gs. with Mr. Crewe that the 69th Reg: has not orders to go to America before this day 12 months'. On 30 January 1779, 'Ld Bolingbroke betts Mr. Long 1 Gn. that we are not at war with Spain this day month'. Bolingbroke (1734–87), who was elected to the club in 1764, features frequently in the book.

Also in 1779, 'Lord Cholmondeley Betts Mr. St. John five Guineas that a Ball fired out of a Cannon pointed horizontally does not rise before it falls – to be decided by a demonstration' (which presumably found for Lord Cholmondeley, but it is one of the frustrations of the Betting Book that it seldom records which party prevailed).

The late eighteenth century was, of course, an era during which men wagered obsessively upon almost anything, and any man who belonged to Brooks's was more subject to the fever than most. On 7 May 1779, 'Genl. Burgoyne gives five guineas to Ld. Ed. Pembroke to receive one guinea for each night His Lordship shall sup in Vaux Hall the ensuing Season'; Burgoyne (1722–92) is today chiefly remembered as the man who surrendered the British army at Saratoga in 1777. A few days later, 'Mr. Fox betts Ld. Northington 100 Gs. The D. of Devonshire has not the Garter on or before the 5th of June 1787'; 'Lord Craven betts Mr. Crewe and Sr. C. Davers one Guinea that Sr. W. Dobson either shoots or hangs himself before this Day twelve months Feby. 28th 1782'; 'Sr. Willby Aston has given Lord Derby sixpence to receive five hundred Guineas if ever he accepts the Post of Groom of the Stole March 17th 1782.'

Mr Clopton was exceedingly unlucky, when Colonel Tarleton wagered one hundred and five guineas to his fifty, on 6 January 1793, that Britain and France would be at war within six months. He lost by four days. Thereafter, the long wars with France provoked a heady succession of bets, most concerning the predicted position of the Allied or French armies on a given date. On 30 April, Mr Fox bet Mr Stepney five guineas that the French would be in Brussels before the Allied powers were in Paris, a sum he presumably collected. A month later, Mr Combe bet Major Maitland 75 guineas to 25 that Lord Howe returned to port without taking a French ship of the line. On 25 June 1799, Lord Holland gave Lord Clermont odds of five to one on a bet of twenty guineas against a Bourbon restoration in France. Holland lived to see the day, but Clermont died in 1806, eight years too soon to collect his winnings.

In our own generation, men occasionally accept wagers to discourage themselves from drinking or smoking. In the first half-century of Brooks's, members offered forfeits to inoculate themselves against the gaming tables. On 9 May 1797, Lord Yarmouth promised to pay Sir John Shelley 500 guineas, if he lost 200 guineas at a single sitting of faro within the succeeding twenty years. In August 1802, Mr Hare agreed to pay Lord Robert Spencer 200 guineas, if he played hazard at Miles's within the year. On 20 May 1811, 'Mr. Motteaux has given Lord G. Levisen one Guinea, and is to receive two hundred if the Latter plays at quinze within one month from the above date'.

Considering the huge sums that were won and lost at the gaming tables, a noteworthy moderation begins to overtake most of the stakes in the betting book in the nineteenth century. Poor Mr Stepney, who bet successfully against Mr Combe in 1805 that Lord Nelson would engage the French before they could regain their ports, was only a guinea the richer for the outcome. In 1801, Lord Peterborough gained only the same sum, by correctly predicting that the Cape of Good Hope would be surrendered neither to the Dutch nor to the French when peace was made between Britain and France.

The decline of the gambling mania that partially characterized the Regency is reflected in the Betting Book. Through the nineteenth century, far fewer wagers are recorded, though the irresistible whimsy remains. In 1852: 'Mr. Bulteel bets Mr. L. Agar Ellis a pony that the present Chancellor of the Exchequer dies a radical'. On 6 July 1896, 'Mr Godfrey Benson bets Mr. Charles Trevelyan £5 that Home Rule will not be granted to Ireland within twenty years. Sir Edward Grey to be arbiter of what constitutes Home Rule'.

On 5 July 1888, 'Lord Moreton bets Mr. Buller £3 to £1 that a certain couple they have in their eye will not have any children before Jany.1 1891. Bet to be off if the husband dies before has been married four months *Sine Posteritate*'; on 2 February 1900, 'Mr. Asquith bets Sir Edward Grey a bottle of Steinberger Cabinet 1868 that Mr. John Morley makes a speech in the debate now proceeding'.

In the early years of the twentieth century, the handwriting becomes more sober, and the Book is dominated by wagers about political developments at home and in Europe. On 20 July 1908, Mr Marsh was rash enough to bet Mr Somerset ten guineas 'that there will not be war between any two great European powers within 20 years'. In November, Sir Hubert Jerningham bets Mr Herbert Weld Blundell ten guineas 'that before 5 years from this date the map of Europe will be so remodelled as to leave England face to face with no other possible allies than France,

Italy and Spain on that continent, the rest of it being divided between Germany and Russia'.

On 1 August 1914, Lord Murray bet Captain Murray ten guineas 'that if, arising out of the Austro-Servian crisis, there is a general European War, there will be no crowned head in Europe except the King of England ten years from the date upon which the war breaks out'. A fair number of surviving monarchs prevented Lord Murray from profiting by his prescience.

Many of the bets on the First World War concerned its likely duration. One imagines that Mr Arthur Pollen collected his £5 from Sir John Fuller, to whom he gave odds of ten to one that hostilities would end within five years. Mr Tollemache Scott lost a guinea to Sir John Fuller, betting on 29 January 1915 that peace would be signed before Christmas 1916. Fuller, who features strongly in the club's military prediction stakes, should have won his guinea, laid on March 1915 against Captain P. Creed, that the German High Seas Fleet would 'come out' before hostilities ended. On 14 March 1916, Mr C.N. Lawrence showed his abiding confidence in the discredited Colonel Winston Churchill, by laying £6 against J. St. Loe Strachey's four, that Churchill would again hold Cabinet rank within a decade. In reality, he only had to wait sixteen months.

The Club's original betting book was closed in October 1924, after more than a century and a half of wagers had been recorded. It is a curiosity that the only entries on the unfilled blank pages thereafter are the signatures of Queen Mary, in February 1938; of Her Majesty The Queen, on 8 December 1954; and of the Princess Royal in 1985, each presumably marking visits to the club. No wagers are attributed to their names.

A new volume was opened in 1924 which, it must be acknowledged, has aspired to neither the quantity nor quality of wagers the first inspired. But there are still some noteworthy entries. There was a nice reflection of popular pessimism, amid growing industrial strife in the country, when Mr Victor Seely laid £5 against the £25 of Mr Cecil Agar-Roberts, who argued 'that H.M.'s troops will not open fire on civilians in London before March 25th 1924'.

In April 1927, Mr Noel Arnott bet Lord Osborne Beauclerk £5 to £1 'that Great Britain will not be at war with Russia on or before April 7/28', which says much for the gloom prevailing in some circles about the threat from the Bolsheviks. In February 1937, Sir Ian Malcolm found himself obliged to pay £5 to Colonel Arthur Murray, after being rash enough to suggest a year earlier that Roosevelt, Hitler and Mussolini would have been shot within a twelvemonth.

The Second World War prompted fewer unfulfilled prophecies by members than the First. Mr Michael Stewart laid £5 with Mr John Lawrence, on 27 January 1942, that Japan would invade Australia within six weeks. Colonel Arthur Murray (obviously an incorrigible seer) bet Mr Archibald Hay £1 that the war in Europe would be over by the end of 1943.

By March 1953, we were back where Lord Osborne Beauclerk left off in 1927, with H. Powys Greenwood wagering £5 against John Wheeler-Bennett that a shooting war with Russia would break out before August. Mr Greenwood was rash enough to offer any member of Brooks's the same terms, and six immediately (and presumably profitably) accepted.

A notorious wager on a notorious court case was struck in July 1963, when Mr Roger Longrigg bet Mr Edward Eyre £5 that Dr Stephen Ward would be convicted of at least one of the eight offences with which he was charged, in the course of the Profumo scandal. The books shows that Mr Eyre paid in October. Ward, of course, was not only convicted, but killed himself.

Modern times invite more cautious wagers, and perhaps more wariness about recording them in club books. In the last thirty years of Brooks's existence, the stakes recorded in the Betting Book have been trifling, certainly by eighteenth-century standards. A succession of political prophets have lost money by expecting events rather too soon. Mr Raymond Bonham-Carter was disappointed in his expectation that President Nixon would be the Republican presidential candidate in 1964; as was Mr Selby Armitage in anticipating the demise of the Greek monarchy by September 1966; and Mr Paniguian in supposing that Britain would join the EEC by February 1967. Mr Michael Forgacs was obviously under-informed about Senator Gary Hart's personal eccentricities when, in March 1984, he wagered £10 that the Senator would become president in November.

Mr Donald Sanne, however, showed exceptional prescience when, as early as August 1966, he laid £1 that Lyndon Johnson would not offer himself for re-election in 1968. Likewise Mr John Page, who laid an even £5 with Sir John Rodgers in January 1975, that Mrs Thatcher would lead the Conservative Party by year's end.

Regency traditions of black prophecy were resurrected by Colonel Dawnay, in July 1969, when he bet £5 that five members of the Fox Club would be dead within five years, a wager that invites some intriguing speculation about the conversation which preceded it.

Even in recent years, the book continues to reflect the spirits and passions of the times, as when Mr E.N. Hallam bets Mr David Colville £10 in 1977, 'that the whole bloody Common Market will have collapsed by 1980'. Some bets seem incapable of satisfactory arbitration, like that of the member who bet five pounds in June 1987 'that the relationship between Lt. Col Oliver North and Ms. Fawn Hall extended beyond the shredder'. The settlement of this one may prove to become a race between the mortality of the members concerned, and the impatience of the subjects of the wager to publish their profitable memoirs.

The Members

Piers Dixon

'LONG Memberships and Family Connections.' That was the title which our predecessors gave to the final chapter of *Brooks's 1764–1964*. The volume ended triumphantly with a catalogue of three score names, which confirmed a legend and perpetuated a myth.

I do not believe that even in the 1960s Brooks's was in any convincing sense still a dynastic club. Certainly this is no longer so today. That is not to say that the Whig tradition is dead. Families disappear into the mists of oblivion. Ideas live.

Our predecessors also laid excessive emphasis on a handful of eighteenth-century families – elderly Spencers, Cavendishes and Russells, descended from young bloods who met in St. James's Street to eat, drink and play cards. If we look at the historical evidence, a different picture emerges. From the beginning outsiders, and indeed occasional *parvenus*, were welcomed.

If there were dynasties at all they were progressively drawn from a much wider circle than the ministries of King George III. Here are the families with the highest scores in elections between 1850 and today:

Smith	33
Buxton	30
Russell	27
Baring	23
Cavendish	14
Whitbread	12

Russells have frequented the place more than Cavendishes – particularly during the early part of this century. This was the nucleus of

Brooks's. Then some bankers arrived. We recruited our first Baring (of German Protestant origin) in 1795 – the elder brother of the fellow from whom all subsequent Barings descend. They were to acquire peerages right, left and centre.

The 'Smith Family Club' still meet to commemorate their forebear, Mr Abel Smith, who set up as a banker in Nottingham during the middle of the eighteenth century. Robert Smith was elected to Brooks's in 1808. Pitt the younger had offered him the choice of an Irish peerage or an English baronetcy (which ranked equally in prestige). Smith opted for the former and emerged as Lord Carrington. His son, the 2nd Lord Carrington and also a member of Brooks's, decided to change his surname to Carington (*sic*), although the rest of his family remained Smith – or became Abel Smith, Dorrien Smith, Hugh Smith, Martin Smith, Vivian Smith.

Meanwhile beer came in. Samuel Whitbread appeared in 1791. Although the first Buxton did not reach us till 1846, that prolific tribe soon swamped the more ancient Whig families during the early part of this century. Whitbreads kept their numbers under control.

Until the second war these six 'dynasties' certainly maintained their presence in absolute terms. But this should be set against the increase in total membership – from 600 to 850 in the hundred years up to 1960. Partly as a result of the merger with St. James' we now have 1420 members. But only twenty-three derive from the six 'dynasties'. The legend is dead.

And yet the Whig tradition survived – epitomized by those early Buxtons. The mirror of Brooks's as it was, they had begun as country gentlemen but soon moved into business and philanthropy – partly through making alliances with Hoares and Peases, Gurneys and Hanburys. Some of their relations had begun as Quakers, although the Buxtons remained firmly loyal to the Church of England. Dividends from the Hanbury brewery enabled them to pursue a benevolent approach to politics. But they also had enough money to live comfortably and maintain younger sons in the army. Men like the Buxtons would with relish fight for Queen and Country but would also humanize the welfare state. Many of them became soldiers and MPs. They were fairly serious and probably did not play cards as much as their predecessors or successors. They would have thought backgammon very odd.

Even so, they were quite jolly when they arrived. Most of them were still in their twenties. During the first decade of this century no less than nine Buxtons were elected. Two brothers were only twenty-four – Harold Buxton (later a colonial bishop) and William Wilberforce Buxton (note the name). When their nephew joined some years later he was only twenty. However, by the time their cousin Lionel Gurney Buxton appeared in 1954 that distinguished soldier and courtier was already seventy-six. By then Brooks's was a different place. Members were older anyway – so he felt at home.

In the period immediately before the amalgamation with St. James' we still had nine Buxtons in the building. Now we have only three. Those Whig families in the reign of the old queen had plenty of sons. Now they ponder school fees.

Is Brooks's really political? And, if it is, what is the bias?

During this century we have nurtured thirty-seven Cabinet Ministers. Macmillan, Halifax and four Chancellors of the Exchequer (McKenna, Anderson, Amory and Jenkins) take first place. Surely this confirms the theory that we are a political club?

But this galaxy conceals reality. In the early 1900s we were thoroughly political. Then came a burst of activity during the 1920s. Since 1930 few men who subsequently achieved high ministerial preferment have appeared in the candidates' book. Nor was Brooks's ever exclusively Whig. Our twenty-five founders included fourteen Whigs, the 4th Duke of Gordon (regularly switching his patronage between Pitt and Fox), Lord de Clifford (former Tory MP) and nine amiable card-players who had no views at all.

During much of the nineteenth century St. James's Street was easygoing. The Carlton and the Reform were the official political clubs. White's and Brooks's, though essentially Tory and Whig, did not press the point.

Then came a change. In 1886 Home Rule for Ireland split the Liberal Party – and Brooks's. We reached a compromise, at least temporarily. During the rest of the century we recruited three men who sat in Unionist Cabinets and four who sat in Liberal Cabinets. Brooks's remained political but not partisan.

When Campbell-Bannerman (Liberal) replaced Balfour (Tory) as Prime Minister in 1905, Grey replaced Lansdowne as Foreign Secretary. Who had proposed Campbell-Bannerman for Brooks's? Surely, if anyone, it must have been someone like Grey? In fact it was Lansdowne. The great Liberal administration of 1905 contained nineteen Cabinet Ministers, of whom no less than twelve were members of Brooks's. Lloyd George and the others would not have wanted to belong anyway. A third of the men who really mattered preferred the Reform – or avoided St. James's altogether.

Brooks's still represented something: the Whig element which, deserted by the Unionists, was now trying to protect the party from Lloyd George. This is not to say that the men whom we elected in the early years of this century derived largely from Whig families. That was certainly Sydney Buxton's provenance, as it was Auberon Herbert's. But the other members who were to reach the Cabinet before the 1920s came from different backgrounds.

Reginald McKenna, of Irish origin, had not been to Oxford or Cambridge. Untypically he chose London. And yet he became Chancellor of the Exchequer. Walter Runciman (Northumberland shipping), Joseph Pease (Quaker from Durham), Alfred Emmott (from a simple London family) and Ian Macpherson (Scotland) had inherited recent industrial money or had made their own way in the world. They all ended up with peerages – with the exception of McKenna, who must surely have been offered one. Here was a new world.

But they had all managed to get a higher education. Emmott preceded McKenna at London. Macpherson moved from George Watson's to Edinburgh University – a standard progression for the bright Scotch lad. Runciman and Pease went to Cambridge.

In 1914 Edward Wood appeared in the candidates' book. This precipitated a more serious confrontation than the events of 1886. Son of Lord Halifax, he was heir to a succession of Whig swells. But he was already a Conservative MP. Here was the man who almost became Prime Minister in 1940. But we blackballed him on the specific charge that he was a member of the Carlton – a particularly obnoxious institution in those days, since it was there that the Tory Party chose its leader. Wood's supporters responded by blackballing Althorp, son of Lord Spencer.

Eventually the two families did a deal: both Wood and Althorp made it.

This was the signal for our recruiting young men with wider political sympathies. The last year of the war saw the admission of Archibald Sinclair (twenty-two and Liberal) together with Osbert Peake (twenty-one but probably already Conservative). Both had been to Eton.

During the 1920s we elected eleven men who were eventually to sit in a Cabinet which was either Conservative or dominated by Conservatives. To these should be added John Seely (who had already served under the Liberals) and Strachey (never actually in the Cabinet but a substantial figure in Attlee's government).

Of course not all the others began as Tories. But with the demise of the Liberal Party they had to go somewhere if they wanted a job. No doubt in more congenial circumstances those ambitious politicians would have sat happily in a series of 'Campbell-Bannerman' Cabinets for another fifty years.

A great change was taking place. Barely two per cent of men arriving in the Club during the first two decades of the century had reached the Cabinet. Now the proportion approached five per cent. Since 1930 it has sunk to one per cent.

Who were these thirteen ministers? The recruits of 1921 were Harrovians – Seely (who though a Liberal was eventually to receive a 'Conservative' peerage as Lord Mottistone) and Donald Somervell (Home Secretary in Churchill's 1945 caretaker government but a reluctant Tory).

1922 was *annus mirabilis*. We elected Strachey and five other men who were to attain high office. Donald Maclean, self-made, remained a Liberal to the end. Edward Hilton Young, who had begun life as a keen Liberal, chose the Tory Party and secured his position in the Cabinet.

John Anderson, Derick Heathcoat Amory and Harold Macmillan were Conservative from the start – at least nominally. Although they all became Chancellor of the Exchequer, we cannot be sure how far they accepted Conservative economic policy. Anderson was forty when he joined Brooks's – and became Permanent Under-Secretary of the Home Office, where he remained for a decade. Unsmilingly he moved on to the governorship of Bengal, a seat in Parliament, the Home Secretaryship and finally the Exchequer. Despite these varied achievements, he seemed colourless to the end. Amory, a much gentler character whom everyone loved, never tried hard. Like Belloc's Lord Lundy, he rose effortlessly from post to post and became Chancellor by mistake.

And so we come to Macmillan himself. What was he like when he appeared in Brooks's in 1922? A rich and rather bookish young man, he had not been born to the purple, but as a boy he had been exposed to the Whig tradition. Harold Russell, a godfather, had provided his Christian name. In 1920 he married Devonshire's daughter – just when his father, Maurice, deserted Brooks's because Managers controlled elections. Within a year he was himself a candidate, the Duke (one of our three Trustees) as proposer; Sir William Garstin (pioneer of African irrigation) as seconder. The building, still full of Russells and Cavendishes, was his natural home. Apart from a ritual membership of the Carlton, the places which he preferred were Pratt's (except for the Proprietor, solidly Tory) and the Beefsteak (gossip). As a very old man he came into Brooks's for the last time, surveyed our new bar and whispered, 'Ah, a Whig club with a Tory carpet!'

Four other men who were to serve in Cabinet with Macmillan joined Brooks's during these years. Churchill's peace-time administration in 1951 brought in Gavin Simonds as Lord Chancellor and Walter Monckton as Minister of Labour.

Brendan Bracken came from nowhere. He was fully grown but without formal education when he booked himself into Sedbergh as a schoolboy; by the age of twenty-eight he was a member of the Club, ready to create the *Financial Times* and befriend Churchill during the wilderness years. David Eccles is now the only political survivor from that golden generation: with the exception of Anthony Pollen, he is our longest serving member.

The candidates of the 1920s differed from their predecessors not only in party affiliation but in education. They emerged from Oxford rather than Cambridge. Five were at Eton (including Strachey), three at Harrow, two at Winchester. Anderson (George Watson's and Edinburgh) approximated to the pattern of the early 1900s. Apart from Bracken, the only one to avoid university was Maclean (son of a cordwainer from Scotland).

The decade 1931–40 saw only three 'Cabinet' elections to Brooks's.

Malcolm MacDonald was the son of Ramsay MacDonald and had been brought up as a Socialist. John Reith, apparently of no strong political conviction, became Minister of Information and created the BBC. George Jellicoe, only twenty-two when elected, was distinctly pink and had to wait another thirty years before entering Heath's Cabinet – still a young man. Clearly convivial, they could not credibly have fitted into White's.

The 1940s gave businessmen the opportunity to shine in politics. Fred Marquis had been created Lord Woolton by Chamberlain, who made him Minister of Food in 1940. But he did not formally become a Conservative until Churchill was defeated in 1945 – as the election results were coming in. Frederick Leathers had been a protégé of Inchcape (himself a member of Brooks's, who introduced him to Churchill during the wilderness years). By 1941 Leathers was a peer and Minister of War Transport, though not a member of the War Cabinet. Woolton had moved from Manchester Grammar School to Manchester University. Leathers got by on elementary education. Superficially this was a return to the Brooks's of the early 1900s. But there was a difference. When we elected them, Woolton was sixty and Leathers sixty-five – elderly men who were already national figures, contemplating a quiet snooze in the morning room.

By 1945 the Conservative Party had in effect become heir not only to the Tories but also to the Whigs and Asquithian Liberals. Churchill's caretaker Cabinet in that year was in complexion not very different from Campbell-Bannerman's. Six of the seventeen ministers had been or would be members of the Club. The 6th Earl of Rosebery, dynastic Whig, had to wait forty-two years between his arrival in Brooks's and his advancement to the Cabinet. Somervell, essentially a lawyer and later our chairman, would have fitted into any respectable government. Anderson had served many masters. Macmillan, romantic Whig if not dynastic, adored Churchill. Bracken was much the same. Woolton confronts us as a latter-day Runciman.

When Churchill formed his first peacetime government in 1951 five of the sixteen Cabinet Ministers were members. If Cyril Asquith had agreed to join the government, there would have been six. In what was by today's conventions a remarkably stable administration, Churchill dropped only two members from his Cabinet – Leathers and Simonds.

But he appointed three others. The survivors when he handed over to Eden were: Macmillan, Woolton, Monckton (wet Conservative), Amory (the same), Peake (traditional Tory) and Eccles. During the 1950s Brooks's brought in only two future Cabinet members: Humphrey Atkins, who served both Heath (as Deputy Chief Whip) and Thatcher (in Cabinet); together with Gordon Campbell, Heath's Scottish Secretary.

By the 1960s Brooks's had ceased to have any obvious political affiliations. Geoffrey Lloyd, a congenial bachelor who had become Colonial Secretary four years earlier, joined in 1961. Peter Brooke sits in the present Cabinet. Robert Carr was Heath's Home Secretary and briefly Leader of the Conservative Party during the *sede vacante* between Heath's disappearance and Thatcher's emergence.

The most remarkable public episode in Brooks's recent history has been the election of Roy Jenkins. Chancellor of the Exchequer and Home Secretary, he would in normal circumstances be today's Bannerman. The only other convincing comparison is with Macmillan: both, like Grey and Halifax before them, Chancellor of Oxford University. That is where Brooks's apostolic succession lies.

We have had many Knights of the Garter in our long history, and some Knights of the Thistle. Today these accolades no longer smother the coat-hangers of Brooks's. Lords Richardson and Shackleton are KG. Our only KT is Lord Thomson of Monifieth.

Both Shackleton and Thomson made their name in the Labour Party. Shackleton (elected to Brooks's in 1982, aged seventy-one), pale blue in his youth, settled down quite naturally as Lord Privy Seal and Leader of the Lords – in both of which offices Jellicoe succeeded him when the Conservatives won the 1970 election. Thomson (1975, aged fifty-four) became Commonwealth Secretary. Neither of these elderly patricians participated in Brooks's during their prime. Like Woolton and Leathers they have retired here to enjoy their old age.

During the 1960s and 1970s we elected no one who is obviously destined to sit in a Cabinet. If the Conservative Party were ever to become wet again, the Club might once more be political.

Of course all politicians rely on civil servants to run the government during the long periods when they are preoccupied with winning elections. Most of them have steered clear of Brooks's – no doubt to avoid their political masters. Those that venture among us tend to be outside the normal pattern. The most eccentric was Edward Marsh, Churchill's private secretary and lifelong confidant, a man of letters rather than a civil servant. Francis Hopwood, after becoming head of the Board of Trade, untypically landed a peerage as Lord Southborough.

Ernest Gowers began as Lloyd George's private secretary, organized the civil defence of London during the blitz and ended his career writing *Plain Words* while editing Fowler's *Modern English Usage*. Warren Fisher, Permanent Secretary of the Treasury for twenty years up to 1939, created the civil service as we know it. In retirement Fisher took on the chairmanship of Brooks's. Since then we have had a few more, notably Edwin Plowden, Chairman of the Atomic Energy Authority and on every sort of committee, and Eric Roll, who contributed substantially to the first round of Common Market negotiations in 1962–3.

In our own generation we have reverted to the quiet manoeuvres of Fisher. The two most recent Cabinet Secretaries, Robert Armstrong and Robin Butler, have commanded the centre of power. Till Antony Acland moved to Washington, we housed both the Permanent Under-Secretary of the Foreign Office and the Cabinet Secretary. That is the first time this has happened.

We elect twice as many diplomats as civil servants. This has nothing to do with St. James', where the Foreign Office tradition was dying before the merger. Many senior diplomats were joining Brooks's anyway. Claude Macdonald represented us in Japan, as did Francis Lindley and Robert Clive. Ambassadors to France have included Oliver Harvey, Pierson Dixon, Nicholas Henderson and John Fretwell. A significant event was our election in 1939 of Orme Sargent, who was to be No. 2 in the Foreign Office during the war and No. 1 thereafter. He confirmed that Brooks's was the building where senior members of his Service should be found.

The cold war saw William Hayter, Frank Roberts, Humphrey Trevelyan and John Killick as ambassadors in Moscow. Patrick Dean, Roger Makins, now Lord Sherfield, and Antony Acland have represented us in America; Roberts and Christopher Mallaby in Germany; John Ward, Alan Campbell and Stephen Egerton in Italy; Dixon, Dean and

Crispin Tickell at the United Nations. Michael Butler has invented the hard ECU.

Nicholas Henderson is not only the sole member of Brooks's to have served as ambassador in Germany, France and America. He is also the only man who has ever achieved this. And he writes charming books. Kenneth James is the first diplomat to be our chairman.

The Empire's disappearance has modified our structure. Young men who would have chosen Africa or the army now seek a living in advertising agencies and picture galleries. During the early decades of the century we elected as many colonial administrators as diplomats. William Garstin, engineer by training, established the economic infrastructure of Egypt and the Sudan. Frederick Lugard ended up as Governor of Nigeria. William Clark, initially a civil servant, became our first High Commissioner in Canada and did the same job in South Africa. Herbert Stanley held governorships in every corner of our far-flung domain.

George Schuster was already forty-six when he joined us, but he still had fifty-five years to go. Meanwhile he became Finance Minister of India and on his return entered parliament as a National Liberal. Others were more Olympian. Lord Liverpool became the first Governor-General of New Zealand – a position in which Lord Cobham succeeded him many years later. They commanded wealth which ensured that they would put on a good show for the locals. Lord Bessborough and Vincent Massey adorned Government House in Ottawa. Appropriately the last of these three proconsular persons was a Baring – Lord Howick. But he was fifty-six when he joined Brooks's and had already spent many years in Africa – governing Rhodesia and Kenya.

Courtiers find Brooks's a safe place. Here we start with a Baring – the 2nd Earl of Cromer, Lord Chamberlain in the days when this swell not only dictated who should come to garden parties and what they should wear, but also decided whether plays were too pornographic for members of the public who would never be seen at a garden party anyway.

For three decades, 1943–1972, the monarch's private secretary was to be a member of Brooks's. Alan Lascelles served George VI, but did not join us until after he left his master. Michael Adeane was only twenty-four when elected – three years before entering royal service as assistant private secretary. By 1953 he was private secretary to the Queen. Clarence House is also well represented. Oliver Dawnay was the Queen Mother's private secretary, and Martin Gilliat still is.

Senior sailors and soldiers have not rushed into our arms, no doubt because London was full of clubs which catered for them. But airmen made an early appearance. In the front rank stands Trenchard, creator of our air force. Edgar Ludlow-Hewitt, Inspector-General of the RAF during the war, bullied Whitehall mercilessly and ensured that we had the resources to smash Germany. William Elliot, who had made his name leading the Balkan Air Force at the end of the Second World War, joined Brooks's when he became Commander-in-Chief of Fighter Command just as the cold war was starting. Ralph Cochrane commanded the 3rd and 5th Bomber Groups and arrived with us shortly after he became Vice-Chief of the Air Staff. These men could have decided England's fate one way or another within a few weeks.

Our only generals of consequence have been Herbert Lawrence and James Marshall-Cornwall. The former, who just missed being CIGS, was perhaps happier in his subsequent career as active and rather political chairman of Glyn's bank. Cornwall, full general who never held an important command, remains a mystery. In his late nineties, while writing his elegant but unrevealing memoirs, he would spend whole days with us. On one occasion he found himself lunching in the Spencer Room with seven members, most of whom he had not met before. A diminutive figure, he got up before the rest of us to return to his manuscript and cheerfully said goodbye, addressing each of us by name. He died at ninety-eight. Can he really have been the man who was in charge of military intelligence during the war?

Sir Roger Backhouse, Admiral of the Fleet and authoritarian First Sea Lord, did for the navy what Trenchard did for the air force, although as his was the more ancient service the intervention may not have been so obvious. Aged sixty-one in 1939, he was poised for battle. Suddenly he died.

No one like these giants has been seen around Brooks's recently. Perhaps they were not typical of their professions anyway. Several of them would probably have preferred to be politicians or academics. In recent years we have suffered not only a general decline in the number of military figures who are members but also the complete disappearance of airmen: they are in the RAF Club – which officers of a certain rank are required to join. When Trenchard and Ludlow-Hewitt were youngsters, an airman could go where he liked.

The merger with St. James' reinforced our soldierly traditions: Major Trevor-Cox, Major McNair Scott and Colonel Demetriadi had joined that club in the 1930s; Colonel Buckley and Colonel Earle during the war. The only regular soldiers who derive from wartime Brooks's are Lord Cathcart and Sir Hereward Wake. Our lone VC, Major Jamieson, came immediately after the fighting ended. The army has since the 1930s been recruiting subalterns from the periphery of the British Isles, often Catholics. They now substantially outnumber our ten sailors, commanded by Admiral Lewis (formerly Second Sea Lord). Our longest-serving naval member is Colin Balfour.

Lawyers have proliferated at Brooks's. When they reach us they are already middle-aged. You do not see greedy young barristers in the backgammon room: they are too busy chasing briefs. Every two years the monarch designates three people to the Court of Appeal. The country contains thousands who have been MPs and hundreds who have been in the Cabinet. Our senior judges form a much smaller pool; there are fewer than a hundred around at any one time. They are England's College of Cardinals. During this century we have admitted four men who have reached the Court of Appeal but have so far gone no further: John Singleton, Henry Phillimore, Anthony Lloyd and Denys Buckley. Lloyd, who exceptionally for a lawyer was only twenty-seven on election, has time on his side. He is certainly within living memory our youngest member who has reached the Court of Appeal

Six of Brooks's judges have moved on to the House of Lords. The first was Oaksey, of Nuremberg fame. He was followed by Somervell, whose doubtful commitment to the Conservative Party in Churchill's 1945 government is confirmed by Attlee's recommendation to the Court of Appeal a year later. Greene later became Master of the Rolls.

Asquith, son of the Prime Minister, was a young man whom Churchill had known since his teens. Goddard had already reached the peak of his profession as Lord Chief Justice when he appeared at Brooks's. Lord

Salmon became chairman of St. James', who elected him in 1960. With the marginal exception of Somervell, these were men who had steered clear of active politics.

The high-flyers, or at any rate the quick-movers, have had a political nose. Simonds, Somervell's friend, went straight to the Lords in 1944. But he was not the only one to leap-frog the Court of Appeal. Radcliffe had caught the eye of Attlee during the Indo-Pakistani boundary commissions of 1947 and two years later became a Law Lord. Wright not only became a Law Lord without apprenticeship but made a deal which allowed him to get the Mastership of the Rolls and then return to the Lords when his time was up. As an old man he spent many months collecting material which Oaksey used at Nuremberg. The most adroit was Parker who, leaping over the Lords, succeeded Goddard as Chief Justice. The two men dominated the judiciary during the 1940s and 1950s.

These fourteen advocates comprised at least ten per cent of comparable judges among their contemporaries, and probably twenty per cent more recently. Brooks's today has as great an attraction for lawyers as for diplomats – and more than for politicians (who avoid us), colonial administrators (who are no more) and intellectual airmen (who no longer come in that form).

But the fourteen do not include the lawyer who may have had the most brilliant intellect of all. John Foster was apparently chosen by Churchill as Solicitor-General in 1951. The Prime Minister got the names muddled up and instead appointed Manningham-Buller, who went on to be Attorney-General and Lord Chancellor. Foster would have been much more amusing on the Woolsack.

A fifth of our members are now non-British by ancestry, at least if their remoter forebears are taken into account. And of the rest barely two-thirds remain English. The amalgamation with the St. James' has merely reinforced a structure which existed from the beginning. Here are the origins of our twenty-five founders in 1764:

English	12
Scotch	8
Welsh	3
Foreign immigrants	2

'Fish' Crawfurd led the Scotch contingent. He did more to give

Brooks's its shape than anyone else, abetted by two Gordons (the 4th Duke and Lord William but not their brother, naughty George), a Lockhart, a Macartney, a Ker (Roxburghe), a Shaw Stewart and a Bowes Lyon (Strathmore, two of whose descendants still belong).

Houghton James, surely a Welshman, would have approved of Kenneth James in the chair, as would Richard Pennant and Mr Wynne.

We have never been an exclusively British club. Our first serious experiments were with Bouverie and Bentinck. The laboratory has been simmering ever since. French-speaking Protestants from sixteenth-century Flanders explain Bouverie's origin. Bentinck (Portland, the Prime Minister) descended from the fellow whom William III brought here to run the government while he was winning battles.

The founders were Anglican. But quite soon a few Catholics were let in, so long as they did not parade their Popery: Lord Petre, Lord Stourton, Lord Shrewsbury and Sir John Throckmorton. Three more Throckmortons arrived before Emancipation in 1829, together with a Mr Fitzgerald, Sir John's candidate and surely Papist – though by no means the first Irishman in the building.

The death of the 'Protestant' Duke of Norfolk in 1815 profoundly influenced our history. The immediate family of his successor, the 12th Duke, had been openly faithful to the Roman Church since the middle of the seventeenth century. We could hardly blackball the new Earl Marshal, who duly joined us a year later. Within a short time several of his close relations followed him, together with Anglican Howards – whom we had been recruiting regularly before 1815. The candidates' book shows that cousins from the two denominations were admitted on the same day.

Norfolk carried the process a stage further. In 1829 he proposed Lord Stafford, who was elected with his two Jerningham sons. Lord Dormer, proposed by Norfolk, arrived in 1830; Thomas Stonor, seconded by him, in 1833; Thomas Fraser, proposed by him, in 1834; and Edward Weld, proposed by him, in 1841.

Meanwhile we had started electing men of Jewish origin though not yet those of Jewish faith. Within a year of Norfolk's election we welcomed David Ricardo (1817), economist and member of an ancient Sephardi family. He was followed by several of his relations, together

The 5th Earl Spencer (1835–1910).
From a mezzotint at Brooks's

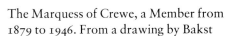

BAKST
1921

The Marquess of Crewe, a Member from
1879 to 1946. From a drawing by Bakst

The Spencer Room : designed as the Eating Room by Holland : altered by Anderson, restored by Richardson

with Sir Ralph Lopes (1834, also Sephardi) and B. Oliveira (1839). Most of these were MPs – which required that they should adhere to the Established Church.

David Salomons (1839) was the first practising Jew to join Brooks's. In 1832 he had founded the London and Westminster Bank (ancestor of Westminster Bank, and eventually NatWest). By 1851 he was an MP but was fined for voting without having sworn on the Bible. Undeterred, he became Lord Mayor of London, ultimately took his seat with full voting rights in 1859 and acquired a baronetcy.

Everyone in London knew the brothers Rothschild: Meyer, the youngest of them (elected in 1841 when only twenty-three), father-in-law of Rosebery the Prime Minister; Lionel; and Anthony. The last two were proposed by Lord John Russell, also Prime Minister, who was later to propose Lionel's son Nathan. At the height of the Baring Crash in 1890 Lord Revelstoke and Lord Rothschild had a place where they could save the banking system unobtrusively.

Clearly Whigs at the highest level were determined that Brooks's should not condone anti-Semitism. This was more like a political demonstration than the casual election of young men who were looking for a place to amuse themselves. In recent years we have elected Rothschilds in the fourth generation – Leo and Victor, the Lord Rothschild who died recently. In 1991 we celebrate one hundred and fifty years of their being in Brooks's. However, candidates of Jewish origin were rare in the nineteenth century and were mostly drawn from families who married outside their community and became Protestant: the first Goschen, Herschell, Jessel, Lehmann and Schuster. We now have some 70 colleagues whose forebears were Jewish in 1764.

Apart from men like these, Germans have not joined us until recently. An exception was Graf von Bruehl, the Duke of Saxony's diplomatic representative here. We have still to elect a German Ambassador. Count Belgiojoso, Austrian Minister at the Court of St. James' and a Milanese, was our first Italian – and Catholic of course. We waited another two centuries before electing the Italian Ambassador in London.

If we exclude descendants of Huguenots, the pioneering Frenchman was 'Monsieur Frances', of whom nothing else is known – not even the identity of his proposer. Was this his Christian name or his surname?

Perhaps he was on Mr Brooks's staff, like Monsieur Champignon the Chef. The Duke d'Orléans decided to vote for the execution of Louis XVI, head of his family, and was rewarded by being guillotined himself ten years after we let him in. Serve him right. Before he became a member, the Duke de Lauzun seduced the sister of Brooks's Duke of Richmond (she had earlier fancied young George III) and fought in America against the British Crown during the revolutionary war. He celebrated the end of hostilities by offering himself for membership. Later, after again commanding revolutionary armies – this time for Robespierre –, he too was guillotined. Count de Flahaut had also fought against us – at Waterloo – but rehabilitated himself by marrying a Scotch heiress. He was the first and last French Ambassador to be a member.

Alexander Raphael, a Catholic of Armenian origin, came from Venice. Vincent Gandolfi (proposed by Norfolk) changed his name to Hornyold. These were our first resident Italians: diplomats like Belgiojoso tend to disappear. Then came Sir Anthony Panizzi, one of Europe's political refugees, of whom we have seen a few more; and Edward Sartoris, an Englishman but surely of Italian descent.

Captain d'Aguilar was our first Spaniard. Pandeli Ralli commemorated a name revered among the London Greeks and was already an MP when he joined us. Although the numbers were not large, a full century before the merger with St. James' foreigners appeared among us at regular intervals.

The most abiding influence has come from Scotland. During the first two centuries of our existence Scots consistently contributed more than one-fifth of our membership – a larger proportion than their presence in the country's population. Here are the most important examples of 740 Scots among the 3,465 men elected up to 1900 (of whom some 3,150 were British):

Stewart	23
Campbell	22
Dundas	19
Douglas	16
Gordon	15
Elliot	14
Graham	13

Cunningham	11
Murray	11
Scott	11
Duff	10
Hamilton	10

These are not families as we understand them in England, but gangs who gathered for protection under a medieval boss. They are Britain's mafia. Clansmen of course concentrate round a central family, but most of them do not descend from the godfather – at least not legitimately.

Inevitably the House of Stewart takes first place. Several of the twenty-three members enjoyed royal ancestry. But the great majority were sons of simple country gentlemen who liked coming to London when it was cold and meeting pretty girls at parties.

Although some of the Campbells were related to the Duke of Argyll (a Highlander), many of them had adopted the surname very recently – in the Lowlands, which provided easier access to the London Assemblies. Even so, every clansman (we still have six of them) instinctively gives a little bow as he emerges from the library under the stern gaze of Lord Frederick.

The Scotch phalanx in Brooks's was not itself representative of Scotland. Highlanders avoided St. James's Street. Scotland's most common surname remains MacDonald. And yet up to 1900 we only elected six, together with four Robertsons – who at home were almost as numerous as MacDonalds and equally impoverished. Maurice Macmillan (1898) must have been the first grandson of a crofter to get here.

The great Cabinet of 1905 contained twelve members of Brooks's, of whom six were Scots. Historians, seeking to explain the bias in Liberal governments, have cited the 'Celtic fringe', which suddenly became self-conscious in the late nineteenth century. A popular movement somehow gave homogeneity to Scotch Presbyterians, Irish Catholics and Welsh Methodists. The reason is more homely and more ancient.

For a hundred and forty years Scots had been strolling into Brooks's to keep warm, drink and play whist. There they met Buxtons, Russells, Cavendishes, Whitbreads and other serious young Englishmen who thought that mankind could be improved through the statute book: politics was not just a game. Smiths, Barings and Rothschilds explained over a glass of port how the Budget could be used as an instrument for social change.

If Campbell-Bannerman needed Ministers he did not have to look far. They were in the coffee room. And many of them had just arrived off the night train from Scotland.

The Irish element has been much smaller – about five per cent. Macartney, one of our founders, may have thought of himself as Irish, although he knew of course that his ancestors were Scotch. And the 140 men whom we elected in 1764 included members of English families who had migrated to Ireland in recent generations: Beresford (Lord Water-ford), Caulfeild (Lord Charlemont), Moore (Lord Drogheda), Temple (Lord Palmerston); together with Scotch Maxwell (Lord Farnham).

More significant was the appearance in 1764 of indigenous Irishmen whose families had conformed to the Established Church. These were not patrician figures. We know that Colonel O'Hara and Colonel Nugent were not Catholic: they would not have been allowed to hold the King's commission if they had been. The same can be said of Thomas Conolly MP and Mr Lynch MP. They represented English seats and must have been thoroughly Anglicized.

The candidates' book became increasingly flooded by FitzGeralds, Fitzmaurices, FitzPatricks, Bourkes, Bellews – and Hely Hutchinsons (almost certainly native Irish). This patrician bias remained much more pronounced than among our English, Scotch and Welsh members: Ireland's middle class was small – and still only partly Protestant.

Catholic emancipation in 1829 changed all this. The most celebrated recruits arrived in that year – the poet Tom Moore and Daniel O'Connell, Liberator of Ireland. They were both Catholic. Indigenous Irishmen increasingly appeared in the Palace of Westminster – and Brooks's. During the years 1764–1900 we elected about 170 Irishmen. Initially they were Protestant. After 1829 they became increasingly Catholic. No less than forty-nine held peerages; together with two Knights of Kerry and The O'Connor Don. Many others were their immediate relations. By contrast our sixty-five Irish members today include only two peers.

Four-fifths of our 1,420 members remain British in the narrow sense – those whose male ancestors in 1764 were English, Welsh or Scotch: we still elect one Scot for every three Englishmen.

The others enjoy more recent origins: Irish (about 65), German (about 35), French (35), Polish (14), Greek (12), Italian (10), Dutch (10). Many of these have been British for several generations. To these should be added 35 men from an assortment of nationalities (Spanish to Chinese) and 15 of indeterminate origin.

The Whig Tradition

Noel Annan

'I'M not a Whig', said Thackeray, 'but, oh, how dearly I should like to be one'. No wonder: to be a Whig was to be born into a magic circle. They were a caste, not a political party. 'It is as difficult to become a Whig,' wrote George Russell, 'as to become a Jew'. Macaulay was one of the very few who worked his way into the circle; Brougham never quite made it; Derby worked his way out of it and became the leader of the Tories. Palmerston was not a Whig. In and out of Whig administrations, he was born and bred a Tory and served in Tory governments from 1807 to 1830. The Whigs thought him vulgar.

The Whigs were regarded by the really old Tory families as parvenus: magnates who had enriched themselves after the Restoration and who dominated politics after they put the Hanoverians on the throne. There were almost as many Whigs in opposition to the Court as there were Sir Robert Walpole's placemen. But they knew who their enemies were. Coke of Norfolk was taken on his knee by his grandfather who said to him, 'Now, remember Tom, as long as you live never trust a Tory'; and he used to add, 'I never have, and, by God, I never will.' The French Revolution divided them. The Cavendish-Bentincks and Cavendishes, Fitzwilliams and Elliots followed Burke: Sheridan, Francis, Erskine and Grey followed Charles James Fox. But the repression that Pitt began was intensified after Waterloo – a clergyman was transported for life because he had signed a petition in favour of parliamentary reform and at Woburn political meetings had to be held after dark by the sons of the Duke of Bedford. The Whigs, however, remained divided until Grey united some of them to vote for the Reform Bill.

At the centre of the circle were the Russells. The first Whig martyr, beheaded in 1683, was a Russell. Lord John Russell was the quintessential Whig. Inside the circle were the Russells' kinsmen: Gowers, Levesons, Howards, Vernons, Capels, Keppels, Grosvenors, Harcourts and Ponsonbys. Attached to the circle were the Greys, Lambtons, Spencers, Fortescues, Fitzmaurices and Lambs: they were not blood relations, and the Listers, Thynnes and Clives married into the circle. The Whigs breakfasted with Samuel Rogers, adopted Tom Moore as their poet and Sydney Smith was their favourite clergyman. When Lord John Russell formed his first administration he was accused of filling most places in it with his cousins. It was all too true; and the Whig who was put up to rebut the charge found the task beyond him.

What did a Whig believe? He declared that all rulers could be removed for misconduct. If a king abused his power, the House of Commons had the right to refuse funds to carry on the government. Queen Victoria once asked Lord John Russell whether it was true that he held the view that under certain circumstances it was lawful for a subject to disobey his sovereign. 'Well, Ma'am, speaking to a Sovereign of the House of Hanover,' he replied, 'I can only answer in the affirmative.' But when as in 1688 or 1714 they installed another monarch, they treated him with decent respect.* Indeed they disliked innovation. No Constitution-mongering for them. They disliked extremists: universal suffrage and annual parliaments did not feature on their agenda. They spoke often with admiration of 'the people'; and indeed they voted for low taxation and spoke against the suppression of habeas corpus and other reactionary measures. Russell urged clemency for the Tolpuddle Martyrs. (Melbourne, who at times barely resembled a Whig, was always notorious among them for his support for reactionary measures and his apathy for reform.) But they were as much against democracy as they were against

---

*Palmerston used to boast that when told at short notice that the Queen desired him to attend her at Windsor, he wrote a letter explaining his absence, giving as his excuse that his horse had taken him to Waterloo instead of to Paddington, and he found himself arriving at his own house instead of at the Castle. A true Whig would have regarded such conduct as impertinent.

despotism; and they advocated and practised enclosure in the countryside.

Nevertheless they believed in freedom. The True Blue, probably the oldest undergraduate club in Cambridge, to this day drink the toast, 'Civil and religious liberty all over the world'. The Whigs disliked the High Church. They wanted toleration, befriended Dissenters, supported Catholic Emancipation and the removal of disabilities upon the Jews. Their contempt for the 'dull country gentlemen' who time and again defeated in Parliament their proposals for the removal of religious tests at Oxford and Cambridge was unbounded. 'The uneducated labourer', wrote Russell, 'beats them hollow in intelligence'.

They made enemies. Arrogant, full of animal spirits often heightened by port; philistine, not above bullying their inferiors, they enraged the ancient Tory families who envied them their wealth. Disraeli pilloried them as a Venetian Oligarchy and Thackeray put them in his *Book of Snobs*. They were snobs. In 1827 they were disgusted at being asked to accept as a colleague in Cabinet one who had been a civil servant. They fought on two fronts against the rows of Tory squires and against the middle-class Radicals. The last Whig to lead his party was Lord Hartington, a true Cavendish if ever there was one, trusted by all and devoid of vanity or ambition. He did not lead it for long. Gladstone returned to denounce Disraeli and discomfit the Whigs. Keen as ever to detect a shift in the political spectrum, Trollope in *The Duke's Children* (1880) pictures young Lord Silverbridge, heir to the great Whig statesman the Duke of Omnium, standing for Parliament in the Tory interest. But it was Ireland that undid the Whigs. In Melbourne's time the Whigs had lost face by making a pact with O'Connell. In 1886, led by Hartington, they left the Liberal Party over Home Rule. To compel Ulster Protestants to be ruled by Roman Catholics was too repugnant to their traditions. But those traditions could no longer sustain a political party. The political creed that had its origin in the struggle between Crown and Parliament had not much to say to the twentieth century.

And yet the aroma of Whiggism lingered. It suffused Lord John Russell's grandson. Bertrand Russell was the uncompromising opponent of tyranny abroad and, at home, of the suppression of the individual's right to express unpopular opinions and advocate pacifism and sexual freedom. There are those who fancy that the Whig tradition passed into the hands of him and Asquithian Liberals such as Maynard Keynes. It is in fact only a fancy and these intellectuals and public servants had hardly anything in common with the old Whig aristocracy. But when Keynes said that on the barricades he would be found on the side of the educated bourgeoisie, he was putting down a marker that he belonged to an élite, who did not pretend to embrace working-class culture and still less accept the claims of the Communists and fellow travellers to be the heirs of the future. Sometimes such élitists among the young would be found on the right of the Labour Party, sometimes on the left of the Conservatives. They were as hostile to Chamberlain and the policy of appeasement as they were to the Marxists and pacifists who opposed rearmament and argued that the Fascist dictators would climb down at the mere mention of the words collective security.

After the Second World War there emerged not so much a political as a cultural consensus between certain members of the Conservative and Labour parties reinforced by those who belonged to no party at all. They were united by their dislike of the old stuffy pre-war *bien-pensants* who in their view had brought about the disaster of the war and now opposed their efforts to extend personal freedom. In the House of Commons Roy Jenkins emerged as the leader of this movement and became the first reforming Home Secretary for many a year. But there were plenty of Conservative sympathizers of his generation such as Edward Boyle or Ian Gilmour. They were willing to reform the laws on divorce, abortion, homosexuality, theatre censorship and obscene literature. Many of them, irritated by the complacent philistinism of life in Britain between the wars, supported those who wanted to persuade boys and girls at school to enjoy and revere literature and the arts. They wanted to spread sweetness and light in Arnoldian fashion through such agencies as the BBC and the Arts Council, the National Trust and the heritage movement. John Betjeman, an authentic Whig eccentric, revived the movement for preserving old buildings.

But the cultural revolution of the Sixties was not for them. The instinctive Whig revulsion from radicalism deflected them: and similarly they blinked in astonishment at the revival of Marxism in intellectual life. They had felt at home in the literary pages of the *New Statesman* before the war: they were less certain about the pages of its successor, the *London Review of Books*. But on the issue of liberty they remained true to form. They regarded with contempt the intolerant, self-righteous manners of protesters and demonstrators. On the other hand, if people wanted to behave in a disobliging fashion, or make love with their own sex, or in heaps, they asked whether they were entitled to do so. If so they saw no reason to stop them; if not they asked whether the laws that restrained such people were reasonable.

But the new self-styled Whigs were to experience a more formidable challenge to their ideals when Margaret Thatcher became Prime Minister. They heard *The Times* and a new generation of publicists asking by what right had this section of the educated classes appointed themselves the guardian of the public's taste? Whom did they think they spoke for? Why should the tax-payer be fleeced to support the rubbish purchased by the Tate Gallery or the snobbery of the *stagione* system of opera at Covent Garden? These élitists dominated the boards of museums and galleries, the State-supported theatres, the quangos set up to preserve the independence of the BBC, the universities and other institutions – they sat on the commissions and committees that examined social maladies, they considered themselves exclusively to be the Great and the Good. Yet had they not betrayed their trust as the guardians of the public interest and become the prisoners of the pressure groups they were meant to govern?

John Vincent and other critics noted how many of these one-time Macmillanites, the breakaway former Labour supporters and the old arbiters of opinion, were repelled by Margaret Thatcher's style. Her style, her manners, the way she treated her colleagues, as much as her policies, offended their sensibilities. Vincent said their dislike of her style was simple snobbery. She stood 'at the point where all snobberies meet, intellectual snobbery, social snobbery, the snobbery of Brooks's, the snobbery of arts graduates about scientists . . . the snobbery of men about career women'.

Brooks's? Whom can he have had in mind? David Astor, Lord Bonham-Carter, Lord Donaldson, Lord Jenkins, Ludo Kennedy, Lord Walston? Perhaps the Duke of Devonshire, a minister under Macmillan who left the Conservative party to join the Social Democrats? Certainly in the list of the club's members one could pick out those who could be classed among the new Whigs: in politics Lord Carr, Lord Jellicoe, Lord Shackleton, Lord Windlesham; in diplomacy Sir Nicholas Henderson and Nigel Clive; among public servants Lord Roll, Sir Richard Way, Lord Zuckerman; among writers Sir Isaiah Berlin, Lord Runciman, Desmond Shaw-Taylor and Philip Ziegler. Not all those who come to mind were necessarily hostile to our first woman prime minister. Sir Jack Plumb, the biographer of that great Whig, Robert Walpole, spoke up for her. But for John Vincent, as for Disraeli, there was a Venetian oligarchy in existence, and his only criticism of Margaret Thatcher was that she had not destroyed it.

Vincent's trope does not bear examination. The political configuration of Brooks's changed when the St. James' Club left Piccadilly and joined Brooks's in St. James's Street. But it is significant that when a populist such as Vincent searches for a symbol to designate an élite he chooses Brooks's. The spirit of Charles James Fox has not vanished for ever. It still lives on in those who may be rumbustious or cynical, but still oppose ideologues and bigots and stand for moderation and reason in public affairs. There are worse toasts than 'civil and religious liberty all over the world'.

PART III

The Tric-Trac Man

Simon Raven

For convenience' sake I shall call him Henry Whybrow. If you should wish to know his real name, you may probably be able to work it out by the time I am finished.

Once upon a time, one winter's afternoon (already nearly dark) in Piccadilly, I came across Henry, whom I had known for decades but not seen for several years; he was hanging about by the entrance of what had once been the St. James' Club, his magenta jowls heaving, his thick lips drooping, his hairy nostrils opening and closing like motor valves.

'What's happened to the Club?' he said.

'It's gone,' I said. 'Didn't you get the letter?'

'I've been abroad for some time.'

'Well, the lease packed in, or something of the sort, and all members were transferred to Brooks's . . . if they wanted to be.'

'What happened to the backgammon sets?' Henry asked.

'They went to Brooks's too. They were set up in a special room with a soothing Turneresque landscape. To keep the players sweet-tempered, I suppose.'

'Ah. I imagine that as a paid up member of the St. James' I was transferred with everybody else?'

'I don't think it was automatic,' I said, 'but I am on my way there now, so you can come with me and see about it.'

Although I had never liked Henry very much, I'd had a soft spot for his wife, Constance, who was long since dead and almost certainly dead of Henry; but I knew she would have wished, not being a vindictive woman, that Henry should be agreeably accommodated with a club now that he had returned (from wherever it was) to London. It was, then, largely out of affection for the memory of Constance that I was now assisting her bulbous relict.

'The Secretary is away,' I said, 'on a Sabbatical Year; but the Club Registrar Incumbent in his place will know the form.'

So through the dank London dusk we went, and down St. James's Street, and up in the lift (belly to belly) in Brooks's, to see the Club Registrar Incumbent. To him Henry Whybrow explained who he was, his absence abroad (where? I wondered again) when the St. James' Club had closed its doors, and his wish to apply, better late than never, to be listed as a Member of Brooks's. I then affirmed that Henry was indeed Henry, that he had been a prominent frequenter of the St. James' before he went abroad, had always comported himself with as much propriety as could rationally be expected of him, and had punctually paid his dues.

'I see no difficulties here,' said the Club Registrar.

'Good,' said Henry, who had cheered up a bit in the last half-hour. 'Now then. I have only been a few hours in England, I have nowhere to stay and no luggage apart from this little bag (as Air Mongol has lost all the rest), and so I should very much like to put up in the Club for a few nights. I am sorry if I seem presumptuous, but needs must when the Devil, et cetera. No doubt you will be requiring my subscription: I shall have to ask you to wait until my assets have arrived from the Orient and are duly credited in Lloyds Bank across the street.'

'We allow a month's grace for payment of subscriptions,' the Registrar said.

'I shall settle with you long before that,' said Henry puffily. 'Let's see, what is the date? November the twenty-seventh? I shall be in a position to satisfy you at the beginning of next month. A matter of days.'

'That's all right then,' I said, as if for some reason my approval were needed.

'And I can have a room?' said Henry.

The Registrar Incumbent hesitated very slightly. Then, 'I can't see why not,' he said. 'I remember the instructions were that members of the St. James' should be admitted without delay or formality. Of course you can have a room, Whybrow – if the porter on duty finds that one is available.'

The Great Subscription Room: designed by Holland in 1776 and largely unaltered. The Dilettanti Society pictures arrived from the St James' Club in 1975

The Library: designed in 1889 by Anderson when the Club was extended. The Dilettanti portraits were installed in 1975, and the room was refurbished in 1992.

That night we had dinner together, Henry and I. His appetite for food and drink, which had always been keen, was now ravenous. He contrived a six course menu for himself, accompanying it with half a bottle of champagne, a bottle of Chambolle Musigny, and about a pint of Château-d'Yquem. Between gulps and mastications he told me a little of what he had been doing abroad.

'I've been all over the Far East,' he said. 'I decided to go when Constance died – get over the loss, you know. She left a tidy sum – I was quite surprised – so I thought: I'll go on a long tour – just the thing to help me get over poor old Constance.

'I didn't have to rough it, of course,' he went on over a quintuple measure of Marc de Provence, 'but every now and then I found myself in some pretty odd places. I was caught by the monsoon once in a garrison town in Mongolia. Complete outpost, hundreds of miles from anywhere. I spent the whole time playing chess and backgammon against the Commandant; funny chap, a combination of Greek, Russian and Amerindian.'

'How muddling.'

'Worse than that. His grandfather had been a Thracian but his father had been born in Georgia, and later exiled to the Arctic Circle, where he married an Eskimo squaw from Alaska. My man was now Colonel Commandant of his hyperborean garrison . . . and, as I say, a very formidable wrangler at chess and backgammon. Taught me a lot about both games, especially tric-trac which was what he always called backgammon – that was the Greek coming out in him, I suppose. I used to think I was pretty good in the old days at the St. James' – but nothing to what I was after a month of playing with him. I picked up every trick in the Asio-Oriental book and a good few extra. Helped me no end on later occasions. And that reminds me: let's see what's going on in that backgammon room you were telling me about.'

I played a couple of games with him myself, lost a few pounds, and passed him on to better players. His method wasn't at all the flamboyant affair which I might have expected from his account of his tuition. I had always understood that the finest exponents of backgammon were for ever on the aggressive, making deployments of hideous menace yet at the same time leaving long trains of 'blobs' which miraculously came together at precisely the moment of crisis. There was nothing of this about Henry's style of play. He didn't even take carefully calculated odds-on risks. He was as dull an opponent as it was possible for a man to be, always making the safe and dreary move, never leaving a lone piece unattended for one second longer than necessary. He never made a flashy move, never showed off. He just proceeded fast and smoothly round the board (but *how*, one asked oneself, with such boring and moderate throws?) and was taking his men off before one had even begun to get one's own strategy together.

'It's a knack,' he said when I congratulated him on his speedy passage. Just you spend a whole month of monsoon playing against a Greek-Russian-Eskimo, and you'd probably get it yourself.'

He had no spectacular triumphs. He was so swift round the board that there was little opportunity to double. 'Better that way,' he said, as we recorded his modest gain and my tolerable loss on the form provided and posted it in the appropriate box for the attention of the Registrar. 'Win a little here and there,' Henry said, 'and there's no hard feelings anywhere. I know how nasty people can be if you take them to the knacker's – I'll never do *that* again.' He did not expand on the theme but moved on to his next opponent, from whom, after five quick games, he had won just twenty pounds. No hard feelings. And then he took on someone else. . . .

At the end of the evening there were only Henry, myself and an elderly spectator left in the room. The elderly spectator, having quietly declined Henry's offer of a game, ordered drinks for the three of us and having thus bought himself a captive audience, began to soliloquize in the relentless and urgent fashion of club *cognoscenti* throughout the kingdom.

'It is interesting to reflect,' he said to us, 'that gambling in the Club went very much out of the fashion for most of the nineteenth century and the first half of the twentieth – was indeed resumed only when you and your fellow-members from the St. James' came here to join us. But of course what passes for gaming nowadays is mere trifling if compared with what went on in the late eighteenth century, when, for example, Mr Brooks first began to manage the club that was later to bear his name.'

Henry's demeanour reminded me of a character called Dead-Wide Dick, Captain of the School XI in the *Hotspur* (a journal I much fancied in my infancy), who spent most of the day apparently asleep but always woke up and went into amazing action as soon as a vital catch came his way or seventy runs were needed in ten minutes.

'Go on,' Henry said urgently, having only a second before appeared to be on the verge of coma; *'please* go on,' he said, rather as though he expected the pandit to reveal the quickest route to Solomon's Mines or Aladdin's Cave.

'Charles James Fox,' said our instructor vibrantly, as if inspired by Henry's enthusiasm, 'Selwyn, Sheridan . . . Wilberforce . . .'

'Wilberforce?' I said.

'Oh yes. He was led astray every now and then. He even ran a Faro Bank on one occasion. He had tremendously good luck – and guilt commensurate with it. Then there was the drunk duellist, FitzGerald, who would insist on playing here though he wasn't a member – everyone was too scared of him to tell him to leave. But perhaps,' said the elderly member, getting his second wind, 'Mr Brooks the Manager was as odd a character as any. He was such a toady that he would always advance large sums, without any security, to any gentleman who was embarrassed for ready money at the tables, cash on the nail being the rule, at least theoretically, at this period. The result was, of course, that Mr Brooks was soon much embarrassed for money himself. So he had a secret passage constructed by the Club servants; it started near the bottom of the present lift shaft and led to a small and secret niche which was excavated under the street. There Mr Brooks would hide when the duns came, well provided with a hamper and a piss pot.'

'Where did he empty it in the event of a long siege?' asked Henry, as if he ardently wished to know.

'Into a pipe that led to a conduit beneath. Mr Brooks became fond of his hide-out, which was just as well, since it was also his last resting place – or very nearly so. When he died, the duns came for his clothes and his cadaver, which in that age would have fetched a handsome price from chirurgeons engaged in anatomical research. So the servants bundled Mr B's body into his niche and battened down the hatches from outside until such time, a very long time, as the duns wearied of the hunt. By some sort of misunderstanding the wretched fellow was entirely forgotten. Only about ten years later, when a member, who had been (like you, Whybrow) many years abroad, ordered a footman to "fetch Brooks your master and tell him to bring two hundred guineas with him", did people suddenly recall that Brooks was still in his niche under St. James's Street. I'm happy to say that he was given a regal funeral to make up.'

Henry rose. Although he had encouraged the soliloquist at the outset, it was plain that he had had enough now.

'I'm off to bed,' he said. 'I need to sleep long hours – some debilitating virus which I picked up in Mongolia.'

'Let me offer you luncheon tomorrow,' said the antiquary, who obviously still had hopes of Henry as an audience.

'I never eat lunch,' said Henry. 'Dinner, if you please . . .'

When I returned to London after a few days in the country, there was a note for me from the Registrar Incumbent asking me to call on him in his office.

'That man of yours, Whybrow,' he began.

'He isn't my man.'

'You introduced him. You should know that he is presenting problems.'

'Oh?'

'First of all, he won't leave his room till late in the afternoon. He locks the door, pins a note outside (on the new paintwork) saying "Do not Disturb until Four p.m. of the Clock", and simply cannot be roused no matter how hard anyone hammers.'

'Why should he be roused?'

'The servants want to make up the room.'

'Then tell them to make it up after he's left it in the evening.'

'The kind of servants who make up the rooms have gone home long before that.'

'Rubbish,' I said. 'If somebody arrives to stay late and unexpected, the servants have to make up a room for him. It's always happening.'

'We have to call on the wrong sort of servants. It is inconvenient, and it is resented.'

'Then charge Whybrow extra.'

'I do,' said the Registrar. 'But here's another thing. He has a very odd way of paying his dues.'

'Is he in default?'

'Not exactly.'

'Either he is,' I said, 'or he isn't.'

'On the first of this month,' said the Registrar, 'about four days after you first brought him here, he came to this office around tea time, and he said: 'By my reckoning I'm well over £270 ahead in backgammon.' Which was true enough. I'd just had all the gaming slips in, as I do at the start of every month, in order to calculate the gains and losses of the previous month. Between his arrival on November 27th and the end of the month's accounting at midnight of November 30th, Henry Whybrow had won £276.80, which included £8 lost to him by you. Here's your statement; take it now and save me the trouble of putting it in an envelope.'

I took it, 'Then what?' I said.

'You pay it.'

'I meant, "Then what about Henry Whybrow?"'

'Whybrow said to me: "Please add up what I owe for my subscription up to December 31st, and for my room, and for all the food and drink I've had. Then deduct it from what I've won and keep the balance for my future credit. I hope to occupy that room indefinitely."'

'"You can't," I said. "Quite apart from the rule which states that no member can occupy a room for more than fourteen consecutive nights, the Christmas break is coming up in ten days' time. You will have to leave the Club from December 23rd to January 3rd. Everybody has to."'

'He didn't like the sound of that,' the Registrar continued. '"Christmas break?" he said. "Since when did the Club close for bloody Christmas?" Then he took a pull on himself. "Sorry," he said: "I mustn't get snappish. So be it. Book me in from January 3rd for as long as you can." "The porter on duty will do that," I said, "if it is possible." "Of course," he said, as mild as milk; "but you won't forget to take what I owe from my winnings – everything, laundry and all? And keep what's left as a credit."'

'"You can have what will be left now," I said, anxious to put an end to this eccentric arrangement; "I'll do my sums and write you a cheque." "Cash?" he said. "I haven't got enough cash," I told him. "Then just you hang on to the balance like a good chap," said Whybrow, "and debit all my dues as before." And with that he was off."

'I don't see what you're grumbling about,' I said. 'You've been paid out fair and square, and he's leaving you some money to pay the next lot. I told you when I introduced him that he was never late in meeting his dues.'

'I just wish he'd pay with a cheque like anybody else.'

'Why?'

'It makes it easier with the books. And another thing, Raven. People are beginning to mutter about Whybrow's winning all the time at backgammon.'

'Does anybody say he cheats?'

'No.'

'Then they're just bad losers,' I said. 'I've watched him play. He doesn't play for a high stake, he doesn't get fierce with the doubling die, he plays an absolutely straight and pedestrian game with no tricks or evasions.'

'Exactly. He doesn't take risks and he concentrates a lot. He works the thing out. People say that isn't very sporting.'

'Simply because they're too idle or too stupid to work the thing out themselves. He finds plenty of chaps who want to play against him – or he wouldn't be winning so much.'

'They're all determined that *somebody* should beat him, that's why. They've become obsessed.'

'And whose fault is that?'

At dinner that evening I sat next to Henry at the Club Table. He enjoyed his food as greedily as ever, but was clearly in a huff.

'What shall I do at Christmas?' he said. 'No meals here, no backgammon, not even a bed.'

'Have you no friends and relations?'

'Not now Constance is dead. And if I had, what's the odds? We'd spend the whole time either simpering at each other or quarrelling about who should do the washing up.'

'You might persuade them to go racing. There's some first-rate meetings on Boxing Day.'

'I can't go racing any more.'

'Surely not warned off?'

'Of course not, or I shouldn't have been let in here.' He evidently disliked the topic but felt, now that it had been raised, that he must make his position clear. 'I find that . . . these days . . . I can't get up early enough.' He looked at me shiftily and gabbled on, 'What I mean is, for midwinter meetings, you have to set off at sparrow's fart.' He paused for a moment to assess the effect on me of this wholly unnecessary gloss, then said: 'Make myself clear?'

'I suppose so. It hardly matters.'

'No. Another annoyance,' he went on crossly, 'about the Club's closing: the night before it closes there's a Dilettanti Dinner, and all the bedrooms have been booked weeks in advance, so I'm now told. As if it's not bad enough having the place shut on the 23rd, I shall now have to find somewhere else to sleep on the night of the 22nd.'

'You'll manage.'

'I dare say.' He grunted and went off to the backgammon room, full of wine of every colour but entirely steady as he went.

I next saw Henry on the night of December 22nd, rather late, nearly midnight, just as I was leaving the Club.

'Want to share a taxi?' I asked. 'If you're going anywhere near my flat?'

'No, thanks.'

He showed no signs of leaving himself.

'I thought you'd been kicked out of your room to make way for some Dilettante?'

'Oh yes. But I'm putting up very near here, only a step or two away.'

'Happy Christmas, then,' I said tactlessly.

Henry said nothing, but turned and walked towards the loo.

I hadn't meant to go to the Club at all on the 23rd. But when I called at Jackson's to pick up my Christmas order of caviare, the fellow said that it had been sent, in error, to Brooks's (where they often sent my stuff for me). The Club had closed at noon, but when I rang the bell, it was opened . . . by a very discomposed Registrar Incumbent.

'I hoped it might be you,' he said. 'I saw an enormous parcel for you. It's just over there.'

'Thank God I could get in. Fresh Beluga goes off pretty quick.'

'Like corpses,' he said.

'Like what?'

'Come upstairs,' he said. 'The duty porter's just getting me some tea and crumpets.'

I looked at my watch. 'Three o'clock,' I said; 'I've got to get down to Walmer in time for dinner. And I want to get that caviare in my refrigerator as soon as I can.'

'Come upstairs,' he insisted.

So up we went in the levitating sentry box.

'You know,' he said, after the porter had deposited the tea tray, 'that I have always been slightly suspicious of your man, Whybrow?'

'He isn't my man,' I repeated from an earlier discussion.

'No. Not any more. He's dead.'

'How? When? I saw him only last night.'

'He'd been dead for long before that,' the Registrar Incumbent said, shaking so much that he dripped butter from his crumpet on the knee of my new suit. 'I've been making enquiries. The answers have just come in. He died in the East. A considerable time ago. Some row over a game of chess or backgammon. The Russian police have made a special report at the request of Scotland Yard. Some row with a Russian officer of some kind.'

'But if Henry Whybrow is dead,' I said, 'the chap we have had here has got to be an impostor. That would explain all the business about not having any money in Lloyds when he joined, and not wanting to sign or receive cheques, and so on and so forth. Just a con man scratching a living.'

'But,' said the Registrar, 'you were so *sure* it was Henry Whybrow. And apparently nothing has happened since he's been staying here to make you think otherwise.'

'I am a rational man,' I said. 'If Henry Whybrow is dead, then I have made a silly mistake, and the man who has been staying in this club has got to be an impostor and a crook. There is no other explanation.'

'Oh yes, there is,' said Henry, coming through the door. 'Sorry to disturb you both. I thought, Registrar, that you would have left by now for Christmas in the bosom of your family; so I just popped up to check

216

on my backgammon winnings for the last three weeks – I imagine you've called the slips in as the place is closed till the New Year, and I shall be needing the credit when the bills come in early in January. But as things have turned out, I am very sorry I came. It is not nice to hear an old friend call one an impostor and a crook.'

'What else can you be?'

'A walking stiff,' said Henry, and laughed rather a lot. 'A zombie, if you like; but not a crook. I agree, however, that I owe you both an explanation.'

'I told you, Simon, about my experience in that Russian Army outpost in Mongolia. Only I left a lot out. The upshot was that I began to beat my mentor at tric-trac, as he called it. What was worse, from his point of view, I also beat him at chess. People get very vain about their chess: King Cnut split the skull of some one forward enough to checkmate him – split his skull with a battle axe. That Russian, cooped up for years in that horrible place, cooped up cheek by jowl with me for weeks of monsoon, finally flipped his lid when I toppled his king, and then toppled me with his sabre. And while I was bleeding to death, he cursed me . . . with a ghastly Thracian curse he'd learnt from his father, who, being Georgian for good measure, was doubly versed in magic. The curse was that I should rise from my grave at dark on the day of my burial and wander the earth – the old Wandering Jew syndrome, you see – wander the earth for ever. And to make matters really foul, I was to endure the torment of never being able to lose at chess or backgammon. You see the point? Theologians say that the most cruel punishment in Hell is being *unable to fail, for ever and ever, amen*; always and for ever having instant sexual success, or writing a masterpiece automatically every time you put pen to paper, or, in my case, being unable to lose at chess . . . or at tric-trac.'

'At least the curse provides you with an income,' said the Registrar sourly.

'That's just the point,' said Henry. 'I've paid my way by tric-trac, under the most hideous and often insanitary circumstances, all the way from Inner Mongolia to the West End of London. Now that I'm here, I am hoping to settle down and play in a civilized and gentlemanly fashion, and otherwise to enjoy a little peace and quiet. And then what happens? You close the Club on me. It's a dreadful thing to ask a fellow to change his whole way of life – or should I say death? – at my age, if only for a few days over Christmas. You've no idea of the problems. To start with, I can only get about when it's dark. And then for as long as the light lasts the next day I have to lie in a sort of trance, like Dracula – though I swear to you I'm not a vampire. But I have a huge appetite for food, because if one is dead one needs immense resources to keep one quick – if you take my meaning. Very often I can't get at food for days, the limitations on my movements being so severe, and so when I can I simply stuff myself like Vitellius. I've been doing that for the last few days to keep me going over Christmas until the Club reopens.'

'I see,' I said; 'and why do you drink so much?'

'For the extra calories. If you're dead, you see, you get no pleasure from it, and you can never get drunk (that's part of the curse), but the calories are an essential item of your heavy diet.'

'This is all very well,' quavered the Registrar, 'but where are you going to spend Christmas? You should have left the Club by noon.'

'Don't be so inhospitable,' said Henry. 'I thought of the bedrooms, but they're all locked and there'll be a relay of porters on duty sniffing round the place, so in the end I decided I'd spend Christmas in Mr Brooks's niche. You remember,' Henry said to me, 'what that old fellow told us about that in the backgammon room on my first night? At dinner the next day I wormed a lot more useful details out of him – the probable approach to the lair, and so forth. As soon as I knew for certain I'd have to leave my room, I reconnoitred the passage and tidied up the cell, and I've just been spending a tolerably comfortable sixteen hours there.'

There was a long silence. Then the Registrar, who had for a time become much calmer, so soothing and sensible had been Henry's mode of discourse, started to shake again.

'But what on earth am I to do with you?' he said. 'Stick a stake through your heart when you're in one of your comas?'

'I told you,' said Henry sternly: 'I am not a vampire. I should just be walking about with a stake through my body, thus creating a scandal. Whereas, if you leave me as I am, nobody need ever know anything derogatory about me.'

'You're not thinking of staying on in the Club?' said the Registrar Incumbent.

'How else am I to li–, er, exist? The Club is the ideal solution. Somewhere to sleep all day – Mr Brooks's niche when I can't have a proper room; excellent food and drink – not that I can actually enjoy it, but the kind of robust country house cuisine you have here is superbly nourishing for one in my condition; and then that agreeable backgammon room in which to make my li–, that is, my means of subsistence. You will have noticed, surely, that I am not being greedy for a guaranteed winner? I know I can't lose, but I only win as much as is strictly necessary for one in my sad situation.'

Henry paused and looked at both of us.

'You wouldn't have the heart,' he said, 'to turn me out?'

And of course, though neither of us really likes Henry, we haven't had the heart to turn him out.

After all, he does no harm. Some chaps like him much more than I do. He has some entertaining tales about the East, and particularly about Mongolia. He makes no demands. The Registrar has found him a flowered chamber pot to furnish the niche when he's in residence, and every now and then I smuggle down a hamper from Jackson's. No; Henry Whybrow is no trouble to anybody. But I thought you might be amused to learn that one of your fellow-members is – well, let's face it, a Ghost, albeit a very mundane one. He is not, as I said at the beginning, actually called Henry Whybrow. I expect you'll guess his real name: a chap who's never seen by day; is always in the Club by night; eats and drinks like Gargantua; has heavy magenta jowls and a proboscis that functions like some bivalvular device; and spends hour after hour in the backgammon room. If you rumble him, don't betray the poor fellow. How would *you* like to be under an eternal curse which never allowed you to get pissed and took all the excitement out of backgammon?

Notes on Contributors

ANNAN, Noel, Baron (Life Peer). Former Provost of King's College, Cambridge; Vice-Chancellor, University of London; Chairman, Board of Trustees, National Gallery. Author of *Leslie Stephen*; *Roxburgh of Stowe*; *Our Age*, etc.

BLAKE, Robert, Baron (Life Peer). Former Provost of The Queen's College, Oxford; Pro-Vice-Chancellor, Oxford University. Author of *The Unknown Prime Minister* (Bonar Law); *Disraeli*; *A History of Rhodesia*; *The Conservative Party from Peel to Thatcher*, etc.

DIXON, Piers. Former merchant banker and Member of Parliament. Author of *Double Diploma*; *Cornish Names*.

FORD, Sir Brinsley. Former Chairman, National Arts Collection Fund and National Trust's Foundation for Art; Secretary of Society of Dilettanti, 1972–1988; President of the Walpole Society. Author of *The Drawings of Richard Wilson*.

HASTINGS, Max. Editor, *The Daily Telegraph*. Former war correspondent and maker of TV documentaries. Author of *Montrose*; *Bomber Command*; *The Battle for the Falklands*; *Overlord*; *The Korean War*; *Outside Days*, etc.

JENKINS, Roy, (Lord Jenkins of Hillhead. Life Peer) Chancellor of Oxford University. President of the Royal Society of Literature. Former Home

Secretary, Chancellor of the Exchequer, President of the European Commission. Author of *Mr Balfour's Poodle*; *Sir Charles Dilke*; *Asquith*; *Nine Men of Power*, etc.

JOLLIFFE, John. Former publisher. Editor of *Raymond Asquith, Life and Letters*; *Neglected Genius, The Diaries of Benjamin Haydon*.

LEES-MILNE, James. Former Adviser, National Trust. Author of *The Age of Adam*; *Earls of Creation*; *Ancestral Voices*; *Prophesying Peace*; *Harold Nicolson* (two vols); *The Enigmatic Edwardian* (Lord Esher); *The Bachelor Duke*, etc.

MILLAR, Sir Oliver. Surveyor Emeritus of The Queen's Pictures. Former Surveyor of the Queen's Pictures and Director of the Royal Collection. Author of several works on the history of the Royal Collection and of the arts in Stuart England, and numerous catalogues of exhibitions, chiefly at the Queen's Gallery.

MORDAUNT CROOK, J. Professor of Architectural history and Public Orator, University of London. Author of *The British Museum*; *The Greek Revival*; *William Burges and the High Victorian Dream*; *The Dilemma of Style*, etc.

NEIDPATH, James, Lord (Heir to 12th Earl of Wemyss). Author of *The Singapore Naval Base and the Defence of Britain's Eastern Empire*.

O'BRIAN, Patrick. Former Foreign Office and intelligence officer. Author of *Picasso*; *Joseph Banks*; the *Jack Aubrey* series; translations of S. de Beauvoir, Colette, etc.

OLLARD, Richard. Former lecturer and publisher. Author of *The Escape of Charles II*; *Pepys*; *Clarendon and his Friends*; *Clarendon's Four Portraits*; *This War Without an Enemy*; *Fisher and Cunningham* etc.

PLUMB, Sir John. Former Master of Christ's College, Cambridge; Professor of Modern English History, Cambridge University; Author of

Sir Robert Walpole (two vols); *The First Four Georges*; *The Growth of Political Stability*; *The Death of the Past*; *Royal Heritage*, etc.

RAVEN, Simon. Former soldier. Author of *The Alms for Oblivion* sequence, *Shadows on the Grass*; *The Old School*; *The First Born of Egypt* sequence; script of *Edward and Mrs Simpson* (TV), etc.

RAY, Cyril. Former war correspondent. Founder and Past President, Circle of Wine Writers; editor of *The Complete Imbiber*. Author of *The Pageant of London*; *From Algiers to Austria: The History of 78 Division*; *The Wines of Italy*; *The Wines of France*; *The Wines of Germany*, etc.

RUST, Graham. International muralist, water-colour painter and illustrator. Author of *The Painted House*.

SEWARD, Desmond. Author of many historical works, of which the most recent are *Henry V as Warlord* and *Napoleon and Hitler: a comparative biography*.

SITWELL, Francis. Younger son of Sacheverell Sitwell. Advertising, public affairs and public relations consultant. Has been Hon. Secretary of the Fox Club since 1985.

WOOD, Christopher. Art Historian and Dealer. Former Director of Christies. Author of *The Dictionary of Victorian Painters* and numerous other books about Victorian art.

ZIEGLER, Philip. Former diplomat and publisher. Author of *The Black Death*; *Lord Melbourne*; *William IV*; *Diana Cooper*; *Mountbatten*; *King Edward VIII*, etc.

List of Subscribers

The Hon. Edward Adeane, C.V.O.
Francis Aglionby, Esq.
Julian Agnew, Esq.
Richard B. Allen, Esq.
Richard J. Allen, Esq.
Charles Amato, Esq.
Robin Andrews, Esq.
The Right Hon. Lord Annan, O.B.E.
The Right Hon. the Earl of
  Annandale and Hartfell
Colin Anson, Esq.
Mahlon Apgar, IV, Esq.
Leonard Appleyard, Esq.
Jonathan Azis, Esq.

Jack Baer, Esq.
Hal Bagot, Esq.
Sir Richard Baker-Wilbraham,
  Baronet
Cdr. Colin Balfour, R.N. (Rtd.), D.S.C.
Antony Barbour, Esq.
Nicholas Baring, Esq.
Peter Baring, Esq.
Henry Barlow, Esq., O.B.E.
Sir William Barlow
The Right Hon. Lord Barnard, T.D.
Antony Barnes, Esq.
Maj. Jan Barnes
Sir John Barnes, K.C.M.G., M.B.E.
Sir Oliver Barnett, C.B.E., Queen's
  Counsel
Andrew Baylis, Esq.
Michael Beaumont, Esq.
Sir Martyn Beckett, Baronet, M.C.

His Grace the Duke of Bedford
Robin Behar, Esq.
Herbert Bell-Syer, Esq., A.F.C.
Sir Andre Benard, K.B.E.
The Right Hon. Lord Benson, G.B.E.
The Hon. Peter Benson
Sir William Bentley, K.C.M.G.
Sir Isaiah Berlin, O.M., C.B.E.
Charles Bingham-Newland, Esq.
Simon Birch, Esq.
Nicholas Blackwell, Esq.
The Right Hon. Lord Blake
Derek Bloom, Esq.
Emmet Blow, Esq.
Duncan Bluck, Esq., O.B.E.
Christopher Boddington, Esq.
Arnold von Bohlen und Halbach, Esq.
The Right Hon. Lord
  Bonham-Carter
Michael Boreham, Esq.
Robin Boudard, Esq.
Aubrey Bowden, Esq.
Neville Bowen, Esq.
Henry Boyd-Carpenter, Esq.
H.R. Boyle, Esq., T.D.
Robert Boyle, Esq.
Julian Briant, Esq.
The Hon. Mark Bridges
Michael Briggs, Esq.
Bartholomew Broadbent, Esq.
Michael Broadbent, Esq.
Donald Brodie, Esq.
Desmond Browne, Esq., Queen's
  Counsel

Lt.-Col. William Buckley, M.B.E.
Anthony Buckwell, Esq.
Claus von Bulow, Esq.
Anthony Burgess, Esq., C.V.O.
Mark Burnyeat, Esq.
Sir Robin Butler, K.C.B., C.V.O.
James Buxton, Esq.
Paul Buxton, Esq.

Sir Alan Campbell, G.C.M.G.
Alan Campbell-Johnson, Esq.,
  C.I.E., O.B.E.
Alain Camu, Esq.
Simon Carey, Esq.
Nigel Carter, Esq.
Antoni Cassel-Kokczynski, Esq.
Charles Cator, Esq.
Sir Peter Cazalet
David Cazes, Esq., D.F.C.
Sir Charles Chadwyck-Healey,
  Baronet
Maj. Nigel Chamberlayne-
  Macdonald, L.V.O., O.B.E.
Charles Cholmondeley, Esq.
Andrew Ciechanowiecki, Esq.
Nigel Clive, Esq., C.M.G., O.B.E.,
  M.C., T.D.
Hugh Cobbe, Esq.
Thomas Cochran, Esq., C.B.E.
John Cochrane, Esq.
Viscount Coke
The Right Hon. Lord Colnbrook,
  Privy Councillor, K.C.M.G.
John Colvin, Esq., C.M.G.
Michael Comninos, Esq.
Neville Cook, Esq.
James Cooke, Esq.
Ian Cooling, Esq.
Robert Copley, Esq.
Patrick Cormack, Esq., M.P.
The Right Hon. Lord Cornwallis,
  O.B.E.

Julian Cotterell, Esq.
Sir John Coulson, K.C.M.G.
John Craig, Esq.
Anthony Croker Poole, Esq.
Prof. Mordaunt Crook
James Cropper, Esq.
Cdr. Sir Michael Culme-Seymour,
  Baronet, R.N. (Rtd.)
Gordon Cumming, Esq.
Sir Andrew Cunynghame, Baronet

William Dacombe, Esq.
Dennis Pehrson Dalberg, Esq.
Philippe Daudy, Esq., C.B.E.
James Dawnay, Esq.
Sir William Deakin, D.S.O.
Basil D'Eath, Esq.
Sir Evelyn Delves Broughton,
  Baronet
Lt.-Col. George Demetriadi, M.B.E.,
  T.D.
Patrick Despard, Esq.
His Grace the Duke of Devonshire,
  Privy Councillor, M.C.
Robert Devoto, Esq.
Kenelm Digby-Jones, Esq.
Prof. David Dilks
Piers Dixon, Esq.
Anthony Doggart, Esq.
John Downing, Esq.
Martin Drury, Esq.
David Duffy, Esq.
Christopher Dunn, Esq.
Richard Dunn, Esq.

Col. Peter Earle, M.C.
Hugo Eastwood, Esq.
Anthony Eden, Esq.
Anthony Edwards, Esq.
Timothy Edwards, Esq.
Sir Stephen Egerton, K.C.M.G.
Karl Eibenschütz

Piers Eley, Esq.

Geoffrey Ellerton, Esq., C.M.G., M.B.E.

John Emmerson, Esq.

Michael Essayan, Esq., Queen's Counsel

Adrian Evans, Esq.

Giles Eyre, Esq.

John Fairbairn, Esq.

The Right Hon. Lord Fanshawe of Richmond, K.C.M.G.

Warren Faris, Esq.

Leslie Farmiloe, Esq., M.C.

James Farrer, Esq.

William Farrer, Esq.

David Ferrand, Esq.

Richard Ferrand, Esq.

Dudley Fishburn, Esq., M.P.

Colin Fitch, Esq.

Alexander Fletcher, Esq.

Sir Brinsley Ford, C.B.E.

Michael Forgacs, Esq.

Jerome Foster, Esq.

David Foston, Esq.

Robin Fox, Esq.

Maj. Reginald Freeman-Thomas

Sir John Fretwell, G.C.M.G.

Alexander Fyjis-Walker, Esq.

Peter Fyson, Esq.

Prince Yuri Galitzine

Barrie Gane, Esq., C.M.G., O.B.E.

William Gardener, Esq.

Hugh Geddes, Esq.

The Right Hon. Lord Geddes

David Gemmill, Esq.

Valeriu Georgescu, Esq.

Philip German-Ribon, Esq.

Geoffrey Gibbon, Esq.

The Hon. Clive Gibson

The Right Hon. Lord Gibson

Graeme Gilchrist, Esq.

Patrick Giles, Esq.

John Gillum, Esq.

Charles Glazebrook, Esq.

Edward Glover, Esq., M.V.O.

Alastair Goodlad, Esq., M.P.

Russell Gore-Andrews, Esq.

Josslyn Gore-Booth, Esq.

Ronnie Gorlin, Esq.

Roderick Gow, Esq.

Robin Gowlland, Esq.

Maj. Sir Charles Graham, Baronet

David Grant, Esq.

Peter Gray, Esq.

Sir Allan Green, K.C.B., Queen's Counsel

Richard Gridley, Esq.

Josceline Grove, Esq.

Count Dominic de Grunne

Benoit Guerin, Esq.

James Guinness, Esq., C.B.E.

John Guinness, Esq., C.B.

Michael Haines, Esq.

Martin Haldane, Esq.

Roderick Hall, Esq.

Sir Ronald Halstead, C.B.E.

The Hon. Robert Hanson

Per Hansson, Esq.

The Right Hon. Lord Hardinge of Penshurst

David Hardy, Esq.

Michael Hargreave, Esq., V.R.D.

Bryce Harland, Esq.

Colin Harris, Esq.

William Harris, Esq., Queen's Counsel

Martin Harrison, Esq.

The Right Hon. Lord Harvey of Tasburgh

Max Hastings, Esq.

Walter Hayes, Esq., C.B.E.

The Right Hon. Lord Henley

Kenneth Hewett, Esq.
John Higginson, Esq., C.B.E.
Myles Hildyard, Esq., M.B.E., M.C.,
  T.D.
Michael Hoare, Esq.
Anthony Hobson, Esq.
Timothy Hobson, Esq.
Michael Hodges, Esq.
Daniel Hodson, Esq.
The Revd. Roger Holloway
The Right Hon. Viscount Hood
David Hopkins, Esq.
Geoffrey Hopkins, Esq.
David Hopkinson, Esq.
Richard Hornby, Esq.
Antony Hornyold, Esq.
Charles Howard, Esq.
Ben Howkins, Esq.
Andrew Hugh Smith, Esq.
David Hugh Smith, Esq.
Neil Hughes-Onslow, Esq.
David Hunter, Esq.
Sir Hugo Huntington-Whiteley,
  Baronet
Robert Hutchinson, Esq.
Robert Hutton, Esq.
John Hyatt, Esq.

The Right Hon. Lord Iliffe
Michael Ingall, Esq.
Simon Ingham, Esq.
Geoffrey Inkin, Esq., O.B.E.
George Ireland, Esq.
Harley Irwin, Esq.

Sir Kenneth James, K.C.M.G.,
  Chairman of the Managers
Alexander d'Janoeff, Esq.
Hugh Janson, Esq.
Nigel Jaques, Esq.
The Hon. Miles Jebb
The Right Hon. the Earl Jellicoe,

Privy Councillor, K.B.E., D.S.O.,
  M.C.
The Right Hon. Lord Jenkins of
  Hillhead, Privy Councillor
John S. Jennings, Esq.
John F.W. Jenyns, Esq.
Charles Jerdein, Esq.
The Hon. John Jolliffe

John Keffer, Esq.
Bernard Kelly, Esq.
David Kelly, Esq.
Laurence Kelly, Esq.
Alan Kelsey, Esq.
Arthur Kennard, Esq.
Sir Francis Kennedy, K.C.M.G.,
  C.B.E.
Mark Kennedy, Esq.
The Right Hon. Lord Kenyon, C.B.E.
Matthew Kirk, Esq.
John Kitching, Esq.
Andrew Knight, Esq.
Jeffrey Knight, Esq.
Kevin Knott, Esq.
The Right Hon. Viscount Knutsford

Cameron La Clair, Esq.
Maurice Lancaster, Esq.
John Langham, Esq., C.B.E.
The Marquis de Lavradio
Richard Law, Esq.
Oliver Lebus, Esq.
Robert Ledsom, Esq.
Julian Lee, Esq.
James Lees-Milne, Esq.
John Leighton-Boyce, Esq.
Peter Lendrum, Esq.
Adm. Sir Andrew Lewis, K.C.B.
Neville Lewis, Esq.
Charles Lillis, Esq.
Sir Anthony Lincoln, K.C.M.G.,
  C.V.O.

Brian Littledale, Esq.
Timothy Llewellyn, Esq.
John Lloyd, Esq.
Roger Lloyd, Esq.
The Hon. Robert Lloyd George
Anthony Loch, Esq., C.B.E.
Sir Donald Logan, K.C.M.G.
Sir Gilbert Longden, M.B.E.
Roger Longrigg, Esq.
William Low, Esq.
Jonathan Lubran, Esq.

Corbett Macadam, Esq.
Ian MacCormick, Esq.
D.C.P. McDougall, Esq.
Roderick McDougall, Esq.
Howard McKinley, Esq.
Andrew McLaren, Esq.
Simon McNair Scott, Esq.
Norman MacSween, Esq.
Bryan Magee, Esq.
Jacques Mallet, Esq.
John Mallet, Esq.
Michael Manser, Esq.
Giles de Margary, Esq.
Sir John Margetson, K.C.M.G.
Peter Martyn, Esq.
Janek Matthews, Esq.
Julian Matthews, Esq.
Hugh Maxwell, Esq.
Sir Ronald Melville, K.C.B.
Z.L. Mieczkowski-Zagroba, Esq.
Philip Mieville, Esq.
Sir Oliver Millar, G.C.V.O.
Jeremy St John Miller, Esq.
William Mocatta, Esq.
The Hon. Christopher Monckton
Martin Monico, Esq.
D.C. Mootham, Esq.
Charles Morland, Esq.
Michael Morley, Esq.
John E.M. Morris, Esq.

John V. Morris, Esq.
Sir Terence Morrison-Scott, D.S.C.
Thomas Mullins, Esq.
Dr Iain Murray-Lyon
Dr Ingo Mussi

Edmund Naylor, Esq.
Paul Negretti, Esq.
Lord Neidpath
Gerald Newfield, Esq.
Timothy Nicholas, Esq.
George Nicholson, Esq.
Charles J. Nickerson, Esq.
Charles L. Nicolson, Esq.
Sir David Nicolson
George Nissen, Esq., C.B.E.
Robert Noel, Esq.
Robert Norgren, Esq.
John Norton, Esq.

Patrick O'Brian, Esq.
Kevin O'Sullivan, Esq.
John Ogden, Esq.
Peregrine Ogden, Esq.
Peter Oldak, Esq.
Richard Ollard, Esq.
Frederick Oppé, Esq.

Anthony Packe, Esq.
William Packer, Esq.
Sir John Page
The Revd. Edward Page-Turner
Andrew Palmer, Esq., C.M.G.,
  C.V.O.
Dominic Park, Esq.
John Parsons, Esq.
Jock Paton, Esq.
The Revd. Canon Arthur Payton
Christopher Peake, Esq.
David Peake, Esq.
David Pearson, Esq.
George Peel, Esq.

Michael Pelham, Esq.
Jeremy Pemberton, Esq.
Sir Peter Petrie, Baronet, C.M.G.
Geoffrey Philips, Esq.
The Hon. Francis Phillimore
Ian Phillips, Esq.
Sir Nicholas Phillips, Queen's
    Counsel
David Pinckney, Esq.
John Pinder, Esq.
George Pinto, Esq.
Desmond Pitcher, Esq.
Sir Edward Playfair, K.C.B.
William Plomer, Esq.
Sir John Plumb
Christopher Ponter, Esq.
Timothy Pope, Esq.
Andrew Powell, Esq.
David Price, Esq.
Jonathan Price, Esq.
Richard Price, Esq.
Derek Priestley, Esq.
Sir Idwal Pugh, K.C.B.

Edward Ram, Esq.
Allan Ramsay, Esq.
William Rathbone, Junior, Esq.
Simon Raven, Esq.
Charles Rawlinson, Esq.
Cyril Ray, Esq.
Jonathan Ray, Esq.
The Right Hon. Lord Reigate, Privy
    Councillor
Alastair Rellie, Esq., C.M.G.
Ladislas Rice, Esq.
Sir Denis Rickett, K.C.M.G., C.B.
David Roberts, Esq.
John Robins, Esq.
Philip Robinson, Esq.
Silvanus Robinson, Esq., C.B.E.
Nigel Robson, Esq.
The Revd. Canon Howard Root

Jeffrey Rose, Esq., C.B.E.
Leopold de Rothschild, Esq., C.B.E.
Martin Russell, Esq.
Graham Rust, Esq.
David Ryott, Esq., T.D.

The Hon. Simon Sainsbury
Timothy Sainsbury, Esq.
The Hon. Piers St Aubyn, M.C.
The Right Hon. Lord St Levan,
    D.S.C.
Count Charles de Salis
Peter Sanguinetti, Esq.
John Saumarez Smith, Esq
The Right Hon. Lord Savile
Konstantin Graf von Schweinitz
David Scott, Esq.
Jonathan Scott, Esq.
Michael Scott, Esq.
Charles Sebag-Montefiore, Esq.
Oliver Sebag-Montefiore, Esq.
Desmond Seward, Esq.
Leopold Seymour. Esq.
Cyril Seymour-Newton, Esq.
Charles Shakerley, Esq.
Sir Brian Shaw
William Shelford, Esq.
David Shellard, Esq.
John Shipton, Esq.
Patrick Shovelton, Esq., C.B.,
    C.M.G.
The Right Hon. Lord Shuttleworth
Martin Simmons, Esq.
Lyddon Simon, Esq.
Francis Sitwell, Esq.
Sir Reresby Sitwell, Baronet
Jeremy Skinner, Esq.
Alan Smith, Esq.
Dr Brian Smith, C.B.E.
Dr Peter Smith
Stephen Sokolow, Esq.
John Southgate, Esq.

W.J. de Souza, Esq.
Adrian Stanford, Esq.
Julian Stanford, Esq.
Peter Stanley Price, Esq., Queen's
  Counsel
George Staple, Esq.
Guenter Steffens, Esq., O.B.E.
Martin Stephenson, Esq.
Timothy Stephenson, Esq.
John Sterling, Esq.
James Stitt, Esq.
Michael Stone, Esq.
Edward Streator, Esq.
Richard Stroud, Esq.
The Right Hon. Lord Sudeley
Richard Surtees, Esq.
Charles Sutcliffe, Esq.
Sir John Swire, C.B.E.
Sir Tatton Sykes, Baronet
David Synnott, Esq.

Peter Tann, Esq.
Mark Tennant, Esq.
Pratt Thompson, Esq.
Ray Thompson, Esq.
Richard Thompson, Esq.
Dr Allan Thomson
Robert Thorne, Esq.
James Thornton, Esq.
Hans Thykier, Esq.
Sir Crispin Tickell, G.C.M.G.,
  K.C.V.O.
Sir Charles Tidbury
Barry Till, Esq.
Alan Tillotson, Esq.
Simon Titcomb, Esq.
The Honorable John Train
Julian Travis, Esq.
The Right Hon. Viscount Trenchard
The Right Hon. Lord Trevethin and
  Oaksey
Peter Trumper, Esq.

Eric Udal, Esq.
Edmund de Unger, Esq.

David Valentine, Esq.
Richard Valentine, Esq.
James Vallance White, Esq.
Thomas Vaughan, Esq.
Xavier Villers, Esq.
Toby Vintcent, Esq.
Claude Virgin, Esq.

J.N. Waddell-Dudley, Esq.
C.P.G. Wade, Esq., O.B.E.
Peter Wake, Esq.
J.P. Harlan Walker, Esq.
Thomas Walker-Munro, Esq.
Roderick Walter, Esq.
Mark Wathen, Esq., T.D.
Adam Watson, Esq., C.M.G.
Alan Watson, Esq., C.B.E.
Ian Watson, Esq.
Harry Waugh, Esq.
Gerard Wertheimer, Esq.
Anthony Wharton, Esq.
Humphrey Whitbread, Esq., T.D.
Samuel Whitbread, Esq.
Mark White, Esq.
Christopher Wigan, Esq.
Ian Wightwick, Esq., M.C.
Francis Wigram, Esq.
Christopher Wilkes, Esq.
Alan Wilkinson, Esq.
Sir William Wilkinson
Geoffrey Williams, Esq.
George Williams, Esq., C.B.E., M.C.,
  T.D.
John Williams, Esq.
Ian Willis, Esq.
Peter Willis, Esq.
Simon Willis, Esq.
David Wills, Esq.
Guy Wilson, Esq.

Michael Wilson, Esq.
William Wilson, Esq.
The Right Hon. Lord Windlesham,
    Privy Councillor, C.V.O.
Peter Winkworth, Esq.
Christopher Wood, Esq.
Anthony Woodall, Esq.

Maj. Francis Yates
David Yorke, Esq.
James Yorke, Esq.
Harrison Young, Esq.
John Young, Esq.

Tadeusz Zablocki, Esq.
Philip Ziegler, Esq., C.V.O.

Index

Index